CHILDREN AND YOUNG PEOPLE
WHO SEXUALLY ABUSE OTHERS

Systems for the protection of children from abuse have been in place for some decades, but only during the 1990s has there been an awareness in the UK that some children and young people also sexually abuse.

Children and Young People Who Sexually Abuse Others brings together leading professionals experienced in working with children and young people and their families in a range of settings. Reflecting the development, achievement and challenges of current practice, they present up-to-date models of policy and practice based on key research findings about incidence, prevalence and characteristics of young abusers. Emphasising the importance of multi-disciplinary working, the book addresses:

- policy and service development in the light of recent legislation and establishment of youth offending teams;
- assessment and treatment work with individuals, in groups and with families;
- issues for young people in out of home settings;
- a programme specifically for working with children under 10 years old;
- female adolescent abusers;
- evaluation of treatment outcomes;
- the challenge of developing empowered and empowering practice in this area of work.

With a practical approach clearly linking theory to practice, *Children and Young People Who Sexually Abuse Others* is an accessible and stimulating book which will be invaluable to all those who want to understand current thinking and practice and will be of particular value to practitioners, managers and policy makers involved in child protection, criminal and youth justice, psychiatry, psychology and counselling as well as to students in the fields of health and social care.

Marcus Erooga is an NSPCC Area Children's Services Manager and a Visiting Research Fellow at the University of Huddersfield. **Helen Masson** is a Principal Lecturer in Social Work at the University of Huddersfield. They are co-editors of *The Journal of Sexual Aggression*.

CHILDREN AND YOUNG PEOPLE WHO SEXUALLY ABUSE OTHERS

Challenges and Responses

Edited by Marcus Erooga and Helen Masson

Foreword by Valerie Howarth

London and New York

First published 1999
by Routledge
11 New Fetter Lane, London EC4P 4EE

Simultaneously published in the USA and Canada
by Routledge
29 West 35th Street, New York, NY 10001

Routledge is an imprint of the Taylor & Francis Group

Typeset in Galliard by Routledge
Printed and bound in Great Britain by Biddles Ltd,
Guildford and King's Lynn

British Library Cataloguing in Publication Data
A catalogue record for this book is available from the British Library

Library of Congress Cataloging in Publication Data
Children and young people who sexually abuse others: challenges and
responses / edited by Marcus
Erooga and Helen Masson.
p. cm.
Includes bibliographical references.
1. Teenage sex offenders–Great Britain. 2. Teenage sex
offenders–Rehabilitation–Great Britain. 3. Teenage child molesters–
Great Britain. 4. Teenage child molesters–Rehabilitation–Great Britain.
5. Social work with juvenile delinquents–Great Britain. 6. Child sexual
abuse–Great Britain–Prevention. I. Erooga, Marcus, 1957– . II. Masson,
Helen C.
HV9067 S48C55 1999
364.36–dc21
99–20647
CIP

ISBN 0–415–19604–3 (hbk)
ISBN 0–415–19605–1 (pbk)

DEDICATED TO CAROLINE,
BILL, SAM AND TOM

CONTENTS

CONTENTS

ILLUSTRATIONS

Tables

Figures

CONTRIBUTORS

Nick Bankes, Team Manager, **Kate Daniels**, Senior Family Therapist and Trainer, and **Carlton Quartly**, Senior Practitioner, are members of ACT, a multidisciplinary team comprising psychology, social work and family therapy staff, funded by Surrey Social Services department. The team offers community-based therapy to children and young people who sexually abuse and to their families. ACT also has a central role in the management of this client group in Surrey and this is achieved through training programmes for staff in various agencies, the development of policies and procedures, as well as consultation to colleagues investigating, assessing or working therapeutically with this client group.

Richard Beckett is a Consultant Clinical and Forensic Psychologist, and Head of Oxford Forensic Psychology Service. Involved with the accreditation of the English Prison Sex Offender Treatment Programmes, he is the author of many associated publications and is currently developing measures to evaluate systematically the impact of treatment on adolescent abusers.

Anne Blues, Children's Services Manager, **Carole Moffat**, Practice Manager and **Paula Telford**, Child Protection Officer, are qualified social workers with post-qualifying training in family therapy, equal opportunities and child protection. Kaleidoscope is a community-based project which provides services to children and young people who are sexually abusing others. They work with boys and girls using individual and family work to help young people and their families understand the behaviour and adopt strategies for changing and controlling it. As well as direct services Kaleidoscope regularly undertakes training and consultation with a range of agencies both locally and nationally.

Alix Brown is a Principal Therapist and Project Manager with the Lucy Faithfull Foundation with special responsibility for clinical work with adolescents, consultation and training. She set up and ran the Shropshire Programme for adolescents (1990–4) and has since acted as consultant to many local authorities and voluntary organisations.

John Burnham is Consultant Family Therapist at Parkview Clinic in Birmingham. He is author of a number of books and articles on family therapy and its applications across service user groups and settings. **Julia Moss** is a Senior Registrar in Child and Adolescent Psychiatry who has combined her clinical work with postgraduate studies in criminology.

Jeff DeBelle, Consultant Paediatrician for Birming-ham Children's Hospital NHS Trust, is also conducting a multi-centre trial of therapeutic interventions for young people who sexually abuse, and evaluation of group interventions.

Ros Jamieson, who originally qualified in medicine and then trained in paediatrics and psychiatry, is Acting Clinical Director at Parkview Clinic.

Linda Butler is a Principal Child Therapist and registered Cognitive Behavioural Psychotherapist. She has undertaken post-graduate training in Child Sexual Abuse at the Institute of Child Health and worked extensively with abused children and their families. **Colin Elliott** is a Consultant Clinical Psychologist and Head of Child Psychology Services in North East Wales. Linda and Colin work in Wrexham Child and Adolescent Mental Health Service, specialising in individual and group cognitive-behavioural therapy, and have considerable experience in running parents' groups for the treatment of conduct disorder and children's and carers' groups for children with problems of impulse control, including sexual aggression.

Kevin Epps is the Principal Clinical Psychologist at Glenthorne Youth Treatment Centre (Department of Health) and Honorary Lecturer in Forensic Clinical Psychology at the University of Birmingham. He has a particular interest in the management and treatment of violent behaviour and sexual aggression and has published widely in this area.

Marcus Erooga is an NSPCC Area Children's Services Manager in the North West and for a number of years has had experience of practice and management of services relating to sexual abuse and sexual offending. He is author of a number of publications on related issues and with Helen Masson is co-editor of *The Journal of Sexual Aggression*. He is a Visiting Research Fellow at Huddersfield University.

Simon Hackett is a lecturer in the Centre of Applied Social Studies, University of Durham. He has extensive experience in work with children and young people who sexually abuse others and was previously Programme Director of G-MAP. He is the author of a number of publications relating to sexual aggression and sexual abuse.

Helen Masson, co-editor and co-author, is a Principal Lecturer in Social Work at Huddersfield University and a founder member of the university's Centre for Applied Childhood Studies. Since 1994 she has been researching policy and practice developments in relation to young sexual abusers and she is the author of a number of book chapters and journal articles on this and related subjects. With Marcus Erooga, she is co-editor of *The Journal of Sexual Aggression*.

Tony Morrison is an independent social care trainer and consultant and a Visiting Honorary Research Fellow at the Centre for Applied Childhood Studies at Huddersfield University. He works with agencies on risk management, supervision, the management of sex offenders, and inter-agency development, acting as consultant to both adolescent and adult sex offender programmes. He is also author of a number of journal articles and books on these subjects.

Bobbie Print is a social worker and a Director of the G-MAP programme, based in Manchester. The programme undertakes assessments, group, individual and family work with young people who sexually abuse others. Bobbie has specialised in this field of work for the past ten years. She has authored a number of publications and has trained extensively in this area of work. She was a founding member of NOTA and a member of the organisation's National Executive Committee until 1998. **David O'Callaghan** has been involved since 1988 in work with young people who sexually abuse. He has held a research grant in this area and published previously on this topic. He is a Programme Director with G-MAP, an independent therapeutic service to sexually aggressive young people based in Greater Manchester. David is a frequent presenter at national conferences and provides training for probation, health and social services.

Eileen Vizard, Consultant Child and Adolescent Psychiatrist, is Clinical Director of the Young Abusers Project, an assessment and treatment service within Camden and Islington Community Health Services NHS Trust and supported by the NSPCC, which has seen over 220 young abusers between the ages of 5½ and 21 years. Dr Vizard has published, researched and taught widely within the field of child care and child abuse. **Judith Usiskin** is a Child and Adolescent Psychotherapist, also based at the Project, whose special area of interest is in learning disability and sexual abuse. She has lectured widely as well as contributing to relevant publications.

David Will is Consultant in Adolescent Psychiatry at the Young People's Unit in the Royal Edinburgh Hospital. He started the first specialist service for young abusers in Scotland in 1989. He has produced some thirty publications, including *Integrated Family Therapy* and papers on work with child sexual abuse survivors and young abusers.

FOREWORD

The most compelling reason for finding ways of successfully treating people who commit sexual offences against children is to protect children from assault, but when the perpetrator is a child should other imperatives also prevail?

ChildLine is one of many agencies facing the day-to-day dilemmas of how to respond to the challenge of children and young people who sexually abuse others. Our telephone counselling service has a policy to respect the confidentiality of children who are abused until they are ready to tell, unless they are in immediate danger. But what happens when a 14-year-old calls about his own sexual behaviour towards younger children he is involved in caring for? How do we balance the need to help him with the imperative to protect other children?

In the year up to 31 March 1998 ChildLine was called by 1,323 children and young people about abuse by other young people: 754 were relatives – brothers, sisters, foster brothers – or boyfriends; 578 were school children; and a further 192 calls were from third parties, parents and friends about abuse by children. One in seven children ringing ChildLine about sexual assault had been abused by another child or young person. The calls reveal a wide range of abuse including unwelcome sexual explorations, frightening sexual threats, sexual assaults, violent sex with young boys and girlfriends and rape – much of which seems to go unreported. There are also more calls now than previously from girls describing unwanted sexual attention from other girls, though the proportion is low, at less than 0.5 per cent of all girls' calls about sexual abuse. Has this, like bullying previously, been accepted as something 'to put up with'? How should we respond to this behaviour?

The calls reveal a picture that is a very long way from the innocence most adults would like to see in children. The following cases speak for themselves.

Mary, 11, told how the next door neighbour, a teenager, had kissed and felt her since she was 6. Now he asked to lick her and asked her to go to his bed. She described being terrified but didn't know how to tell.

A 12-year-old girl called frightened and uncomfortable. An older girl was following her into the toilet and touching her vagina. She wanted it to stop.

A mother called to talk about her 7-year-old son, who complained of an older friend 'sucking his penis'. The same child had been touching a little girl in a similar way and both mothers had shared concern, but didn't know what to do next.

The search for answers about how to help both young victims and perpetrators has been slow. Dilemmas have been shared and islands of good practice developed but little, in this country, has been written in an easily accessible form. When the NCH, together with the Department of Health, set up a *Survey of Treatment Facilities for Young Abusers* which reported in June 1992, quotes like 'this is only just becoming recognised as a massive problem', and 'my guess is that there is an awful lot of what I consider sex offending going on which isn't seen as such by the family, and abuse is not being recognised' were common. In many areas the situation remains much the same. There are pockets of excellent practice, but wide gaps in understanding exist over how to tackle the very wide range of sexually deviant behaviour that workers encounter. Even when the offence is clear, the response is somewhat uncertain.

One mother called to say that her daughter had been sexually assaulted by an 8-year-old boy. She reported the incident immediately, but was not seen until the next day – a Friday. Her daughter had been distressed by an examination by a male doctor, but was told that someone would visit to talk about a video interview. No one came. When the mother rang the family support unit, her contact had gone home. She wanted to know what to do to protect her child's rights and how to support her through the process of investigation. She felt that the assault was not being taken seriously because it was by a child.

We should ask ourselves would the response have been different if the abuser had been an adult?

The development of positive programmes to help young sex offenders is in the early stages, but it has always been clear that if intervention comes early enough, there is far more likelihood of success than with adult abusers. However, we need more research and better dissemination of research findings and practice knowledge, in order to develop a multi-faceted approach capable of responding to the diversity, as well as the complexity, of this phenomenon. The recent publication *Sexually Abused and Abusing Children in Substitute Care* by Farmer and Pollock (1998) is a welcome addition to the available body of knowledge, but there remains a huge gap regarding the identification and treatment of young people in the general population. Issues such as how to treat young people who have been abused and confess to abusive behaviour themselves; how to meet their emotional needs, whilst separating out their abusive behaviours and holding them responsible for their actions and how to understand and manage the societal reaction to sexually deviant and abusive acts in our young, all require further attention. Contributors in the following pages address these issues with clarity, and readers will find their thinking on these matters challenged and progressed.

This book, *Children and Young People Who Sexually Abuse Others: Challenges and Responses*, is timely. It seeks to extend knowledge, not only of the nature of the problem, but also on how the very special needs of these children and young people can be brought back into focus within a child protection framework. Whatever feelings are engendered about their offences, these are children with special needs and, as such, should be provided with appropriate services. If these young people are to experience any kind of normal adult life, they will require the help of highly skilled professionals, people who understand detailed risk assessment, the distorted thinking pattern of the young abuser, the effects on their family and on their victims. They have a right to regain their childhood.

Valerie Howarth, Chief Executive – ChildLine

PREFACE

Systems for the protection of children from abuse have been in place for some decades in this country. However it is only during the 1990s that there has been a developing awareness of the possibility that children and adolescents can also be sexual abusers of others. Whilst much of the early research into sexual abuse by children and young people came from North America, research in the United Kingdom has provided evidence that up to a third of reported sexual offences are committed by under 18-year-olds (NCH, 1992). Availability of services for these children and young people is still patchy across the UK, in contrast to the more comprehensive provision now in place for adult sex offenders (HM Inspectorate of Probation, 1998).

In 1994 Routledge published *Sexual Offending Against Children: Assessment and Treatment of Male Abusers*, co-edited by Tony Morrison, Marcus Erooga, and Richard C. Beckett. Primarily a book about adult male abusers, it included one chapter on adolescent sexual abusers by Dave O'Callaghan and Bobbie Print. The book as a whole was very well received and has made an important UK contribution to literature on the subject of male sexual offending. This current volume, co-edited by Marcus Erooga and Helen Masson, develops the focus to concentrate on the issue of children and young people who sexually abuse others, with contributions from nationally known practitioners, clinicians, academics and researchers.

The book is intended for a number of audiences across a range of agencies and organisations involved in child protection, criminal and youth justice, psychiatry, psychology and counselling. Practitioners, who have often been in the forefront of recognising the existence of young sexual abusers, will, it is hoped, find this volume relevant and helpful in developing their understanding and practice. Similarly, their managers and those responsible for policy will find the book useful in illuminating the practice complexities and dilemmas which their staff face and outlining the issues which organisations and systems need to resolve, as well as offering guidance on best policy and practice. The book will also be of value to students studying in the health and social care fields and to educators involved in professional training.

The authorship reflects the book's firm commitment to the importance of multi-agency and inter-disciplinary collaboration and the content addresses work in both community and residential settings. Although there are differences in perspective and emphasis between chapters, the editors see this as healthy and inevitable given the relatively recent emergence of this area of work and its complexities. Indeed it is hoped that the rich diversity of theoretical and practical perspectives contained within the book will offer stimulation and food for thought for readers with both more and less experience in working with young sexual abusers.

In chapter 1 key research findings about the incidence, prevalence and characteristics of young sexual abusers are reviewed and relevant theoretical models discussed, providing a basis for subsequent chapters. It is therefore suggested that this is the starting point for the reader, before exploring the remainder of the book. Chapters 2 and 3 focus on policy and service development both at national and local levels whilst chapter 4 provides an overview, at a broad, macro level, of issues relating to placement provision for these children and young people. Included here is consideration, from a systemic perspective, of the formal and informal processes which impact on decision-making about choice of placement.

Chapter 5 addresses the difficult balancing act involved in minimising the risk of further acts of sexual abuse and victimisation, whilst also ensuring that young sexual abusers' developmental, educational and therapeutic needs are addressed. Chapter 6 covers the purposes, content and process of assessment work with children and young people who sexually abuse before chapters 7, 8, and 9 overview methods of intervention, covering individual psychotherapy, groupwork and work with families. Chapter 12 critically reviews the complex area of evaluating treatment outcomes in relation to young abusers and the final chapter analyses the many aspects which contribute to empowered and empowering practice in this area of work.

The balance of content in the book reflects current understanding of the known population exhibiting this problem, hence the primary focus on interventions with and the management of young males over ten and their families. However it has also been a priority to include a chapter on young female abusers (chapter 10) and on sexually aggressive children under ten years (chapter 11). Whilst it has not been possible to include a specific focus on issues for black children and young people, or those with learning difficulties, and thus does nothing to ameliorate the paucity of literature relevant to the needs of these groups, it is hoped that anti-discriminatory and anti-oppressive perspectives are apparent throughout the book.

The book has been written at a time of major debate and change both within child protection and youth justice systems with significant pieces of legislation such as the 1997 Sex Offenders Act and the 1998 Crime and Disorder Act only recently implemented. The potential impacts of these changes on the identification, management and treatment of young sexual abusers are anticipated and discussed. More than once the point is made that, as a society and as professionals, we continue to struggle with how to respond best to sexually aggressive or abusive children and young people who are often in need of both care and control, youngsters who are both victims and persecutors.

One fundamental issue which has properly been the subject of considerable debate and analysis has been on the subject of definition, how to distinguish those sexual behaviours exhibited by children and young people which are abusive from those which are either experimental or simply inappropriate. This task is made more difficult when many adults still find it uncomfortable to conceptualise children as sexual beings and when normal sexual development in childhood and adolescence is not fully understood (Hanks, 1997). Differentiated categories of sexual behaviour are addressed more fully in chapter 3; however, as an overarching orientation, the following, slightly modified, definition originally suggested by Ryan and Lane (1991) is our starting point:

> The juvenile sex offender is defined as a minor who commits any sexual act with a person of any age (1) against the victim's will, (2) without true consent, or (3) in an aggressive, exploitative, or threatening manner.
>
> (p. 3)

The editors have also been very much aware of the need to maintain consistency in terminology given the range of phrases used to delineate children and young people who are sexually aggressive or abusive towards others, phrases which have fallen in and out of favour since the early 1990s. In the hope of providing clarity for the reader the phrase 'sexually aggressive child or children' is used specifically to denote children under the age of 10, that is, under the age of criminal responsibility in the UK (although some North American research includes children under 12 within this category). A number of similar descriptors, for example, young sexual abusers, adolescent or juvenile sexual abusers, and young people who sexually abuse refer to children and young people of 10 years and above. Unless specifically addressing young female sexual abusers the pronoun 'he' is used throughout, in recognition of the fact that the bulk of sexually aggressive children and young sexual abusers are male.

At the conclusion of the process of drawing the book together we would want not only to thank the chapter contributors for their expertise and their forbearance with our enthusiastic editing, but also to express our thanks and appreciation to Liz Saville who has provided invaluable secretarial support during the preparation of this volume. Finally we would want to acknowledge our respective long suffering partners who have, once again, provided all the hidden support, without much complaint, whilst we were absorbed in 'that book'.

1

CHILDREN AND YOUNG PEOPLE WHO SEXUALLY ABUSE OTHERS

Incidence, characteristics and causation

Helen Masson and Marcus Erooga

Introduction

Sexual abuse by children and young people has emerged as a problem in the United Kingdom during the 1990s. Correspondingly the number of related professional publications has increased (NCH, 1992; Hoghughi *et al.*, 1997; Farmer and Pollock, 1998), as has public awareness. A measure of this heightened awareness is the regularity of reporting of instances of such alleged abuse in the media, with discussions in the more responsible press about, for example, the rights and wrongs of trials of young children in adult courts in instances of the most serious allegations, such as rape (see, for example, *The Guardian*, 1998). This introductory chapter will review and discuss issues of incidence, prevalence, and the characteristics of young sexual abusers. Current theoretical models and concepts which seek to understand the behaviour of such youngsters and which inform the assessment and intervention approaches considered in subsequent chapters will then be outlined.

Incidence and prevalence of sexual abuse by children and young people

The latest available criminal statistics for England and Wales, those for 1997 (Home Office, 1998) give the recorded level of sexual offences as 33,200 – comprising less than 1 per cent of all notifiable offences. Of the 6,400 individuals subsequently cautioned for or found guilty of sexual offences (interestingly a steadily decreasing annual number from the 10,700 recorded in 1988 and 1989) approximately 23 per cent (1,500) were between aged 10 and under 21 years of age. Of the 1,900 or so of these offenders who were cautioned (the vast majority of whom were male) approximately 10.5 per cent (200) were aged 10–13 years, 26 per cent (500) were aged 14–17 years and 10.5 per cent (200) were aged 18–20 years. In other words, children and young people aged between 10 and 21 years accounted for 47 per cent of all cautions for sexual offences. Approximately 4,500 males were found guilty in a court of a sexual offence of whom 9 per cent (400) were aged 14–17 years and 4.5 per cent (200) were aged between 18 and 20. A much smaller percentage of young people (13.5 per cent) accounted for findings of guilt as a result of court process.

These statistics, which refer only to offenders over the age of criminal responsibility and only reported offences, represent just a small proportion of sexual abuse committed by children and young people, particularly as much abuse goes unreported or is not recognised or dealt with as such. Various studies have, therefore, tried to estimate the extent of sexual abuse by young people. In a major retrospective study of adults concerning their experiences of abuse in childhood, Finkelhor (1979) found that 34 per cent of women and 39 per cent of men who recalled having a sexual encounter during their childhood with someone five or more years older than themselves reported that the older partner was aged between 10 and 19 years. Other studies (Fromuth *et al.*, 1991 and Ageton, 1983) suggest that about 3 per cent of all adolescent males have committed sexually abusive acts whilst Abel *et al.*, (1985) found that approximately 50 per cent of adult sex offenders reported that they began their sexual offending during their adolescent years. Considering these kinds of research findings together, overview reports (for example, NCH, 1992 and Openshaw *et al.*,1993) conclude that there appears to be a consistent finding that between about 25 and 33 per cent of all alleged sexual abuse involves young (mainly adolescent) perpetrators.

Development of sexually abusive behaviour

Whilst there has been research into the significant proportions of adult offenders who report the onset of arousal to children during childhood or adolescence and concern that adolescents who abuse may continue to do so into adulthood there has been relatively little consideration of why young people develop sexually abusive behaviour in the first place. The traumagenic model developed by Finkelhor and Brown (1986) on the dynamics of the effects of sexual abuse on children and young people gives some clue as to the mechanism by which some abused children go on to abuse others as part of their response to their own abusive experiences.

They suggest that as part of the *traumatic sexualisation* following abuse, inappropriate sexual behaviour and sexualised responses may be 'rewarded', either literally by the abuser, or psychologically or physiologically. Thus closeness, intimate relationships and power may become sexualised. The sense of *powerlessness* which may form part of the abuse can lead to a need to control or dominate events or people, and so lead to the re-enactment of the abusive behaviour itself in order to remediate the feelings associated with their own experiences. Feelings of *betrayal*, which may also be a consequence of the abuse, may diminish the ability to form appropriate relationships and may engender feelings of hostility and distrust and possibly a desire for retaliation. Finally *stigmatisation* resulting from abuse can further corrode the self-image and generate a sense of isolation which increases the effect of the other factors.

Additionally, Skuse *et al.* (1997) have identified factors which increase the risk of sexually abusive behaviour irrespective of early childhood experience of sexual victimisation: being a victim of physical violence; witnessing physical violence; discontinuity of care possibly compounded by rejection by their family, all contributing to a lack of experience of forming good enough attachments.

However, being abused is far from being a predictive factor in becoming abusive, and only around 50 per cent of young abusers have themselves experienced sexual victimisation (Bentovim and Williams, 1998). Other issues therefore also appear to be significant. Becker (1988) proposes a model which includes a broad range of factors which may contribute to the development of sexually abusive behaviour, at an *individual* level: social isolation; impulse conduct disorder; limited cognitive abilities and a history of physical and/or sexual abuse; *familial* factors: carers who engage in coercive sexual behaviour; family belief systems supportive of such behaviour and carers who have poor interpersonal skills and lack empathy; and *societal* factors: society which is supportive of coercive (male) sexual behaviour; society which supports the sexualisation of children and peer groups who behave in antisocial ways. The main theoretical frameworks currently influencing treatment models, which will be addressed later in this chapter, draw on aspects of these factors.

Characteristics of male adolescent sexual abusers

As the criminal statistics for 1997 (Home Office, 1998) suggest, reported young sexual offenders are predominately males in their middle to late teenage years. There are significant concerns about other groups of youngsters involved in sexually aggressive or abusive behaviour and an outline of their characteristics will be provided below. Initially, however, our focus will be on the largest category of young sexual abusers, adolescent males.

Despite the fact that most research into young sexual abusers has focused on adolescent males there are many aspects of this population which warrant further study. Existing studies are often flawed in that they do not adequately compare adolescent sexual abusers with either normal adolescents or, for example, with violent and non-violent delinquents. It is also not yet known whether young male sexual abusers can be subdivided into meaningful typologies, nor is it empirically established which of these adolescents are most at risk of continuing to commit sexual offences as adults.

Early thinking, as reported in the NCH Enquiry report (1992) and implicit in the central government guidance *Working Together* (DoH, 1991b), was that unlike other juvenile delinquents who typically grow out of their offending, young sexual abusers were more likely to continue in their abusive behaviour unless treated, preferably under some kind of civil or criminal legal mandate. More recent findings, largely based on North American studies, suggest, however, that the large majority of such adolescents do not progress into being adult abusers (ATSA, 1997). In a climate of scarce resources, an imperative must be to try and identify those factors which contribute to long-term sexual offending in order to target those youngsters most at risk of pursuing such a career. Chapter 12 on evaluation issues provides an overview of current research and knowledge about factors associated with long-term sexual offending.

However, based on existing studies a generalised pen picture of male adolescent sexual abusers and their offences can be developed. The victims of such offenders are usually younger by a number of years, are both male and female children and are usually known to the abuser as a sibling or through a babysitting relationship, although in cases of rape the abusers are less likely to know their victims. Although the full range of sexually abusive behaviours is perpetrated by such youngsters, Ryan and Lane (1997) suggest that:

> The modal offence scenario most likely involves a seven or eight-year-old victim, and more likely a female who is not related to the offender by blood or marriage. The behaviour is unwanted, involves genital touching and often penetration (over 60 per cent), and is accompanied by sufficient coercion or force to overcome the victim's resistance.
>
> (p. 7)

In terms of their characteristics young male sexual abusers seem to have a number of social skills deficits, often being socially isolated, lacking dating skills and sexual knowledge, and experiencing high levels of social anxiety (Shoor *et al.*, 1966; Becker and Abel, 1985; Fehrenbach *et al.*,1986; Awad and Saunders, 1989). Not surprisingly this lack of social competence often results in low self-esteem and emotional loneliness. It is worth bearing in mind, however, that low self-esteem may be a consequence of contemporary events, for example, being apprehended and punished, although for others it may be a problem which is long-standing and chronic. Thus Marshall (1989) has suggested that problems of early emotional attachment contribute to a failure to establish intimate relationships in later life and subsequent low self-esteem and emotional loneliness.

Graves (1993) found that about three-quarters of his study sample reported or were rated as lacking heterosexual (dating) confidence, experience and skills. In contrast, adolescents who assaulted peers or older victims were only half as likely to report similar problems. Problems of heterosexual competence may exist at a number of levels. Adolescents may, for a variety of reasons, be apprehensive about members of the opposite sex. This may be due to a lack of sexual knowledge (Crawford and Howells, 1982), feeling unattractive, and having expectations of ridicule or rejection. These problems may exist in addition to general social skills problems, for example in relation to initiating and maintaining conversations with peers they find attractive, and ensuring that sexual relationships are mutual and consenting. Homosexual youths may have additional problems associated with adjusting to and accepting their sexual orientation, anxiety about the reactions of family and friends, and the practicalities of finding homosexual friends.

Young male sexual abusers may well be doing poorly at school both in terms of behaviour and educational attainment (Kahn and Chambers, 1991) and like adult male sexual offenders relatively high proportions of them (between 25 per cent and 60 per cent, depending on the study cited) report having been victims of sexual abuse themselves (O'Callaghan and Print, 1994). A number of studies, therefore, also suggest that the families of such youngsters may have a number of difficulties in terms of their stability and intra-familial dynamics (Ryan and Lane, 1997). Most young adolescent male sexual abusers in treatment are white but this finding may, as with black adult sex offenders (Cowburn, 1996), reflect the racist bias inherent in the criminal justice and other systems which result in young black offenders being dealt with more punitively and having less access to treatment facilities.

Emerging groups

Female adolescent sexual abusers

In their overview of female youth who sexually abuse, Lane with Lobanov-Rostovsky (in Ryan and Lane, 1997) comment on the very disturbed backgrounds of the young female abusers with whom they have worked, noting high levels of both sexual and physical victimisation, problematic relationships with parents, family separation, problems at school and with peers in particular. However they also comment, 'Many of the developmental experiences are similar to those identified in the history of male youth, although they may be experienced differently by female youth based on gender, socialisation and role expectations' (p. 348).

They suggest that young female sexual abusers may well benefit from the same kinds of treatment approaches as young male sexual abusers although they comment that issues of autonomy and the consequences of female socialisation experiences may well be useful additional foci. Chapter 10 discusses in more detail the similarities and differences between male and female adolescent sexual abusers and one project's approach to work with these young women.

Pre-adolescent sexual abusers

As regards younger children, one of the earliest descriptions of sexually aggressive children in treatment (forty-seven boys aged 4–13 years) was provided by Johnson (1988). Of these boys, 49 per cent had themselves been sexually abused and 19 per cent physically abused by people they knew. The boys all knew the children they abused, in 46 per cent of cases the victim was a sibling and 18 per cent were members of the extended family. Compared to adolescent sexual abusers it appeared that these sexually aggressive children used less coercion and more enticement to secure the compliance of their victims. The mean age of the boys at the time of their sexually aggressive behaviour was 8 years 9 months; the mean age of their victims 6 years 9 months. There was a history of sexual and physical abuse in the majority of the families of the boys, as well as a history of substance abuse.

In one of the few studies of female sexually aggressive children, also by Johnson (1989), it was found that all of the sample of thirteen girls (aged 4 to 12 years, with a mean age of 7.5) who were in treatment had been subjected to prior sexual victimisation of a serious nature, often with close relatives, and had usually received little support and

6

validation from other family members when they had disclosed their abuse. Also 31 per cent had been physically abused. All had used force or coercion to gain the compliance of their victims and 77 per cent had chosen victims in the family. The mean age of their first known sexually aggressive behaviour was 6 years 9 months and the average age of their victims was 4 years 4 months.

In a larger, more recent study of 287 sexually aggressive children aged 12 years and under (Burton *et al.*, 1997) 79 per cent of the children were male and 21 per cent were female, with the average child living in a two-parent home. In 70 per cent of their families at least one care-taker was chemically dependent; 48 per cent had at least one parent known to have been sexually abused; and 72 per cent of the children were sexually abused themselves (60 per cent by a carer). The children with known sexual abuse histories were younger at the first sign of sexual aggression than those without known sexual abuse histories. Lane with Lobanov-Rostovsky (in Ryan and Lane, 1997) have surveyed the issues and concerns raised by young children with sexually aggressive behaviour problems. They have worked with some 100 young children whom they divided into two treatment groups (7–9 years and 10–12 years). The majority of these children were male and two-thirds were white. Nearly half of the children were living at home at the point of referral and over two-thirds had a history of sexual, physical or emotional victimisation or abandonment experiences. One third exhibited psychiatric, learning or medical problems and about a quarter had been involved in what would be considered other delinquent activity if they were older. The treatment approach they adopted was eclectic, drawing on a modified version of the abuse cycle concept outlined later in this chapter, complemented with work on the children's own child-hood traumas and involving collaborative work with family and other caretakers.

The authors of Chapter 11 describe a somewhat similar treatment approach in a UK context, based on cognitive development theory, in their 'Stop and Think' group for young children exhibiting sexually aggressive behaviour.

Young abusers with learning difficulties

Lane with Lobanov-Rostovsky (in Ryan and Lane, 1997) comment in relation to this group:

> Clinical observation indicates numerous similarities but also
> some unique differences between sexually abusive behaviour

of disabled and non-disabled youth. The range of behaviours, the types of sexually abusive behaviours, and the elements of the behaviour appear similar, while the associated cognitive processes, the context of the behaviours and the level of sophistication exhibit some differences

(p. 342)

What little research has been undertaken seems to suggest that there may be a more repetitive, habitual quality to the behaviour of these youngsters in terms of victim choice, location and frequency of behaviour, they may have greater difficulty understanding the abusive nature of their activities and may justify what they've done against what they perceive to be normal male behaviour. They may also exhibit more impulsivity and a more childlike need for immediate gratification. Stermac and Sheridan (1993) suggest that they are significantly more likely to display inappropriate, non-assaultive 'nuisance' behaviours such as public masturbation, exhibitionism and voyeurism and that they are less discriminating in their choice of victim, choosing male and female victims equally. Their behaviour also has to be understood in the context of societal prejudice towards such disability, a general lack of attention paid to issues of sexuality in relation to this group and their increased vulnerability to being the victims of sexual abuse themselves. Clearly management and treatment of these young people have to be planned in the light of careful assessment of their cognitive and social functioning so that, for example, treatment delivery attends to issues such as shortened attention spans, more experiential styles of learning and the need for careful use of language and repetition of messages.

Rationale and philosophy for involvement and intervention with children and young people who sexually abuse

It is important that the rationale and philosophy which underlies our understanding of, and involvement with, young people who sexually abuse others is clear. The list which follows is adapted from a NOTA (National Organisation for the Treatment of Abusers) briefing prepared in 1995 by Tony Morrison and Bobbie Print, both contributors to this book. The phrase 'young people' is used here to denote both children and adolescents unless otherwise specified:

- Sexual abuse by young people accounts for a significant proportion of all sexual offending;
- It is harmful to victims;
- It involves the misuse of power and breaching of the victim's informed consent by the abuser for his/her psychological and sexual gratification;
- The causes of sexual abuse by young people are multi-factorial involving socio-cultural, environmental, familial, inter-personal and developmental elements. These are unique in each case;
- Adolescent sexual abuse is reinforced by low esteem, poor social skills, distorted thinking, sexual fantasy and masturbation. Sexual behaviour is learned;
- Intervention needs to be based on an accountability approach, recognising that all sexual abuse is unacceptable and when committed by adolescents is also illegal;
- Children and adolescent sexual abusers are children and adolescents who sexually abuse and not sexual abusers who happen to be children and adolescents;
- The overarching goals of intervention are:

    - The protection of victims
    - The prevention of further offences
    - The development of self-control

- No single agency can manage young people who sexually abuse. Child protection, child welfare and criminal justice agencies need to collaborate;
- Intervention must recognise the young person in his/her total context, in particular the role of families;
- Young people who sexually abuse may be of either gender, any race, culture, class, sexual orientation and learning ability. The position of an abuser as a member of an oppressed group does not take away from his/her individual responsibility for the abuse;
- Oppression is always a block to effective intervention. However, work with young people who sexually abuse which leaves victims vulnerable and risk factors unchallenged can never be anti-oppressive. The opposite of oppression is not collusion;
- Adolescent sexual abusers are unlikely to engage in treatment unless there are significant negative consequences for them not doing so;
- Intervention should be at the least invasive level commensurate with the protection of actual or potential victims.

Theoretical frameworks

As has already been stated, sexual offending is largely perpetrated by males and any explanation of such offending has to be considered within a context of much larger, unreported rates of 'normal' male sexual aggression against females. Kelly *et al.* (1992) argue that research on convicted offenders and theories of behaviour emerging from a clinical focus have tended to maintain the dominance of the medical/pathology perspective in relation to particular individuals. In doing so they fail to address social constructions of masculinity and prevalent societal attitudes and beliefs which condone or justify sexual violence against female adults and children which, if changed, would result in the transformation of family power relations. Whilst acknowledging the importance of developing this much broader perspective our analysis focuses on existing theories and models of treatment for addressing sexually abusive behaviour.

Key models of sexually abusive behaviour

During the early 1980s models were developed in North America which have remained extremely influential in the UK in understanding sexually abusive behaviour. The two most widespread and commonly used models for understanding sexually abusive behaviour in adolescents are the four-preconditions model developed by David Finkelhor (1984) and the sexual abuse cycle developed by Lane and Zamora (1982, 1984) and subsequently developed further by Sandy Lane (1991,1997). This section will review those models and outline some of the key concepts that both assist in understanding sexually abusive behaviour and are usually components of a treatment programme.

Finkelhor's four preconditions model

A researcher and academic, Finkelhor was seeking a comprehensive theory that addressed the range of knowledge about sexual abusers without being specific to a particular school of thought. He proposed a model which related primarily to adult male abusers but which is frequently adapted in practice for use with adolescents (see figure 1.1).

In summary the model suggests four *preconditions* which must be met before sexual abuse can occur. The potential abuser needs to:

1   Have some *motivation* to abuse – this may be because the victim meets some important emotional need and/or sexual contact with

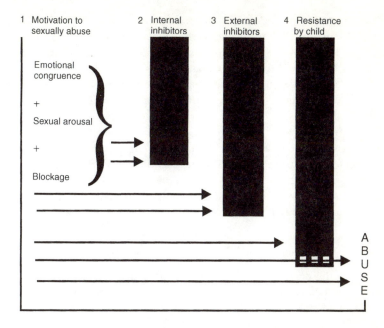

Figure 1.1 Finkelhor's four preconditions model of sexually abusive behaviour
Source: (Finkelhor, 1984)

the victim is sexually gratifying and/or other sources of sexual gratification are not available or are less satisfying;

2   Overcome any *internal inhibitions* against acting on that motivation – commonly this is by way of 'cognitive distortions', self-serving distortions of attitude and belief, whereby the victim, either individually or as a 'category' comes to be seen as in some way consenting to or responsible for their own abuse.

3   Overcome *external inhibitors* to committing sexual abuse – gaining the opportunity to have access to the potential victim in an environment where the abuse is possible. In the case of child victims this may relate to the supervision the child receives from others. Those interested in pursuing further the issue of non-abusing carers and their significance as deterrents to abuse are recommended to Gerrilyn Smith's chapter 'Parent, partner, protector', in Smith, 1994, which includes an adaptation of the four preconditions model and to the current authors' own description of running groupwork programmes for mothers of sexually abused children (Masson and Erooga, 1989);

4   Overcome or undermine a *victim's possible resistance* to the abuse. Writing in relation to child victims Finkelhor emphasises this is not an issue to be regarded simplistically but may relate to a complex set of factors involving personality traits which inhibit the targeting of a particular child as well as more straightforward resistance to the abuse itself. These concepts are equally applicable to peer or adult victims.

What can be seen, therefore, is that there are a number of potential barriers to abuse, the first two relating to the abuser and the third and fourth relating to factors external to the abuser. The model offers a way of beginning to understand something of the dynamics of the abuser as well as the abuse process, also a feature of the cycle model.

Compulsive behaviour cycles of sexual abuse

Prior to the development of models of compulsive sexual offending in the early 1980s a common view of such behaviour was that it resulted from uncontrollable urges. Practice experience with adolescents (Lane and Zamora, 1982, 1984) led to the development of the concept of sexual abuse cycles involving dysfunctional responses to problematic situations or interactions. In these models responses are based on distorted perceptions relating to power and control which then become sexualised. This framework is now regarded as generally applicable irrespective of age or intellectual or developmental functioning and is reported to be in use, with appropriate adaptations to meet individual circumstances or need, in the majority of treatment programmes (Lane, 1997).

This widespread use of the concept both for young people and a separate but similar model independently developed for adults (Wolf, 1984) clearly indicate the intuitive and practice-based appeal of this concept for exploring and understanding patterns of sexually abusive behaviour – a tool which is experienced as helpful both to those trying to understand and change their behaviour and those trying to help them to do so. However, the question of the validity of the model has yet to be firmly established. Lane (1997) reports that whilst not entirely empirically validated, research has begun to confirm various elements of the cycle concept, most recently the link between negative affective states and deviant sexual fantasy.

The sexual abuse cycle for adolescents (Lane, 1997) represents cognitive and behavioural progressions prior to, during and after sexually abusive behaviour. When applied to an individual, the details of the components of the cycle will vary, but common elements of the overall pattern are still apparent, with common abusive behaviour patterns, types of gratification and styles of thinking which support the behaviour.

However, in using the model it should be noted that it describes a process of events, not a causal representation. It is represented cyclically because of the repetitive compulsive nature of the behaviour sequence and because of indications that previous offence incidents often parallel and reinforce the subsequent offence pattern.

As shown diagrammatically in figure 1.2, the young person's life experiences, outlook and beliefs predispose them to respond to an event, interaction or problem with feelings of helplessness (the event), experienced as stressful and now anticipated as unsafe (negative anticipation). Feelings of hopelessness are accompanied by a desire to avoid the issue, the feelings and the anticipated outcomes (avoidance). Not being successful in this leads to feelings of resentment and defensiveness and attempts to exert power over others in a non-sexual way as compensation (power/control). Whilst effective, the duration of the effect is temporary, leading to thinking about further power-based behaviours and other behaviours which might feel good, such as sex (fantasy). The exertion of control or dominance is eventually expressed sexually (sexual abuse). There is then a need to cope with the knowledge of the behaviour and fear of external consequences of being caught (fugitive thinking). Inability to tolerate this anxiety or discomfort leads

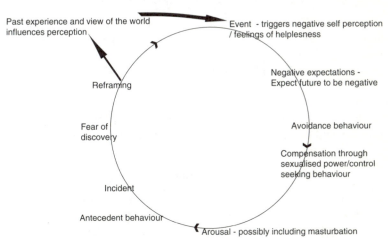

Figure 1.2 The sexual abuse cycle

Source: (Lane, 1997)

subsequently to the behaviour becoming assimilated through a series of cognitive distortions or 'thinking errors'. The cycle therefore represents a series of maladaptive coping mechanisms that temporarily alleviate discomfort but do not resolve the problem.

Progression through the cycle is not necessarily consistent, thus an individual will seldom progress through the whole cycle a step at time, nor will each trigger of the cycle lead to a sexual offence. Lane describes interruptions or delays in the cycle as plateaux, suggesting that in response to repeated triggers the young person may progress to the same plateau several times, not moving on to the next until the current one is not effective in relieving anxiety or countering negative self-perception. She points out that whilst the stress may seem to dissipate temporarily, in fact it accumulates over time. The rate of progression will also vary, though it does appear that the more frequently the maladaptive response pattern is used, the faster the rate of progression becomes. Thus the more habituated to the use of the cycle the lower the individual's tolerance to precipitating events or problems and the further into the cycle the progression of the initial response. An assessment implication may therefore be that the speed of progression may be indicative of the length of time the maladaptive behaviour patterns have been used, though this is not synonymous with the length of time that abusive behaviour has been perpetrated.

Treatment issues

The treatment implications of the models will be apparent. By becoming aware of their pattern of thinking, and emotional and behavioural responses through use of the cycle model, the young person can then consciously develop other methods of coping with stress or abusive stimuli and thus decrease the likelihood of further abusive behaviour.

In coming to understand sexually abusive behaviour, however, a number of other issues need to be understood as contributing to the problem and addressed as part of a programme of intervention.

Minimisation, denial and projection of blame

Inasmuch as the offending behaviour itself is a dysfunctional response which serves to avoid emotional discomfort so minimisation and denial of the existence of a problem or, at the point of detection that the behaviour occurred at all, is a logical response. Denial is a dynamic, rather than a static state, thus the nature and level of denial is likely to change with the anticipated consequences, emotional and external, of being disclosive. Similarly, there is not a single phenomenon which can be labelled denial, rather there is a continuum of minimisation or denial on which the young person may place themselves at various times. Thus the response may range from outright denial of the abusive act(s) through denial of responsibility for the behaviour: 'I was drunk'; denial of intent: 'I just got carried away'; to minimisation of harm or seriousness: 'It wasn't anything bad I did'.

Cognitive distortions

Distorted cognitions, also described as thinking errors, refer to pro-offending beliefs or attitudes that justify, rationalise or support the sexually abusive behaviour. They commonly distort the role of their victim in the abuse, portraying them as in some way responsible for encouraging or initiating sexual contact.

> Some ... support a ... belief in the victim's willingness or need to engage in the sexually abusive behaviour, some shape the perception of the victim as obligated to meet the needs of the perpetrator, some construe the (abusing) behaviour as helpful and still others allow the youth to objectify or depersonalise the victim.
>
> (Lane, 1997, p. 89)

They may also serve to reassure the abuser that they have done nothing wrong and certainly not something harmful. Typical examples would be:

- She must have wanted to – she never said no.
- I liked it when it happened to me.
- I did no more than what happened to me.
- I wouldn't have forced him but he didn't try and stop me so it was OK.
- I paid for her Coke so she owes me.
- Women are all the same and I know what they want.

Once again, whilst the patterns of distortion may be common to many abusers the specific details will vary according to individual experience and personality, though clues to individual distortions may be heard in explanations offered by the abuser 'I knew he wanted to by the way he looked at me' or echoed by victims in their statements 'he said he was only doing it because he loved me'.

Deviant sexual arousal

The first of the Finkelhor preconditions *motivation to sexually abuse* may relate to deviant sexual arousal for some individuals. Whilst this is an important factor in consideration of adult sex offenders, this is less well established in adolescents. Hunter *et al.* (1991) found less correlation between adolescent sexual offenders' measured sexual arousal and their offence histories than has been reported in the literature on adult offenders, and cautioned against interpreting adolescent sexual arousal patterns in the same way as one might interpret adult data. Nevertheless, it is likely that as research progresses, the presence of deviant arousal to children or to non-consenting sex will emerge as an important factor in work with adolescent abusers.

Victim empathy and victim awareness

For many offenders a lack of empathy with the experience of their victims will be an important element in becoming sufficiently disinhibited to abuse and there is therefore a significant relationship between lack of victim empathy and cognitive distortions, as it is the latter which contributes to the absence of understanding, cognitively and emotionally, of the impact of their abusive behaviour. The two main components of victim empathy training focus upon developing the client's intellectual appreciation of the impact of sexual abuse and applying this to their own victim, and, secondly developing their capacity for emotional sensitivity and responsiveness to victim distress (Beckett, 1994a).

Whereas victim awareness is an intellectual process of understanding, victim empathy describes the emotional connection with the victim experience. It is important not to confuse the two, as whilst awareness may soon be learned, there may be considerable emotional investment on the offender's part to resist making the more difficult connection. These separate aspects may be most effectively addressed in different ways. Awareness may require a didactic approach whereas empathy may be best achieved through experiential techniques.

Rape prone attitudes and beliefs

Studies of adult rapists and violent men have identified certain attitudes and beliefs associated with both sexual and general violence. Groth's (1979) study on rapists emphasised the role of hostility towards women as both a motivator and disinhibitor for rape. Burt (1980) suggested that individuals who endorse 'rape myths' and have sexual beliefs and attitudes which endorse the use of violence against women are also more prone to rape behaviour. Whilst this research has not been replicated with adolescents these attitudes are likely to inform rape behaviour in young people.

Relapse prevention

Whilst avoiding relapse is a goal of intervention from the outset, the young person's active participation in that process can increase as their understanding of their own process increases. When an offender understands his own cycle, he should then be able to share this knowledge with relevant others, by developing his own alert checklist (North West Treatment Associates, 1988). To do so requires a high level of accountability for thinking and personal choices, recognising internal and external high-risk factors (Ryan and Lane, 1997). He needs to understand all aspects of his cycle and the implications for his feelings, thoughts and behaviour, as well as the relevant implications for his victim and his partner at the time. He should be helped to develop a relapse prevention plan with identified triggers, danger situations and strategies to cope with these prior to concluding any programme of intervention. Pithers and Gray (1996) have suggested that motivation to learn and use relapse prevention strategies increases once victim awareness and empathy work has been completed.

Conclusion

From the above it will be appreciated that whilst sexually aggressive behaviour is experienced by both those who commit it and those who encounter it as confusing and disturbing, during recent years we have made considerable progress in coming to understand the extent of such abusive behaviour, those most at risk of perpetrating it, the dynamics which lead to the behaviour and enable its progression; and ways of responding effectively. The chapters which follow are intended to address these issues further by considering the contexts which are needed for effective responses, both in legislation and policy and more specifically in terms of placement and intervention; assessment issues; treatment approaches within individual and group settings as well as work with families; specific issues in work with young women and children who abuse; evaluation strategies and empowerment issues for workers.

The 1990s have seen progress in this area of work that few expected ten years ago. It is hoped that by use of the knowledge and expertise reflected in this volume sexual abuse by children and young people can be identified, managed and treated more effectively and the endless ripples of distress and suffering it causes can thereby diminish.

2

'IS THERE A STRATEGY OUT THERE?'

Policy and management perspectives on young people who sexually abuse others

Tony Morrison

Introduction

In a recent workshop for practitioners, participants were asked to depict their experience of working with young people who sexually abuse by making a physical model using a range of craft materials. One model comprised a small figure, the worker, walking on a high wire between two parapets, balanced only by a wide pole. Behind her, waiting to take their turn to attempt this high wire act, were several more workers, on the ground prowling around underneath was a bear. Several of the other presentations used wild animals or monsters to depict a sense of danger and threat. In contrast workers were typically represented by small, isolated figures, in one case, simply by a small piece of blue tac. Another group introduced their presentation by throwing a 'hot potato' around.

These images left a powerful impression. Whilst the reality may be more differentiated, with some workers operating in more supportive and better organised environments, for a significant number these pictures represent an accurate portrayal of their experiences of isolation, anxiety, fear, disempowerment and deskilling. Few if any of the models created included a supportive manager or supervisor. Despite these difficulties, workers across the country are striving to address the problems of this population of young people and children who sexually abuse other children.

This chapter seeks to provide an overview, in so far as available information allows, of the current state of development of work with young people who sexually abuse. It takes as its starting point the National Children's Homes (NCH) Report (1992) into children and young people who sexually abuse and asks how far things have progressed since then. The chapter considers:

- the principal findings and recommendations of the NCH report;
- issues concerning philosophy of intervention;
- issues concerning policy and co-ordination, with particular reference to the Crime and Disorder Act 1998;
- current levels of service provision, and issues in service delivery;
- strategic imperatives in this area of work.

Size of the problem: the need for intervention

Chapter 1 indicated that criminal statistics represent only a proportion of the sexual abuse committed by young people and children. Researchers have estimated that between a third and a quarter of child sexual abuse is committed by young people under 18 years (Horne *et al.*, 1991; Kelly *et al.*, 1991; N. Ireland Research Team, 1991).

On 31 March 1994 there were 10,071 children on child protection registers because of sexual abuse in England and Wales (Department of Health (DoH), 1995a). Dividing that by a quarter suggests that some 2,500 children would have been abused by someone under 18. However, as the British Crime Survey (1988) shows, sexual assaults are grossly under-reported. In 1988 only one in six assaults was reported. If, therefore the 1994 child protection figures were then multiplied by six it would suggest that over 10,000 children were sexually abused by a young person or a child in 1994.

Abel *et al.* (1985) found that half of adult sex offenders reported the onset of sexual offending in their adolescence. Taking this as a guide, we can apply it to Marshall's estimate that in the UK in 1993 there were at least 260,000 men aged 20 or over who had been convicted of a sexual offence (1996). This would mean that approximately 130,000 men in 1993 had committed sexual offences in their adolescence. It is thus clear that the contribution of young people to the sum total of sexual abuse is considerable.

NCH and Department of Health Reports in 1992: establishing a baseline

Published in 1992, the NCH Report provided the first comprehensive picture of how young abusers were being managed in the UK. It painted a gloomy picture of:

- conflicts over definitions of juvenile sexual abuse;
- a lack of a co-ordinated management structure with agencies frequently intervening without reference to others and decisions often made about disposal without the involvement of professionals experienced in sexual abuse work;
- an absence of policy and uncertainty about the legitimacy of the work;
- clashes of philosophy especially between juvenile justice and child protection approaches;
- inadequate data about the nature, scope and effects of the problem;
- an absence of internal and inter-agency policy and practice guidance;
- a lack of clarity about assessment and intervention models;
- an absence of services for young abusers;
- placement problems and risks arising from victims and abusers being placed in the same accommodation;
- inadequate supervision and training;
- alienation for front-line workers trying to tackle the problem.

The report concluded that:

> uncertainty about the legitimacy of the work, and the complex consequences of denial combine to create great pressure on staff who can easily be made to feel scapegoats. Management denial of the need to work with young abusers can leave staff isolated, and unclear whether or not this is a legitimate area for them to be involved in.
>
> (p. 27)

It also suggested that ignorance, denial, fear, minimisation and collusion about the problem existed in all agencies, at all levels of management, within the legal profession and within society in general.

The report's recommendations were that:

- an overall systematic approach should be developed;
- agencies should define their areas of responsibility;
- inter-agency policies and communication should be established;
- the work be placed within the scope of Area Child Protection Committees (ACPCs) and that annual reports should comment specifically on progress;
- the work be located within the child protection system;

- police and social service departments should jointly investigate such cases;
- separate case conferences for the victim and the young abuser should be held;
- abusers should not be placed in foster care with younger children;
- a continuum of care services ranging from local/community to secure/regional therapeutic facilities should be developed;
- national good practice guidance should be developed through government departments;
- an integrated training strategy be devised, including a strategy for increasing the number of skilled supervisors for this area of work;
- further research should be conducted to explore incidence, causality and intervention.

Department of Health Strategic Statement 1992

The other important document issued in 1992 was the Government's Inter-Departmental Group on Child Abuse Strategic Statement on Working with Abusers (DoH, 1992). This stated that: 'adolescent abusers are themselves in need of services because evidence suggests that appropriate and early intervention will bring abusive behaviour under control' (p. 2).

The strategic objectives, which were to be implemented at a local level via ACPCs, were listed as:

- formulating a coherent policy for the management and treatment of abusers;
- building a better understanding of abusers;
- viewing sexual abuse as a problem requiring assessment and treatment both for the abuser and the victim;
- promoting a multi-disciplinary approach to the problem;
- encouraging local and national resources, in recognition of the high demands of the work;
- educating both the public and professionals about this problem.

Work was to be firmly located within the child protection system and the primary objective of intervention was to, 'seek to prevent suspected or known abusers from harming potential victims' (p. 4). So the stage was set, the problem had been officially identified and an outline policy framework at a national level had been established.

Progress since 1992

Fine words and reports are not enough, however, as the practitioners' presentations described at the beginning of this chapter illustrate. Unfortunately the absence of any systematic data base, and the paucity of national research make it hard to provide a clear national picture of what has happened since 1992. None the less it is possible to piece together enough to provide an overview under three main headings: philosophy of intervention; policy and co-ordination; provision of service.

Philosophy of intervention

Despite the government's clear statement that the management of these young people should fall within the child protection system, there remain tensions between and within professional groups as to how the problem should be defined and over philosophies of intervention. Whilst there has been a growing recognition that some form of intervention is required, significant debates exist over questions surrounding whether the young person is seen as victim or perpetrator; the need for mandatory intervention or not; the degree to which juvenile abusers can be held responsible for their own behaviour; the extent to which the young person or child understands his or her sexuality; the likelihood he or she will grow out of the abusive behaviour; and the need to treat or to punish.

These issues have been explored by Sanders and Ladwa-Thomas (1997) in a survey of the attitudes of fifty practitioners from three social work settings (child protection, children and families, and youth justice), probation officers and police in one Welsh authority. The greatest diversity of opinion was on views as to whether juvenile abusers should be seen as victims rather than perpetrators. Child protection specialists felt they should be seen as victims, in contrast to youth justice workers and police officers who felt they should be seen as offenders. The police sample in particular was much less inclined than the other groups to regard this group as 'children in need'. Another difference was over the question as to whether a register of young abusers would be useful, with child protection and children and family social workers being strongly opposed, in contrast to police respondents who were strongly in favour, and youth justice and probation staff who were somewhat in favour.

Despite these areas of disagreement, Sanders and Ladwa-Thomas concluded that: 'most social work agencies have much in common so there are no major obstacles to overcome in collaborating over work with young abusers ... police staff were most frequently at odds with the other agencies' (p. 270). Secondly they concluded that the other area of potential difficulty was between interventionist and diversionary approaches. These tensions have wider significance in the light of other changes currently unfolding which include:

- the refocusing of child protection systems;
- the current consultation process (DoH, 1998) in relation to the revision of existing guidance on inter-agency working in child protection contained in *Working Together* (Department of Health, 1991b);
- the Sex Offenders Act, 1997;
- the Crime and Disorder Act's provisions for the future prevention and management of youth crime (HMSO, 1998).

Each of these developments will be explored and their implications for the management of juvenile sexual abusers.

Refocusing of child protection work

This has its roots in the publication of *Messages from Research* (DoH, 1995b) which summarised the findings of twenty research programmes commissioned following the Cleveland crisis (Cleveland Inquiry, 1988). Amongst its conclusions was the view that too many children and families were being unnecessarily caught up in the child protection process, causing stress to those families and alienation from services. The gradual process of net-widening in the child protection system was, it suggested, in need of reversal in order to divert families not presenting significant risk of harm, out of the system, so as to address their needs in a less invasive and less formalised manner. The key to this was a philosophical shift that would see such children as primarily 'children in need' under the Children Act, 1989, rather than 'children at risk'. Although social services departments and Area Child Protection Committees (ACPCs) have responded to the initiative in a very unsystematic and disparate manner, overall it has resulted in an increased emphasis on diversionary approaches.

Consultation paper on working together to safeguard children

Whilst the consultation paper (DoH, 1998) endorses the need to avoid drawing families into the child protection system unnecessarily it confirms the view that: 'handling juvenile sexual abuse cases within ACPC procedures will continue to provide the most effective way of tackling the problem' (para. 5.17).

However, it also invites discussion on whether, and when, juvenile sexual abusers should be subject to a child protection case conference or placed on a child protection register. It does, however, state that juvenile abusers should be the subject of a written inter-agency plan.

This wording suggests then that professionals will be left to decide whether such cases should be managed through the child protection case conference process or diverted into some other form of Section 17 inter-agency case planning process. Finally the document states the need for new guidance in order to address the inter-relationship between child protection and the new criminal justice processes for youth crime contained within the 1998 Crime and Disorder Act.

The Sex Offenders Act 1997

The aim of this Act is to increase the ability of criminal justice agencies to monitor and share information on sexual offenders, and by doing so to develop more effective risk management plans in order to prevent re-offending. Indeed the Act is based on the premise of the high risk of recidivism in adult sex offenders. In some cases the Act has already resulted in the use of intensive surveillance and other methods to prevent the offender having access to potential victims.

The Act places a requirement on all adults and juveniles, convicted or cautioned for certain sexual offences, to register with the police within fourteen days:

- their names, and any other names they use;
- their address, and any subsequent change of address;
- their date of birth.

The Act applies to all those convicted or cautioned from the date of its implementation and to all those who, at that point, were under the supervision of criminal justice agencies, or in custody for a specified sexual offence. The length of registration depends on the nature of the original sentence, varying from five years for a caution, to life for sentences of thirty months or more, or if committed to hospital under a restriction order.

The only distinction made for juvenile offenders is that their registration periods are half the length of those aged over 18 years, and that there is a duty of notification on their parent or guardian. Discussions are currently in progress about the need for further consideration about the application of the Act to juveniles. For example, the wide geographical variation in cautioning and prosecution practice will result in very inconsistent patterns of registration. Overall, based on the 1997 crime statistics (Home Office, 1998), had the Act been implemented then it would have resulted in 700 young people between 10 and 17 being cautioned for sexual offences, and 400 who were convicted, being registered.

The Act also enables, but does not require, the police to disclose their information about a sexual offender to third parties, mainly other professionals in criminal justice and child protection settings, but also potentially to members of the public. This provision for disclosure is linked to the police making a risk assessment to determine when and to whom any disclosure will be made. In many authorities, the process of disclosure has been formalised through inter-agency protocols providing for the convening of risk management panels, either by the police or probation services.

In the case of juveniles the likely response of parents to registration requirements, and potentially to any suggestion that there might be public disclosure will be critical. In a recent case the family of a 15-year-old boy in a groupwork programme was subject to an attempted arson attack on their home when neighbours discovered what he had done and they eventually had to move out of the neighbourhood. If the registration system serves to increase the apprehensions and resistance of parents to engage in treatment work because they feel it is they, as much as their child, who are being 'blamed', then the Act's potential gains will have been more than outweighed by the alienation of the group most critical to the monitoring and management of juvenile offenders, their parents. This is not to suggest that registration is not appropriate for some juveniles, but that such decisions should be made on a case-by-case basis, through a process of multi-disciplinary decision-making.

The Sex Offenders Act 1997, and its lack of flexibility in the case of juveniles, demonstrates the way in which interventionist philosophies and research with adult sex offenders permeate criminal justice approaches to juveniles. In doing so the Act fails to recognise that juvenile offenders are 'children in need' under the 1989 Children Act, not just offenders, and in many cases are also victims of harm themselves. More recently professionals in North America have become concerned that assumptions about adult recidivism should not be used to guide legislative policy with juvenile offenders. In 1997 the Association for the Treatment of Sexual Abusers (ATSA) issued a position paper on the legal management of juvenile sexual offenders which argued for a careful balancing of criminal justice and rehabilitative elements, appreciating the differences between adult and juvenile offenders:

> Recent research suggests that there are important distinctions between juvenile and adult sexual offenders, as well as finding out that not all juvenile sexual offenders are the same. There is little evidence to support the assumption that the majority of juvenile sexual offenders are destined to become adult sexual offenders, or that these youths engage in acts of sexual penetration for the same reasons as their adult counterparts.
>
> (ATSA, 1997, p. 1)

The workings of the Sex Offender Act 1997 with regard to juveniles may then increase the potential professional tensions identified earlier between criminal justice and social work philosophies of intervention.

The Crime and Disorder Act 1998

This Act had its origins in research by the Audit Commission on youth crime and its management (Audit Commission, 1998). Significantly there was no mention of juvenile sex offenders in this report, although these young people will be affected by the Act, as are all professionals working with them. Discussion here will be confined to the implications of the Act for juvenile sexual abusers, but it is worth stating its broader intentions as expressed in the summary to the White Paper *No More Excuses* (Home Office, 1998b). This recommended the development of a clear strategy to prevent offending and re-offending; that offenders and their parents face up to their offending behaviour, and its effects on families, victims and communities; that offenders take responsibility for their behaviour; that earlier, more effective intervention when young people first offend should be developed, with the aim of helping young people develop a sense of personal responsibility; faster, more efficient procedures from arrest to sentence; and partnerships between all youth justice agencies to deliver a better, faster system.

The Act's effects will therefore be a move away from well-established diversionary approaches to youth crime and a return to a more interventionist, and net-widening approach, particularly in terms of crime prevention work (Hibbert, personal communication, 1998). Thus the Act includes child safety orders and child curfew orders which can target children under the age of 10. Cautions are replaced by reprimands and final warnings, the latter of which can trigger services from the new youth offending teams (YOTS).

The emphasis on accountability and personal responsibility is also clear from the title: *No More Excuses*. This is reflected in a range of new sentencing provisions including:

- re-sentencing for an original offence on breach of a supervision order and allowing courts a full range of sentencing disposals;
- reparation orders through which offenders will be expected to undertake specific reparation to their victims, including a supervised meeting with the victim;
- action plan orders – short-term task focused orders;
- parenting orders which require parents to attend a number of specified sessions aimed at improving their parenting skills.

Finally Clause 2 of the Act makes provision for the police to seek sex offender orders on convicted sex offenders whose behaviour demonstrates a risk of re-offending, and to obtain a civil injunction to monitor and restrain the offender's movements. It also provides for extended sentences to be imposed on sexually violent offenders. Once again, although these last two sex offender provisions are aimed at adults, they have the potential to affect juvenile sexual offenders.

Looking at the overall philosophy of the Act, there are elements which fit comfortably into existing approaches to juveniles who commit sexual offences, for instance the emphasis on responsibility, awareness of consequences for the victim, and a new form of cautioning which can trigger service provision. Indeed the move away from a diversionary approach with juvenile sex offenders has become quite a well-established principle.

However, few new resources are to be released to implement the wide ranging nature of this Act, with the main changes in delivery of services being effected through the establishment of youth offending teams, discussed below. The question of resources may therefore block some of the potentially beneficial provisions of the forthcoming Act for juvenile sexual offenders.

In summary young abusers are being managed in a context in which there are growing ideological strains, at least at a national policy level, between welfare approaches based on the 'child in need' concept, and criminal justice approaches based on an accountability principle. Added importance is given to this debate because of the growing body of research which emphasises the role of early attachment deficits, problems of self-esteem, and the capacity for empathy in the aetiology of sexually abusive behaviour by juveniles (Barbaree *et al.*, 1998; Ryan, 1998). In other words research is pointing more and more to the necessity of understanding abusive behaviour in the context of early life and family experiences.

Moreover given that the vast majority of juvenile sexual offences are not the subject of a criminal investigation, let alone cautioning or prosecution, the likely result is the development of an increasingly double-track approach, dependent on whether cases enter child protection/child in need, or criminal justice/offender-orientated systems. This will have consequences not only for how the behaviour is regarded, but also for its management and the type of services that are considered appropriate. Government guidance will be crucial in seeking to reconcile these different pathways within an ideologically coherent framework for intervention.

Policy and co-ordination

Helen Masson's important research (1997) in this area has certainly indicated some progress in terms of policy development. The research indicated that by 1994 of 106 ACPCs surveyed, 20 per cent had drawn up inter-agency procedures whilst a further 44 per cent had working parties working on the issue. Different models were identified designed to integrate child protection and youth justice approaches. Indeed there have been some very good examples of local policy development (STRATA, 1997). However, it is salutary to note the contrast with policies in respect of adult sex offenders. ACOP's survey of probation services in 1995 (ACOP, 1996) revealed that 98 per cent had strategies for the management of adult sex offenders. One explanation for this difference lies in the fact that probation services are clearly lead agencies with regard to the management of adult sex offenders. The question of who is/are the lead agencies in relation to the management of juvenile sexual abusers remains a major unanswered question.

Whilst welcoming such ACPC policy developments as there have been, it is worth asking how many of these inter-agency procedures constitute a commitment to service delivery, and resources as opposed to agreements simply about the need to work together? For example, an experienced primary school teacher sought consultation about the following circumstances:

> The distraught mother of a 5-year-old boy in her class reported that her son, Ash, had told her that two older boys in the school had on several occasions had oral sex with her son. The mother had tried to report this, without

> obtaining any response, to the local social services depart-
> ment, the police and a voluntary agency. Her concern
> was heightened because the summer holidays were
> imminent and the two boys, who were alleged to be
> responsible, lived only a few houses away from her.
> When the teacher had raised the issue with her head-
> teacher, who carried the designated child protection role,
> he advised her not to pursue the matter as her job was
> to teach!

Sadly this occurred in an area in which the ACPC had only recently issued new guidelines for the management of juvenile sexual abusers.

As the case example illustrates, the road from policy to practice is a long and winding one. It also illustrates that *multi-disciplinary* work where committed individuals from different disciplines work together is not enough. What is crucial is *inter-agency* collaboration, where *organisations* work together. How many inter-agency committees or task groups for young abuser projects in fact bring together interested individuals rather than committed agencies?

Galvanising this organisational level of commitment is not easy. The role of ACPCs in placing and holding this issue on the agenda is crucial, and they have played an important role in instigating a number of service developments. However, as a non-executive and non-operational body ACPCs cannot be expected to carry this work alone, without any national strategy or allocation of resources. Unfortunately thus far neither have Children's Services Plans provided a framework for a more systematic analysis of this group's needs at local level, nor any substantial commissioning of services for them.

These concerns have been powerfully echoed in one of the major conclusions of the recent *Thematic Inspection of the Work of the Probation Service with Sex Offenders* (HM Inspectorate of Probation, 1998). The report expressed considerable concern about the absence of any systematic framework for the management of juvenile sexual offenders, or for the planning of services for them. The initiative and the responsibility have been left almost entirely at a local level, resulting in a patchwork of uncoordinated policies and services.

Youth offending teams and the Youth Justice Board

One of the major consequences of the Crime and Disorder Act 1998 is the creation of youth offending teams (YOTs) at a local authority level.

These teams are responsible to the local authority's chief executive and comprise a manager, police, social work, probation, education and health staff. Together their task is to prevent offending by children and young people (Home Office, 1998a). In addition to the provision of direct services, the team is required to formulate a local youth justice plan, based on audits of the types and needs of young offenders, and services. The guidance specifically mentions sex offenders amongst the type of offenders who could be included in this audit. The guidance also mentions the need to develop effective information systems to monitor the outcomes of intervention.

At a national level, a Youth Justice Board has been established with a remit to:

- establish national standards;
- maintain a rolling programme of inspections;
- approve local youth justice annual plans;
- initiate training; and
- identify and disseminate good practice.

(Home Office, 1998b)

Whilst the question of resources looms large over the implementation of the new youth offending teams, the emphasis on auditing local need, combined with the establishment of a strategic national-level Board, does provide a real opportunity to develop a more coherent set of standards and practice in relation to juvenile sexual offenders. Of course there will be many competing priorities, but it will be up to professionals concerned with this field to seek to influence the agenda at both national and local levels, through bodies such as NOTA, the National Organisation for the Treatment of Abusers. This opportunity will however, need to be grasped firmly for in the short term much time and energy will be consumed in establishing and making these new and potentially very diverse multi-disciplinary teams work.

Provision of service

Probably the easiest thing to say is that we do not know what the current level of provision is, in part because we have no real idea what the level of need is. Anecdotally the picture suggests that services remain extremely patchy, with a predominant focus on working with the young person, and far less emphasis on working with their family. Professionals often have to seek treatment and residential provision from services that are at great distances from the young person's home environment. There appear to be massive gaps in the geographical spread of services.

The most comprehensive picture comes from a recent survey of services in Scotland (Skinner, 1997). This identified eighteen programmes across Scotland for all sex offenders offering a total of 299 places. Of these, however, only seven programmes offered places to young people under 16 years, and only two programmes were dedicated to this group. For England and Wales there is no current information on the extent of provision. The recent *Thematic Inspection of the Work of the Probation Service with Sex Offenders* (HM Inspectorate of Probation, 1998) found that in less than half of the ten probation service areas inspected was there any provision for juvenile sex offenders. By contrast Becker (1998) reported that there were more than 800 specialised treatment programmes in the United States in 1993.

Monck and New's (1995) survey of voluntary agency treatment facilities for fifty-five young perpetrators reviewed eleven centres. Three of these provided services to thirty-four of the young people, whilst in contrast five centres saw only one young person during the research period. Only ten out of the fifty-five boys were subject to any form of legal order, seven of whom were under probation orders. It is thus clear that even within specialist settings the level of provision varies considerably.

The increase in multi-agency partnership projects since 1992 involving both voluntary and independent sector organisations has been encouraging. However, there have been a number of examples where funding has evaporated after three years, at a point when the programmes had only just become fully established. This is echoed in comments made by centre managers in the Monck and New study (1995), and elsewhere, about a number of concerns in relation to service delivery including:

- financial insecurity;
- difficulty in recruiting experienced staff;
- uncertainty about aims and who services are to be targeted at;
- uncertainty about likely levels of service demand and take-up;
- a lack of consistent assessment as to the suitability of referrals;
- tensions between how social services departments, paying for a service, and the specialist service see the needs of a case;
- a pressure to focus on assessment rather than longer-term work;
- a reluctance by the commissioning authority to include provision for work with other family members;

- how to fit existing services to victims alongside new services to young abusers.

There is also a danger in expecting that only specialist provision can manage young abusers. That route will only lead to a marginalisation of the problem, and a deskilling of the generality of the workforce who actually undertake the majority of the work with these young people. Specialists will make little headway seeing an adolescent in care once a week, if those who care for and live with him day by day do not feel confident in playing their vital part in creating a therapeutic and non-abusive environment. Specialists must be a catalyst for practice, and a resource to develop the workforce, not a dumping ground for difficult cases.

Finally it is important to remember that whilst the focus of research studies tends to be on groupwork programmes, for the large majority of staff working with a young person, such a resource is not available. The vast proportion of work is carried out on an individual basis, and it is often these workers who feel the most isolated and unsupported.

The absence of any systematic data base means that we know little either about the extent of need, or the extent of provision. In this context we must ask ourselves how equality of opportunity to services can be secured for black and female clients and those with special needs, particularly learning difficulties. The answer is that as things currently stand, provision for these groups is even less developed, with the consequence that these groups will either receive no service, or in the case of black young people, be at greater risk of prosecution.

Four strategy imperatives

Since 1992 the picture has been very mixed. Undoubtedly there has been a significant growth in professionals' awareness and commitment at an individual level to address the needs of young sexual abusers. There has been a corresponding increase in training available and a gradual increase in relevant literature. In many parts of the country this has been supported to varying degrees by policy development at managerial and inter-agency levels. There have also been a number of funding initiatives shared between voluntary and statutory agencies.

But there remain glaring gaps at the level of national strategy, national policy, practice guidance, funding, and standard setting which are impeding future developments in this field. Some programmes simply cannot get out of first gear, and yet others can only progress through considerable personal or localised effort to overcome the barriers and inertia that threaten to overwhelm already hard-pressed agencies when they think about addressing the needs of these young people. What then are the critical next stages if work in this field is to truly take off?

Plainly there are no quick fixes to be had, but this chapter concludes with four strategies through which the effectiveness of this work can be increased at both national and local levels:

The creation of a standing conference on the prevention of sexual aggression

This could act as an umbrella group to lobby for resources, legal changes and to act as a focus for public campaigning and education. The public needs to be much more informed about the problem and prevalence of inappropriate or abusive sexual behaviour by children and young people, and how parents can play a preventive role.

Development of inter-agency protocols for the management of juveniles who commit sexual assaults

This needs to be established on a national basis, in order to promote greater consistency of response, particularly in determining when child protection processes should be entered or exited, and how the interface with criminal justice processes should be managed. It would provide an inter-agency framework for the vast majority of juveniles who do not enter the criminal justice process. Such protocols would also need to consider the needs of children under the age of criminal responsibility, 10 years, and how they should best be managed on an inter-agency basis. Protocols would also need to clarify the roles and responsibilities of the various agencies, and in particular to identify lead agency functions.

Youth Justice Board: national survey, strategy and standards for the management of juvenile sexual offenders

The establishment of a Youth Justice Board with a quality assurance role provides the most important opportunity since the 1992 NCH Report to develop a national strategy and standards for this field. The Board could collate a national survey of needs and services via the annual reports from local youth offending teams. This in turn would provide a strategic framework at a local level, whose implementation and progress could be monitored on a national basis. The Board could establish a task force in this area, to which organisations such as NOTA could contribute, or carry out work on its behalf. It could also publish and disseminate examples of good practice and commission training at a national level.

Reviewing the legal options for the management of juvenile abusers

Whilst the new reprimand and final warning provisions may be helpful they will still not provide sanctions for non-compliance with any services offered. Given the major problems for child witnesses giving evidence, and the reduction in the numbers of juvenile abusers being prosecuted, there is a need to develop diversion schemes based on a plea of guilt for a selected group of offences, with powers to determine the programme to be attended, where the juvenile lives, and contact arrangements with children. Failure to comply would result in a return to court for sentencing on the original offence.

There is also a need to review the implications of the 1997 Sex Offenders Act, with a view to providing discretionary criteria for inter-agency decisions about the registration of juvenile sexual offenders.

Conclusion

It was Oscar Wilde who suggested that a map of the world without Utopia was useless. Despite the many challenges ahead, it is important to remind ourselves that both nationally and internationally the management of sexual offenders is still a very young field. By such criteria this field is still in its infancy, and barely into toddlerhood at best! But, like toddlers, those involved in this field will not retreat quietly into the shadows, for we have learnt enough already to know not just that this work is vital, but also that it needs to thrive.

3

WORKING WITH YOUNG PEOPLE

Linking policy and practice

Alix Brown

Introduction and overview

Adolescents who exhibit sexually abusive behaviour constitute a group who both can and should be provided with services, particularly as their stage of development makes them more likely to be amenable to change than adults, who are also likely to have been offending for longer periods of time. Other factors, specific to young people, which will be outlined in this chapter also make it imperative that intervention in a given geographical area is provided in a consistent way. Recognition of this means that provision for appropriate services should be included in local policies and procedures. It will be argued that opportunities can be created for assessment and intervention work with young people, ideally whilst maintained within their community or in the local area, and that such programmes need not be resource-intensive but do require commitment from agencies and workers.

Issues specific to young people

Whatever models are used to describe abusive behaviours and their reinforcement (see chapter 1), young people who abuse will be developing ways of behaving which, over a period of time, can become addictive or compulsive. However, because they have not been involved in abusing over long periods, such behaviours will probably not be as entrenched as they are for adult abusers. In addition, young people, particularly as they approach and pass through puberty, are developing their own understandings of sexual behaviour and their own sexual feelings. How these understandings develop depends very much on the young person's past and present experiences of sex. These will include whether or not they have had access to appropriate sex education; the attitudes of their family to sexual matters; whether they have experienced abuse themselves; and how they have been, or are being, introduced to sex among their peer group.

Bolton *et al.* (1989) describe environments which can help young people to develop healthy understandings about sex and relationships and those which distort understanding and make it difficult for the young person to relate to others as they become involved in sexual behaviour. For many young people, the inconsistencies or misunderstandings created in their own families are corrected through educative work in school. However, not all schools provide the same standard of sex education (the curriculum for which is decided by school governors) or emphasise practical considerations for young people, together with wider issues of relationships and respect and responsibility for others. Such wide-ranging sex education, provided at age and developmentally appropriate times, enables a young person to grow up with clear ideas about sex and to approach the formation of relationships with confidence.

Notwithstanding the often 'hit and miss' formal sex education most children receive, there is much helpful material available, including videos such as *Sex – A Guide for the Young* (Multi-media Film Foundation of Canada) and books (for example Fisher, 1991 and Butterworth, 1993) which are presented in ways which are easily accessible to young people.

For young people who have suffered sexual abuse, their views about sex will have been strongly affected by that experience, although the way in which this manifests itself will vary immensely. Some young people will retreat, perhaps become withdrawn and isolated and may be further victimised in future; others will act out their feelings either violently or criminally and a few will turn to abusing others. Many will lose (or not develop) the ability to empathise with others (Ryan, 1996) because they cannot cope with their own pain.

With a young person whose own experiences of abuse are still very recent and may be a significant part of their own self-harming, criminal, violent or sexually abusive behaviours, therapeutic work should involve not only their current behaviours but also issues which tie in with their earlier abuse and their understanding of it. This is different from work with adult abusers, where control of their patterns of behaviour is the primary focus in order to prevent further offending, rather than issues around their own abuse.

In addition, most young people have no understanding of the effects of abuse either on others or on themselves, and need this information before they can even begin to make appropriate choices about their abusing behaviours. This means that work with young people who abuse is often very different from work which might be carried out with an adult who would be expected to have a wider understanding of the damage caused by abuse. Young people cannot be assumed to have an adult understanding: working with them on the basis that they have is usually unhelpful and may push the young person into increasing resistance to intervention.

Avoidance of labelling

It is essential to avoid labelling or stigmatising young people who commit sexually abusive behaviour. The phenomenon of labelling is familiar to those who work in youth justice and its existence provided the rationale for policies of diversion of young people away from the courts and formal process. There is evidence (for example, Hartjen, 1978; Schur, 1971) that young people tend to 'take on' and internalise labels, so that continual talk of a 10-, 12-, 14- or 16-year-old as a 'sex offender' may leave them feeling that they cannot change. It is also likely to have similar ongoing repercussions in their family and with other agencies involved. It is more helpful to describe them as 'young people who show sexually abusive behaviours' with the implication that, whilst they are responsible for their behaviours, those can be changed. Similarly it is more helpful for projects which work with such young people to have a neutral name, rather than one which emphasises the 'offending' aspects.

In child protection case conferences, where a number of agencies may be represented, using the most helpful terminology does not mean minimising the facts of the abuse but may enable other workers to enhance the motivation of the young person to change. Condemnation by labelling may, from the outset, tend to block change and make it harder for the young person to accept responsibility for their behaviour and undertake a programme of intervention.

Sexual and sexually abusive behaviour in young people

Clinical experience over a number of years suggests that young people's sexual behaviour can be conceptualised in four categories although these are not mutually exclusive. Nevertheless it is helpful to view their behaviours in this way not only as a means of making sense of the interventions which might be proposed, but also as a means of identifying the policies and resources needed to ensure that all young people receive an appropriate service. The categories are:

1   Appropriate adolescent sexuality;
2   Inappropriate adolescent sexual behaviour;
3   'Acting out' of external sexual abuse pattern;
4   Creation of young person's own sexually abusing patterns.

Appropriate adolescent sexual behaviour

This refers to young people's need to experiment with sex and sexual activity and to reach their own understandings (Hirst, 1994; Moore and Rosenthal, 1993). This behaviour, which may involve a great deal of sexual innuendo, sexual touching of peers (often in a situation with several other pairs of young people) and much boasting about sexual activity (real or imagined) can often leave adults feeling uncomfortable and concerned. It can also fall outside the law as, for instance, when two 15-year-olds mutually consent to sexual intercourse. While there is often no difficulty with this behaviour when the young person is not alleged to have committed any other sexual offences, there is a concern that a young person who has abused in another context may find their appropriate sexual outlets proscribed because of the perception that this behaviour also reflects abuse.

Inappropriate adolescent sexual behaviour

This is also not necessarily serious in itself although it is always important that it is recognised so that some appropriate intervention is provided. Such behaviour varies widely. It may follow on from the first category in that behaviour which began as mutual exploration is then taken too far. A colleague has described this behaviour as 'appropriate inappropriate behaviour' recognising that, while it is abusive, it is also behaviour which, if dealt with quickly, need not continue into adulthood. Some examples of this behaviour might be bottom-pinching, 'pinging' bra-straps or attempts to kiss or grab a girl (or, indeed a boy, as both male and female adolescents can show this behaviour) without their consent and/or in a violent or forceful way. This behaviour can arise from a lack of social skills and understandings or (especially in the younger age group) from having observed apparently similar behaviour between adults but not necessarily having understood the full context of that behaviour. Such behaviour would be predominantly directed at similar age peers or, occasionally, older individuals. Unchecked, it could lead to the development of abusive relationships in adulthood, as potential partners are increasingly 'objectified' and seen merely as providing for the abuser's sexual or power-based needs.

In other circumstances, inappropriate adolescent sexual behaviour is potentially much more serious. For example, a young person may have become obsessed with a particular type of sexual activity to the extent that they attempt to carry it out on an inappropriate partner (this may be a peer, or an older or younger person). Initially this behaviour, although it is likely to appear serious, would not necessarily be accompanied by extensive fantasy. If it continues for any length of time, fantasy may be built up around the behaviour and a repeating pattern will be created. Clearly a thorough initial assessment (see chapter 6) is required in order to ascertain the background to the observed behaviour and the potential for continued risk. There may also be links here for young people who have suffered abuse (not necessarily sexual) and are meeting some of their own needs by choosing to indulge in the abusive behaviours.

'Acting out' of external sexual abuse pattern

This clearly relates to a young person who has suffered sexual abuse of some kind and is repeating the behaviours which operated during that abuse. Where the abuse committed by the young person against a younger child is extensive and sophisticated and where there has been detailed thought and planning about the abuse, it is likely that the young person carrying out the abusing is either repeating or re-working abuse which they have suffered. It is also possible, and especially for the younger age-group (6–10 years), that abuse which they have suffered but not clearly recalled, is 'acted out' against other children without much conscious knowledge of the precursors (Terr, 1991). Often, however, the earlier abuse is not disclosed (or its extent is not known) and it is sometimes difficult to separate this category from the fourth group although ongoing work with such a child or young person can facilitate disclosure of their own abuse at a later stage.

Creation of young person's own sexually abusing patterns

The fourth category includes all those young people who have found that the sexually abusive behaviour is meeting their own needs (for example, for comfort, closeness, power, sex) and who are beginning to develop their own ways of abusing and their own specific fantasies. Those from categories two and three may well, if their abusing behaviour continues over a period, move into this category. Clearly, without intervention, young people who have reached this stage are likely to continue to abuse in future, but early on in the process, when the patterns are still not firmly fixed, changes are possible provided that the young person is motivated and that ongoing intervention is available.

Many young people who come to the notice of the authorities because of sexually abusive behaviour will exhibit elements of all four categories and it is therefore of paramount importance to be able to separate out the behaviours at an early stage. This avoids young people either having no help because the abuse is deemed to be 'experimental' or convicting many young people, whose behaviour is relatively easy to understand and to change, of sexual offences which leave them subject to legal penalties, including registration under the Sex Offenders Act 1997.

Prosecution, caution or no further action: the impact of the Sex Offenders Act 1997

Whilst in law the police and the crown prosecution service have the power to decide which young people shall face caution or prosecution, in fact in most areas this decision is informed by a multi-agency panel, juvenile liaison bureau or juvenile panel of some kind. Enabling the local authority (or, in some cases, the probation service) to advise the police and the crown prosecution service appropriately at an early stage serves a number of purposes and avoids prosecutions for minor offending while ensuring that the behaviour itself can be seen to be taken seriously.

In the past, prior to the implementation of the 1997 Sex Offenders Act, the best result for many young people showing sexually abusive behaviour was that they received a caution for the behaviour and, through a child protection case conference or a 'caution-plus' programme (some input usually provided through a youth justice worker following a police caution), made a commitment to intervention to consider their behaviour in detail. Surprising though it may seem, this route was the preferred one (and was apparently successful) for nearly half of the young people facing prosecution for sexual offences in Shropshire over a four-year period (Brown, 1995). Having committed themselves to a period of assessment, only one young person in a sample of fifty who received cautions dropped out and this because of family pressure. Accepting the caution meant that the young person had admitted to at least some of the behaviour (albeit in some instances a very small part) and this provided a safe basis from which to explore much of what had happened.

As described in chapter 2, with the introduction of the 1997 Sex Offenders Act, young people who admit and are cautioned are registered. Indications are that, as a result, many young people are more reluctant to admit to anything at an early stage. This situation, in itself, enhances their denial of the offending and makes it more difficult for the young person to admit later in intervention. It also removes a useful option for those young people whose offending comes very much within the 'appropriate but inappropriate' end of the second category and can relatively easily be confronted and dealt with. Currently most of these young people appear to simply deny their behaviour, with the risk that they may then be prosecuted and have a conviction which carries longer registration under the Sex Offenders Act, and has significant implications for them in the future. Alternatively, no further legal action may be taken and the young person and their family, still in denial, will thus not receive (or accept) any input. There may be other factors involved in such denials (most often issues around family perceptions and family responses) but it seems likely that the threat of registration, along with all that this implies to the young person about being seen as a 'sex offender' by their local community, is having a significant impact.

The implementation of the 1998 Crime and Disorder Act with its warnings and final reprimands for young people as alternatives to cautions does not alter the situation, as Section 65(9) of this Act makes clear that cautions under the 1997 Sex Offenders Act will be construed as including such warnings and reprimands.

Child protection case conferencing and registration of young people with sexually abusive behaviours

There is no specific provision in the Children Act 1989 relating to young people who abuse others. Section 47, which requires local authorities to make enquiries so as to decide whether or not they should take action to safeguard a child's welfare, assumes that this would be to protect the child as a victim of abusive behaviour rather than as an abuser. In addition, there is still diversity in the approach of local authorities to young people who abuse, with some areas favouring avoidance of formal processes and others suggesting that a firm legal mandate is required in order to carry out intervention work. However, there does appear to be consensus about the need for intervention which focuses on the sexually abusive behaviours, whether or not this is achieved via a legal mandate or by agreement at case conference. Young people may well be offered similar interventions in different local authority areas but some may also be convicted for sexual offences where peers, in a neighbouring area, may have no such official record yet have committed similar or more serious offences.

Working Together (Department of Health, 1991b) provides encouragement for local authorities to work with young people who show sexually abusive behaviours. They are advised to hold a child protection case conference in respect of such young people, separately from the victim(s), and to have a proper assessment available. The guidance also recommends psychiatric assessment, although advances in this field would suggest that this would most appropriately be undertaken by someone (social worker, youth justice worker, probation officer, psychologist or psychiatrist) specifically trained in working with young people who sexually abuse. Very few such young people show symptoms of a mental disorder but many exhibit behaviours characteristic of young people who have been victims of severe sexual, physical or emotional abuse.

If a local authority is to case conference all young people alleged to have committed sexually abusive behaviours, then it is essential that any assessment is able to recognise the different aspects of that behaviour. Thus it is important to separate out what is appropriate and developing adolescent sexuality and fantasy from inappropriate and abusive behaviours, some of which may be linked directly to a young person's own abusive experiences. It is equally essential that the process does not end at this point and that interventions recommended within the assessment report are able to be implemented in order to minimise the risk of repeated abusive behaviour. Without intervention at this stage, it may be difficult for a young person to really understand or to permanently change their behaviour.

Currently *Working Together* is being revised (Department of Health, 1998) with discussion and consultation taking place about child protection case conferencing and possible child protection registration of young people who abuse. It can be strongly argued that it is important to case conference all such young people in order to mark the fact that this behaviour needs to be taken seriously and also to enable appropriate input to be provided to the young person and the family, as well as, of course, to the victim.

The desirability and feasibility of including these young people on local authority child protection registers is much less clear. These registers are held for children and young people who are at risk of significant harm by physical, sexual or emotional abuse or neglect. Some areas have introduced an additional category on their register to cover those young people who may abuse others. However, unless registration actually leads to the provision of services, it is probably irrelevant except in cases where the young person is also at risk under one of the pre-existing categories.

A disadvantage of a policy of child protection registration for young people who have sexually abused is that those involved in what are apparently more minor offences may not be registered at all and may, as a consequence, fail to access any services as it is usually the case that priority is given to those cases on the register. Apparently minor offending can hide more extensive patterns of abusive behaviour which do not emerge in therapy until significant trust has been built up between the young person and their worker. As the extent of sexual offending therefore often becomes known gradually during a period of intervention, this could mean that some who have abused quite extensively are missed.

Systems to manage young people who show sexually abusive behaviour

In setting up a system which can work with all young people involved in sexually abusive behaviours, it needs to be accepted that this behaviour does not fall within the remit of, for example, youth justice agencies alone or indeed of child protection services alone. Some young people will become known through direct reporting to the police either via a child protection/police enquiry team or to the local police station. Others may emerge through behaviour observed while in residential or foster care, or even, especially with peer abuse, through incidents in local schools. Some of these young people will receive a caution, others may be charged and, for many, the behaviour will be effectively ignored.

It therefore makes sense in policy terms to be able to refer young people to a central system within a local authority area which is able to deal with referrals from any source but which links in with individual workers in youth justice or children and family teams, for example, to work jointly with the young person and/or to feed back information about risk, placement and prognosis. Such a system can be set up in several ways. The implementation of the 1998 Crime and Disorder Act, with its youth offending teams, may well provide a clearer approach than has heretofore been possible. In the past, different local authorities have produced different solutions, some of which have apparently provided an effective resource. Nevertheless, however the service is provided, the important issues to be addressed remain the same:

1 Provision (either through the same resource or several different ones) of a service to cover all children and young people who show such behaviour (from 5 to 21 years if possible);

2   Ensuring that, whoever does the work, local social service workers, police, education welfare officers and probation workers have some understanding of the issues involved and that there is a clear route for referral, preferably via a child protection case conference;

3   Systems of accountability to the referring worker(s) in relation to reports of progress and indicators of risk, placement issues and other issues which affect the work with the young person;

4   Provision of specialist reports for court (civil and criminal) and for those working with the young person to attend reviews and case conferences relating to them;

5   Ensuring that local magistrates and solicitors are aware of the issues involved in this type of behaviour and in the therapeutic work so that magistrates can have some confidence in the reports they receive and solicitors advise their clients appropriately;

6   Ensuring that appropriate therapeutic work will be available following an initial assessment of the young person and that this work is properly and fully resourced and financed;

7   Appropriate systems for the support of workers, with frequent training up-dates, good supervision and clear directions from management (whether this be a single agency or a multi-agency system);

8   Systems for the support of carers – natural families, foster carers and residential workers – so that each placement supports the work being carried out with the young person;

9   Systems for the support of other agencies, for instance schools, in relation to particular cases.

Given the multi-agency nature of the work, local Area Child Protection Committees (ACPCs) can usefully take a lead in supporting and recognising such developments. Indeed NOTA (the National Organisation for the Treatment of Abusers) recommends that ACPCs are actively involved in co-ordinating work with both adult and adolescent offenders (NOTA, 1993).

There must also be a recognition of the need for such a service and some understanding of the work at the highest level within the agencies which provide management support. Workers must feel (and be) supported both in terms of training and supervision provision, and also by stated agency policies. There should, for instance, be a clearly stated policy on the use of sexually explicit material possibly based on the helpful guidance produced by NOTA (1994). This would address its use in work with the young person on appropriate fantasy and in sex education programmes. Management must recognise the usefulness of such material and support the workers who are making use of it, within guidelines which are acceptable to the agency (and which may have to be negotiated by the workers concerned).

Clarity about the procedures to follow when a young person who is being worked with discloses further abuse, either by themselves or against them, is also essential. This should, in most instances, be covered by existing child protection policies, or by specifically agreed policies, where necessary, in the case of multi-agency projects. More generally, agency approval and recognition of this work, which can be emotionally taxing on the workers, needs to be made clear and explicit. This also gives a local programme credibility with local judiciary and ensures that information about the programme is disseminated at the highest levels to all relevant agencies.

In Shropshire (Brown, 1995) the Adolescent Sexual Offences Programme was social services led and managed through the child protection team, simply because multi-agency working was less easy to organise in the county in the period 1988–1990. The funding for the co-ordinator's post, however, while devolving back to social services after two years, was initially provided by joint health, education and social services funding. The other programme workers were recruited from area teams and residential work and worked with one or two young people at a time. Their cases were supervised by the co-ordinator and they met regularly for ongoing support and training. This model enabled understanding of the issues to be passed on via those workers who were involved, to other colleagues in their teams. Thus this model was not resource-intensive, nor did it de-skill workers.

Other models are possible, however, including statutory agencies working on their own, multi-agency projects, or projects where a voluntary organisation, such as Barnados, NCH or the NSPCC, takes the lead role in partnership with, or part-funded by, social and/or probation services. Resources may also be health based, possibly through child and adolescent psychiatric services. Where such services already exist, discussions will be needed with the new youth offending teams (YOTs) to avoid duplication of work and to ensure that appropriate services are provided for a wide range of young people.

Specialist projects may seem attractive but they may also have their drawbacks. Local workers referring to such a programme may get little or no feedback on the work carried out, may feel 'de-skilled' and consequently be less likely to react to potentially dangerous situations or to recognise when the young person is at significant risk of re-offending. Whilst there is now an emphasis on social workers as 'case managers', allocating resources rather than carrying out the work themselves, workers who lack reasonable knowledge and understanding of the need for focused intervention work are likely to miss obvious referrals and to fail to prioritise intervention work appropriately.

The advent of youth offender teams may enable provision for assessment and intervention work to be developed in areas where, up to now, this has been carried out in an *'ad hoc'* piecemeal fashion by those workers who have had the time and interest and have been prepared to pioneer a new service. However, whilst a young person who receives a 'final warning' must now be referred to the local YOT for a rehabilitation programme, and thus can undergo intervention without necessarily having a conviction for sexual offending, there will still be those who have engaged in sexually abusive behaviours which have not attracted a 'reprimand' or a final warning from the police. They may also require intervention but are likely to be low priority.

Whilst there appears, therefore, to be a potential role for these new teams in providing a reasonably comprehensive service for young people who abuse, it also seems likely that some of this work, perhaps with a younger age group, will continue to be carried out in local authority children and family teams and through the child protection system. Thought needs to be given as to how this work is allocated and organised, although, as already indicated, it need not be resource-intensive and can utilise existing workers for service delivery, providing appropriate training and support are given.

Co-working is often seen as essential in working with young people who abuse. It can indeed be very helpful for those staff who are embarking on this area of work and it does provide useful insights, especially in difficult cases, which may be missed by a single worker. However, as expertise is built up, and provided there is good supervision, a single worker may be more able to form a helpful therapeutic relationship with a young person. Setting up co-working situations clearly requires more time and is thus more resource-intensive. It also requires co-workers to have a good understanding and to be able to work closely together. Experience suggests that it does not seem to be essential to have a male and female co-worker and it is likely to be counter-productive if two workers who are not familiar with each other's way of working are placed in that situation simply because it is agency policy to always co-work with a male and female worker.

In the early stages of assessment and intervention, using video to record the sessions may be as effective as using a co-worker and is additionally helpful in supervision and in training other workers. It might also be possible for some thought to be given to 'live' supervision (using one-way screen or video link), although this is also more resource-intensive.

Carrying out the work – training needs

Whilst work with young people who show sexually abusive behaviour is specialised and requires training in intervention techniques, there is no reason why workers from a variety of professional backgrounds, across field and residential settings, should not be involved. However, safeguards are necessary so that roles and responsibilities do not become confused. For example it is suggested that residential workers should not undertake interventions with a young person in their own establishment and similarly, it is helpful if a social worker working with a young person is not also the social worker for the child's family. It is difficult to focus on therapeutic work when other issues, such as school, family or statutory duties, impinge and the excessive caseload of many workers is likely to mean that therapeutic interventions are not delivered consistently. The message then received by the young person (and by their family/carers) is that this input is not important and the abusive behaviour is thereby inadvertently colluded with.

By the end of training, the key requirements are that staff involved demonstrate:

1 An understanding of and ability to work with adolescents on sexual issues;
2 An understanding of the issues involved in sexual abuse, both by adults and adolescents and recognition of the effects upon the victims;
3 Confidence to carry out a work programme with a young person who may be reluctant to engage, at least initially.

In addition it is crucial that such staff have access to regular supervision from a supervisor with some knowledge of the work and/or access to specialist consultation as required.

Current thinking in working with young people who show sexually abusive behaviours (see chapter 1) would suggest initial assessment and ongoing intervention work should cover issues of responsibility for the abuse, relapse prevention work, victim empathy, work on sexual fantasy and sex education, confidence-building and social skills work as well. In addition, for many young people, it is essential to deal with their own victim issues and provision needs to be made for this work to be done concurrently with the focus on the offending behaviour.

This spread of issues suggests that workers will need access in training to a range of information and skills, some of which they can utilise possibly through linking with other agencies such as education and health promotion. Thus there are advantages in these agencies having an investment in the project, not just for the workers with the young people, but also in the reverse direction, when the workers can provide general awareness training around sexually abusive behaviour for education and health workers who may not otherwise receive such specific input. This, in its turn, makes it more likely that young people with difficult behaviours will be recognised and referred early, thus enhancing their chances of significant change during intervention.

Evaluation

As discussed in chapter 12 evaluating programmes working with young people who sexually abuse, is notoriously difficult. It is recognised, for example, that measures of re-offence rates are inadequate as most sexual offending is secret and often not disclosed. In addition because most young people are well supervised once identified, any further offending may not occur until well after they have left the remit of social services.

It can be helpful to consider, over the period of assessment and intervention, the general behaviour and maturation of the young person. This can often be done on a subjective basis, using those who have the day-to-day care of the young person and see him/her in ordinary situations. In addition, some evaluation (either through questionnaires or interview) of the young person's changing understanding of programme content and their perception of their own behaviour is useful. It is also helpful to build in to programmes a recall at, for example, six months or twelve months after involvement has formally ceased. This recall may involve completing further questionnaires relating to knowledge and understanding and/or some subjective evaluation from parents, carers, teachers and significant others about the young person's behaviours in general. Keeping good records of referrals, the numbers who are cautioned or convicted and the numbers who drop out prior to completion of a programme is important, as well as regular up-dates for all agencies involved and the local ACPC.

Conclusion

Provision of a service for young people who show sexually abusive behaviours is of paramount importance if their behaviour is to be tackled with the prospect of some change or, at the very least, appropriate monitoring and risk reduction. The rationale for such a service is very simple: young people are much more open to changing their behaviour because it has often not taken on a fixed pattern. Such a service can be provided on a multi-agency or single agency basis and without highly specialised, but appropriately trained workers who are well supported by agreed policies and reasonable resources.

A service of this type needs to be accessible to referrers however the young person's behaviour emerges, as not all young people will be identified through standard youth justice or child protection routes. The service also needs to be able to respond appropriately, for example, with specialised court reports or recommendations for case conferences. A high level of accountability both to referrers and to the young person and their carers is essential if therapeutic work provided by the service is to have any credibility or, indeed, any lasting effect on the behaviour of the young person. But, however the service is provided, the potential cost of failing to work with adolescents who show abusive behaviour is, in contrast, likely to be extensive, both for their victims and themselves.

4

PLACEMENT PROVISION AND PLACEMENT DECISIONS

Resources and processes

Nick Bankes, Kate Daniels and Carlton Quartly

Introduction

This chapter has been written by members of ACT – a Surrey social services multi-disciplinary assessment, consultation and therapeutic service for children and young people who sexually abuse and their families or carers. An important part of ACT's function is to advise social workers on appropriate placements for young sexual abusers at the point of referral and investigation through to the termination phase of therapy.

In the first part of this chapter resource issues pertinent to the placement of young sexual abusers are outlined, drawing on the experience of ACT's work. In the second part anonymised case examples are used to examine the processes whereby practitioners make placement decisions and suggestions are made for ways in which some of the pitfalls inherent in these processes can be avoided. This is followed by a brief concluding section which reviews the main issues raised in the chapter.

Placement provision

Accommodation is one of the most pressing needs identified for this client group but the current picture in the United Kingdom is one of poor and patchy service provision (Masson, 1995). Generally there is a lack of placement facilities and an often uncoordinated and *ad hoc* response by professionals. A report cited by Araji (1997) documented that nearly 50 per cent of sexually aggressive children were not in a placement of choice but rather in the only placement available. It is clear that there is little spare capacity, with service systems not having enough appropriate placements for those children and young people who should be accommodated because of their sexually aggressive or abusive behaviour. Worryingly too, many young people are often allocated to resources without a formulation of their difficulties or a thorough understanding of what led to the abuse. Thus some young people are in expensive and scarce residential programmes without due attention being paid to their specific needs.

Where no alternative placement can be found the young person may have to be maintained within their current situation although this can be far from satisfactory. In one case involving an 11-year-old boy this resulted in an increase in sexualised and aggressive behaviours, with concern expressed about the physical safety and emotional well-being of his carers. Cover stories may also be used by professionals as part of their attempts to get a young person placed. In such cases the young person's presenting behaviour can either be minimised or ignored altogether, leaving carers or residential workers unprepared and uninformed in dealing with any potential risk.

> In a case recently publicised in the media (Clark, 1997) a local authority was sued because it was claimed the social worker had failed to tell the foster carers that a 15-year-old boy placed with them had a known history of sexual abuse. The boy subsequently sexually abused four other children in their home. The local authority claimed they did not have a duty of care towards the family to provide the information. The family was told he was a bully and a liar, labels used to mask the seriousness of his sexually abusive behaviour.

Conversely some descriptions may be exaggerated, for example labels such as 'sex offender' may be applied to young people, to heighten professional anxiety and obtain appropriate resources despite the dangers associated with the use of such negative labels (see chapter 3).

A principle of the Children Act 1989 is that children and young people are best cared for in their own family, wherever possible. This is equally applicable to young sexual abusers. There is an orthodoxy, however, that suggests that in all cases of intrafamilial abuse the perpetrator should be removed from the home (Ryan and Lane, 1991). Such a stance can be too prescriptive and at times unworkable. Temporary separation of the victim and the abuser may be necessary but professional approaches to families at the point of disclosure should be refocused to ensure a more differentiated response based on a thorough assessment (see chapters 6 and 9).

When consideration is given to keeping a young person in their home setting, parents must be supported and educated more effectively than they often are currently. Professionals need to engage with and listen to parents or carers who may be experiencing significant split loyalties and be acutely upset. Intervention is required not only to help them understand and deal with their own difficult feelings but also to help them manage the young person in the household by creating appropriate boundaries to protect actual and potential victims.

Although many young people who sexually abuse can remain safely placed in their family home, a new environment may be required for some young people if there has been an adverse reaction from the family towards the abuser, or where problems within the family are so great that the changes they need to make in order to protect, supervise or contain cannot be made either in the short or long term (Bentovim, 1991). In addition young people may be vulnerable themselves and may face retaliation from the family, community or placement.

> Adam, a white, 15-year-old boy charged with sexual offences against neighbourhood children, needed to be moved from his foster home when he and his carers received threatening calls and were harassed by members of the community. He was subsequently moved to a residential unit but his offence behaviour again became known and he was ostracised and scapegoated by fellow residents. There being no other alternative accommodation available he was placed in bed and breakfast accommodation where the possibilities for monitoring his behaviour were dangerously minimised.

Similar incidents have been reported in the national media (see, e.g., Campbell, 1998).

Our care system is one that is changing and evolving but perhaps not in line with increased research and knowledge about the nature of sexual abuse by children and young people (National Children's Homes, 1992). Over the last decade there has been a move towards the phasing out of residential care for young people with more emphasis placed on fostering provision. Utting (1997) argues, however, that residential provision does have its place, providing the necessary intensity of therapeutic support, as well as a role in containment. This is inevitably an expensive option and one that local authorities are therefore often reluctant to fund. Moreover there are only a few residential units in the United Kingdom specialising in this area of work which means that the involvement of the family in therapeutic work becomes difficult if the child or young person is in a unit which is geographically distant.

Where a young person has been accommodated, reunification is seen as an important goal. As far back as the early 1970s research has been providing evidence that it is much more difficult to rehabilitate children with their families after time has lapsed (see, for example, Rowe and Lambert, 1973) but the very nature of work with young people who abuse often means that intervention is of a long-term nature. In addition many young people have a history of repeated moves and breakdowns within the care system. A general review of young people accommodated in Surrey (Surrey Children's Services, 1998) demonstrated that return home rates within a year are low, at approximately 20 per cent. Short-time fostering becomes long term and rehabilitation and integration back into the family of origin becomes a more difficult task. These problems are exacerbated when the young person is known or alleged to have perpetrated abuse.

Bengis (1986) promoted the idea of developing a 'continuum of care', a notion that received further support in the British context through the publication and recommendations of the NCH Report (1992). Such a continuum suggests that service provision needs to be sensitive to the range of young people who abuse and the risks they pose: from less restrictive/intensive environments for those deemed to be low risk, to secure accommodation and custody in some cases where there is a need for greater community protection. Within this range of provision should be included community-based options such as the young person living at home, in the extended family, in foster care or in supported lodgings schemes where there is some degree of monitoring and supervision. Decisions about which is the most appropriate placement should be made in the light of an assessment of risk, as well as an assessment of the young person's therapeutic needs and motivation for treatment. Additionally it should be borne in mind that the placement chosen should comprise the least restrictive environment available commensurate with these factors.

Risk has become a key criterion for determining resources (Morrison, 1998) and decisions about which is the most suitable placement are often closely linked to the degree of risk that the young person presents in his own home or in the community. However, risk is difficult to determine and our approaches and models have not been empirically tested. Deciding on the risk which a young person may pose within the community can be daunting and it is easy to over-react. Decisions may not be made in a thoughtful and rational way. For example, studies by Doughty and Schneider (1987), Maynard and Wiederman (1997) and Harnett (1997) demonstrate that practitioners often rate the danger-ousness of their client as higher than it actually is. In general these studies report that professionals hold more negative attitudes to sexual offenders than non-sexual offenders with sympathy reserved for victims and not perpetrators. Risks also need to be managed appropriately over time. As work progresses with a young person the 'perceived' risk may rise rapidly (and cause panic) as more information becomes available. In fact the actual risk may have significantly decreased because the young person's behaviour is better understood and can be monitored more effectively. Further guidance is needed and use made of the lists of risk factors that might influence placement and therapeutic treat-ment decisions which have been provided by several authors (Ross and Loss, 1987; Wenet and Clarke, 1986; Perry and Orchard, 1992; Hoghughi et al., 1997).

Providing the right type of accommodation is very important in terms of avoiding relapse. Preventing re-offending often starts with the external constraints and careful monitoring that can be provided by the environment in which the young person lives and by the people who care for him. However, as work progresses with the young person this external control should give way to internal controls, insight and a real change in behaviour and thus a change of placement which enables the young person to exercise these internal controls may be appropriate.

Through a survey of referrals to ACT it has been identified that a significant proportion of all sexual abuse is perpetrated within the envi-ronment in which the young person lives. Powerful dilemmas are therefore raised about whether it is deemed necessary to remove the young person for a period of time and, if so, what alternative resources are available. The survey indicated that many young people did remain at home but without recourse to a risk assessment to establish the extent to which the young person may place others at continued risk. For others their sexually abusive behaviour facilitated removal to general residential care where there were children who were particu-larly vulnerable because abuse had already become an integral part of their history. Whilst there was a great deal of skill and commitment from staff in the residential sector, they appeared to be inadequately prepared and trained to deal with the type of behaviour the young person might exhibit. This often resulted in placement breakdown and the move of the young person to a more contained and specialist setting. Many carers and accommodation providers encountered in the survey described a heightened sense of anxiety when managing this client group. What is required in these situations is commitment from agencies to train and support residential staff and foster carers so they are clear about the focus of their work and to provide effective, complementary educational and therapeutic services.

For a small proportion of young people, their level of dangerous-ness was such that a more specialist residential environment was the only realistic option. These placements are costly. For other young people who were particularly difficult to place, a specialist community option was developed in Surrey where a single young person's place-ment was staffed around the clock by a team of residential workers. This is a short-term solution as it can be seen as isolating for the young person. In the survey, foster care was an under-utilised option, primarily because there was a lack of available carers without younger or developmentally less advanced children in placement. It may well be, however, that the family environment and parenting which such placements can offer have the potential to fulfil many of the needs of these young people.

In relation to children and young people who sexually abuse, our own local authority has made significant use of placements in the private and voluntary sector to meet specialist needs, but is now looking at local cost-effective alternative provision. In line with this a number of options have been identified by the authors which would meet the placement needs of young people who abuse. Based on the concept of a 'continuum of care', a range of available services are recommended with increasing levels of supervision commensurate with the level of risk. These suggestions – specialist foster care, development of a 4/5 bedded residential unit and a supported lodgings scheme – may be of relevance to readers considering alternative accommodation models in their areas.

Space precludes detailed discussion of the first two options, the content of which are hopefully self-evident. As regards the supported lodging scheme this would build on an existing model used with young offenders, the plan being to select from existing private land-lords six who would provide supportive accommodation for either adult or young sexual abusers. They would be trained for the role and supported by a specialist worker. It is hoped that the scheme will develop as a tripartite arrangement between social services, the probation service and the voluntary sector with the last providing the set-up and lead-in costs.

It is vital that there is sufficient provision within the system to ensure that children can be matched to placements by need rather than by available resources. Whilst it is recognised that with limited resources a continuum of care may not be possible within a small geographical area, this may be achieved by utilising and combining resources across county or local authority boundaries.

In summary, in working with children and young people who abuse, professionals have largely focused on the investigation and treatment phases of work whilst the issue of accommodation has largely been ignored and constraints on budgets have led to constrictions in resources available. As others are also recommending (Farmer and Pollock, 1998) it is argued here that the range and flexibility of accommodation must be increased, together with improvements made in the quality of services offered, through training, support and consultation. Effective links between different agencies within the community are needed to develop services which are appropriate to the needs of service users, in the context of a strategic vision and over-arching policies which dovetail with national policy and provision, as discussed in chapter 2.

Making decisions about placements: process issues

A key issue in making placement decisions is the decision-making process itself. Successful management of cases involving children and young people who sexually abuse relies on a coherent and consistent response from all agencies working with such cases. It involves the exercise of professional judgement and authority by those who have been allocated power over the lives of others. The appropriate use of such power and authority in cases of sexual abuse where power has been abused is crucial. However, the application of such principles of good practice is not always easy and the decision-making process can be fraught with misunderstanding and confusion.

In looking at the interactional aspects of the decision-making process it is important to distinguish between content and process. In the decision-making process the *content* might be described as the issue of how and where a young person who sexually abuses is placed. John Burnham describes process as: 'patterns of negotiation that develop gradually through trial and error' (Burnham, 1986, p. 11).

Such patterns can be formulated explicitly according to agreed rules about hierarchy, roles and responsibilities or lines of communication. However, other patterns also develop and emerge outside the awareness of those involved. This might mean that as professionals with different agendas, attitudes and expectations seek to negotiate a common belief system and a way to proceed, so covert relationships and communication processes develop which can cause the decision-making process to founder.

The capacity for the professional system to mirror the dysfunctional processes in the client family has been well documented (Berkowitz and Leff, 1984; Britton, 1981; Dimmock and Dungworth, 1985; Furniss, 1991; Reder, 1986). Reder suggests that: 'this process appears most pronounced when the central family has problems with organization and authority' (Reder, 1983, p. 24).

This is demonstrated in the case of Bertie where disarray in the judicial and care proceedings tended to reflect the disarray in Bertie's family. Bertie is a white male of 12 who had been systematically abused by an uncle from the age of 3. In addition his behaviour to other children was described by his teachers as sexualised and abusive. The family and uncle were investigated and Bertie was removed from his home. He was placed in the most immediately available children's home. Due to contested care proceedings Bertie was subjected to a variety of assessments without any coherent plan involving his family or his overall needs. Throughout the process, relationships and patterns of communication between professionals became increasingly problematic.

Alliances were formed between professionals who agreed on certain courses of action. Those who held alternative views felt excluded. Sensing this they then attempted to introduce *their* opinions and views in unhelpful ways. As coalitions were established, the open forum for sharing of ideas was replaced by more covert discussions. Roles and tasks overlapped and boundaries became diffuse as those working with different aspects of the case sought to apply their points of view and support the interest of those they felt they represented. The social worker holding the case coped with a variety of conflicting agendas and injunctions from associates by allying himself closely with Bertie and so losing the much needed opportunity for an overview of the whole case.

> The effect of such incoherence was that professionals became stuck with their own processes and were unable to formulate a clear plan for Bertie's future. A systemic paralysis set in.

A key feature highlighted by this example is that of escalating confusion. The more workers tried to deal with the case according to their own ideas and beliefs, the more problematic things became. Instead of taking time to consider alternative solutions collectively, workers, operating from within their own belief systems, applied their own particular approaches more rigorously and thus the attempted solutions became the problem (Watzlawick *et al.*, 1974).

In order to explore how such processes occur within the professional system it is important to look at the contexts that define and organise behaviour. One influencing context may be the client family with which the professional system is engaged. Equally the belief systems of the workers' agencies and families will inform the way workers undertake their respective tasks and interact with professionals and clients.

The model of the Co-ordinated Management of Meaning discussed in chapter 9 provides a frame for considering the way multiple levels of context are hierarchically organised and operate reflexively in loops of reciprocal influence. Each level of context is influenced by the one above (contextual force) and to a lesser degree asserts influence upwards on the above context (implicative force).

One can see how contexts defined behaviour in this recursive way in the case of Bertie. A pervading atmosphere of alarm about the degree of the abuse Bertie had sustained, coupled with alarm about his own sexualised behaviour, instigated his summary removal from home and the institution of care proceedings. Bertie's family, working in accordance with their own rules about family closeness and loyalty, promptly contested the care proceedings and sought to maintain contact with Bertie. Isolated from his family and confused by events, Bertie looked for comfort and intimacy via behaviours deemed inappropriate. In the absence of any assessment that took into account the contextual influences on his behaviour, Bertie was labelled a high risk, contact with his parents was seen as dangerous and they were refused access to him and so the atmosphere of alarm was perpetuated.

It could be argued that unless workers are aware of the dictates and rules, and the belief systems generated by the multiple contexts in which they operate, they are more likely to be subject to the unhelpful, and largely unconscious processes that can arise in cases such as sexual abuse.

The following discussion looks at the aspects of three significant contexts which can unhelpfully organise the way in which professionals engage in decision-making about young people who sexually abuse. It explores the way in which these contexts can help to produce the rigid or entrenched positions among workers that mitigate against useful therapeutic manoeuverability and successful professional collaboration (Morrison, 1998; Bentovim, 1992; Menzies, 1970).

Community, media and society – the atmosphere of alarm that surrounds sexual abuse

Social and cultural attitudes to sexual abuse by young people provide a powerful over-arching context within which professionals in this field address their work. In any case where risk to others is involved there is a requirement for social workers to assess that risk and act decisively and with some speed to protect those who are vulnerable. This can be experienced by practitioners as pressure and in cases of sexual abuse the sense of pressure is compounded. Sexual abuse is a highly emotive subject. The notion of young people as sexually abusive can inspire fear, repugnance and alarm at a most primitive level (Olafson *et al.*, 1993) and these attitudes are commonly presented and indeed almost encouraged by the media. The community does not want its children to be at risk or to be seen as a risk and the media will quickly denounce those guardians who fail to sanitise or to protect. Blanchard (1995) suggests that constant exposure to the media and public opinion may lead to a less than humanistic attitude in professionals. Media censure is a powerful organising force. Workers in abuse cases often feel this pressure – not only to 'do something quickly' but also to 'get it right'. Such imperatives can easily contradict each other. Workers making placement decisions require time and an atmosphere of calm in which to share and consider all the information available. In the absence of such a context they make decisions with the paralysing fear that they may be responding too quickly or not quickly enough.

Creating a space for the decision-making process is vital. Part of this involves raising awareness of the fact of sexual abuse by children and young people. Where there is little or no knowledge, there often tends to be an unrealistic fear. In the imagination of the uninformed and through the messages of the media, children are transformed very quickly from innocents to evil monsters (James and Jenks, 1996). Organising training events and liaison with community groups, associated professional bodies, carers, families and at a management level in agencies is the only way to help forestall the paralysing atmosphere of fear and alarm that can hinder the management of such cases.

The professional context: agencies' different belief systems

Alarm and anxiety in the community about sexual abuse by young people raises questions of responsibility. Work with young people who sexually abuse usually involves a number of different agencies as well as carers, and a sense of alarm can impact upon all of these bodies. Each agency involved in the work and the decision-making process will have a different perspective on the case, a different set of responsibilities and different statutory or discretionary powers (Bentovim, 1998). It is in this professional context that one recognises the tension that is inherent in the decision-making process between meeting the thera- peutic needs of the young person and their family, ensuring the safety of those who are potentially vulnerable and responding to society's need to see that decisive and retributive action is taken. In cases of sexual abuse the opportunity for disagreement and difference of opinion between involved professionals is considerable. This is most evident in the area of risk. Workers can polarise in their views.

One GP who saw a young person, Carl, and his family, dismissed any concern saying that the young person's actions had been no more than sexual experimentation. The parents of the child who had been abused did not see it that way and neither did the social worker. In contrast, in another case a boy, Dion, who had sexually abused his younger siblings and was receiving therapy, was hastily removed from a residential establishment because he had been discovered engaging in mutual masturbation with peer-aged boys.

It is possible that some of the difficulties that these cases provoked could have been avoided if a forum had been available in which ideas, anxieties and opinions could have been aired. Unfortunately case conferences are unlikely to provide such a forum, being content rather than process oriented (Bacon, 1988). They are also likely to include parents and so may well be an inappropriate context for workers and professional carers to explore their own anxieties and differences.

If workers feel vulnerable and isolated they are more likely to become entrenched in their views and to seek the safety and certainty of a particular position (Morrison, 1994). This might mean forming an allegiance with the client they represent and/or an antipathy towards someone else in the family (Justice and Justice, 1993; Mintzer, 1996; Reynolds-Mejia and Levitan, 1990; Preston-Shoot and Agass, 1990). Such partisan positions are unhelpful in terms of gaining the emotional distance required to make holistic and collaborative assessments.

A meeting of professionals should afford workers the opportunity to express their fears; to explore the pressures they feel; to consider the ways their agencies' agendas might conflict with each other and also to explore the risk factors in the case, imagined, real or possible. It is only through this initial process of sharing information, expertise and feelings that collaborative decision-making can be undertaken.

Personal – the workers' own experiences of and responses to the subject matter

The third defining context is the personal one. There are a number of reasons why workers may choose to hold certain views or take a particular position on a case with which they are working. Such choices are not always informed by conscious, professional assessment. Again the subject matter is at the heart of this. Every individual working with cases of sexual abuse among young people will bring to that work their own sexual development, sexual knowledge learned in the context of family rules, their own understanding and interpretation of cultural rules and their own emotional reactions. A worker's emotional position on the subject of sexual abuse by children and young people will almost inevitably inform their assessments and practice. Unless workers are afforded the opportunity to explore and to understand their own material on this subject there is a risk that it may continually intrude on their work in unhelpful ways.

Using Karpman's model of the Drama Triangle (Karpman, 1968), Carr looked at the way workers in such cases can take different roles with their clients in response to their own unresolved experiences within their family of origin or unresolved issues relating to their own sexuality (Carr, 1989). He points to the way these counter transference reactions can create therapeutic impasses in the working teams: 'When one member experiences a countertransference reaction, another member usually experiences a complementary countertransference reaction, for example if one worker begins to rescue a child, another will try to rescue the parents' (p. 95).

He goes on to suggest that these counter-transference reactions operate at an unconscious level and if not brought into conscious awareness 'may influence, in a dramatic way, assessment and decision-making about families where child abuse has occurred' (Carr, 1989, pp. 94–5). He also describes the process whereby splitting and polarisation in the professional network may often mirror the splitting and polarisation within the family.

In the case of Bertie, discussions took place about the hostile feelings of the social worker towards the young person's family. His attitude was not shared by his associates in the case and this became an issue. Professionals trying to decide whether the young person should return to live at home were stuck with their different views and it seemed impossible to take the discussion forward. The subsequent information that Bertie's social worker had been abused himself by his father threw some light on the suspicion with which he viewed Bertie's father. It was a courageous decision for him to bring this experience into the professional discussion, and it proved to be helpful in opening up a new and more productive dialogue.

It has already been noted that workers who feel embattled or victimised by their own work system may over-identify with a particular client in the case. This may occur when a worker has an experience of having been embattled within their own family or of being the family fixer – always having to sort things out (Malan, 1979; Loughlin, 1992). In one such case it became evident that the female workers dealing with the case were feeling overwhelmed by the material and unsupported by their male associates who were also involved in the case. This was a direct reflection of the dynamics in the client's family and it transpired that it was also the family experience of the women workers. Whilst one might argue that such gendered dynamics can occur in any kind of work, in cases involving sexual abuse by young people the distress levels that arise can create a much more heightened response which impacts on professionals in different ways according to their personal histories (Kennel and Agresti, 1995; Little and Hamby, 1996; Morrison, 1990).

Engagement and collaboration with the young person's family is fundamental to the decision-making process but can be severely hindered by the worker's personal reactions to the case. This can be demonstrated in the way professionals decide whether or not a young person remains at home. As was suggested earlier, the decision may of course be made in the light of limited resources. However, it may also be informed by a worker's feelings about the client family. A worker who has difficulty with their emotional response to the abuse or to the client's family may wish to remove the child from that family in an attempt to provide himself, the worker, with some distance from the emotional unpleasantness and complexity of the case. This attempt to sanitise can be rationalised by emphasising the family's severely dysfunctional nature and the need to work individually with the young person. If the goodwill and co-operation of the client family are not enlisted then a process as described in the Bertie case can arise, whereby the family's attempts to maintain family authority and family rules with their child are viewed by the professional system as manipulative and dangerous. Power sanctions are then invoked by the professionals and an escalating conflict occurs leaving the young person further bewildered and confused about issues of power and authority.

It would be unrealistic to assume that professionals' personal responses to the abuse, to the family and to the young person can be avoided. They can however, be acknowledged, explored and used appropriately.

> In one case where two workers found themselves struggling with a conflict of attitudes towards a young person's behaviour, they realised through discussion that they were adopting the conflictual positions of the young person's parents. The female worker minimised Eric's offence and like his mother wanted to rescue him. The male worker, taking the father's position, felt deeply alarmed by the offence and angry with the young man. Their different reactions had threatened to disrupt the possibility of any successful plans being made for Eric's placement. Once these had been acknowledged and discussed the workers were able to use the insights these reactions offered to help their client. They expressed their dilemma to him and together explored with him the way this dilemma worked in his family. It was the beginning of a therapeutic conversation.

In order for workers to feel that they can expose and explore their own sensitivities and responses to sexual abuse in this way they must have confidence and trust in the support of fellow team members. Supervision which takes such material into account is imperative. However, work like this within a team should not simply take place around individual cases.

Team-building and consultation should be ongoing and should incorporate inter-agency team development. There is also an argument for professionals in this sort of work to receive additional out-of-agency consultation or therapy as discussed in chapter 13.

Conclusion

The preceding analysis highlights the dilemmas that face many helping professionals when dealing with the vexing issue of placing children and young people who sexually abuse. Practice does not exist in a vacuum and the delivery of services to this client group is influenced by social, professional, personal, political and financial agendas. In the light of these pressures, professionals can lose objectivity and the fundamentals of good practice can all too often be compromised.

In the first part of this chapter the placement needs of this group of young people have been highlighted, ranging from remaining at home to secure accommodation. Fostering, specialist residential provision, semi-supported lodgings and living within the extended family all fall within this continuum. Decisions about the most appropriate placement should be made in the light of a risk assessment. In order to provide appropriate accommodation for these young people, it has been suggested that, at both local and national levels, consideration of financial, political and professional constraints should be addressed and strategies and guidelines produced to assist practitioners in making appropriate placement decisions. Equally, combining resources between agencies and local authorities may well be a more cost-effective way of providing some of these resources.

All the resources in the world will not necessarily result in appropriate placements. In the second part of this chapter the discussion has focused on how the decision-making process itself is beset by various conscious and unconscious agendas at societal, agency and personal levels which can result in inappropriate decisions being made. It has been recommended that practitioners and managers are courageous enough to acknowledge and explore these processes.

With the recent outcry for community protection the fear of many professionals is that young sexual abusers will become labelled and stigmatised in the same manner as adult paedophiles despite the fact that the intervention and management issues are very different. Social workers act as intermediaries between young abusers and a society that wishes to condemn them. The dilemma is simultaneously to provide for the needs of the young person whilst protecting any potential vulnerable victims of sexual abuse within a context of limited resources.

5

LOOKING AFTER YOUNG SEXUAL ABUSERS

Child protection, risk management and risk reduction

Kevin Epps

Introduction

This chapter explores some of the problems inherent in looking after a child or young person who is known to have engaged in some form of sexually inappropriate or sexually abusive behaviour with another child. The chapter is structured around a central theme: how to minimise the risk of further episodes of abuse (a child protection issue) whilst at the same time helping to promote the development and welfare of the young abuser (a child-care issue). This is not an easy task, requiring a balance to be maintained between three sets of factors: the young abuser, the context in which he lives, and access to potential child victims. The balancing task is made more difficult by the dynamic nature of each of these factors; children develop and change, and do not physically stay in one place. Consequently, the risk a young abuser presents is always open to change. The process of managing risk therefore requires planning, monitoring and evaluation, sometimes over a period of several years. In addition, in common with all other management tasks, it involves making decisions; for example, about where the young abuser should live, or about the most appropriate types of therapeutic intervention. Decision-making requires information, and it is the quality of this information, and the decisions and actions that flow from it, that are fundamental to the management of risk.

The remainder of the chapter is structured around the information-gathering and decision-making processes that guide the management of young abusers and the protection of other children. A framework for managing and evaluating risk is developed, in which emphasis is given to the various types and sources of information required to inform decision-making.

Although the chapter will focus on issues arising once an allegation of sexual abuse has been made, it is worth noting that the first step in preventing abuse, and indeed in managing children who have previously abused, must be to acknowledge and accept the possibility that there may be a risk of abuse, and to take action to prevent it. For many people the notion of sexually abusive children remains alien and unthinkable so that, for example, it is not uncommon in fostering and residential care situations to find children with an unknown history placed together in the same bedroom, with no consideration of the possible risks involved. As will be emphasised in this chapter, appropriate supervision and careful thinking through of potential risks are essential to children's safety.

For the sake of simplicity, the term 'child' is used to refer to children and young people up to the age of 18 years, beyond which children can no longer be subject to legislation under the 1989 Children Act. In addition, although it is recognised that female children also abuse (see chapter 10), the pronoun 'he' is used throughout the chapter.

Immediate priorities when abuse is discovered

Collecting information about current risk and the need for child protection

One of the immediate concerns of many social workers, parents, and other adults with responsibility for looking after a sexually abusive child is the provision of some form of therapy to help stop the child abusing and to provide some insight into why the abuse took place. Many people struggle to understand abusive behaviour and the question 'why?' is an understandable reaction. However, the view taken in this chapter is that in the immediate and short term the emphasis must be on protecting other children; ensuring that the young abuser is safely looked after in a stable, structured environment; and collecting information about the abuser, his family, and his abusive behaviour. As soon as this can be achieved, within a matter of days in some cases, and weeks, months or even years in others, therapeutic plans can be developed to address abusive behaviour.

Chapters 2 and 3 overview the kinds of actions that should be pursued at the point when allegations are made that a child has been sexually abusive. These actions typically involve undertaking an investigation and initial assessment, managed through child protection and/or criminal justice systems. The main priority is to secure the safety of victims, current and potential. At a minimum, information is required about the likely amount of contact between the perpetrator and the victim(s) of abuse and the extent to which this is controlled and supervised. It is also desirable to have information about likely contact between the abuser and other children and the extent to which these may be at risk from the abuser.

If the safety of children cannot be guaranteed within the current living arrangements, the abusive child, or the victim(s), may need to be removed to another setting where the risk is reduced. There is clearly room for error here; for example, an abusive child may be removed unnecessarily, or placed in a setting where other children may be put at risk or, alternatively, in a situation where he is at risk from various types of abusive experience, perhaps in a poorly supervised setting with older, delinquent children.

Currently, there are insufficient resources to deal with sexually abusive children. Children who continue to abuse because they are inadequately supervised often find themselves moving from one child-care placement to another, creating more victims along the way. They may also lose faith in adults and become even more socially isolated, possibly withdrawing even further into a world of sexual fantasy which increases the risk of further abusive behaviour. The development of specialised, local, fostering resources, with high levels of supervision and awareness of the need to protect other children would help to overcome these problems, allowing further assessment to take place in a safe environment (see Lee and Olender, 1992). This helps facilitate the development of longer-term plans for care and intervention. Chapter 4 addresses these issues in more detail.

Meeting the needs of the young abuser

When it becomes apparent that a child is at risk of abusing other children, a range of other problems needs to be addressed in addition to child protection issues. Consideration has to be given to meeting the needs of the young abuser, with a view to ensuring minimal disruption to his welfare and education. As noted earlier, the lack of specialised resources often leads to a considerable degree of disruption. Young abusers are sometimes placed a considerable distance from home, making family contact and school attendance difficult.

Consideration needs to be given to the amount and type of family contact that is appropriate, especially if the victim of abuse is a member of the family unit, as other children in the family could be at risk. Initially, all family visits may need to be supervised to ensure that there is no inappropriate verbal or physical behaviour between the young abuser and other children, and to make an assessment of parental and family interaction. Information is also required about parental attitudes to the disclosure of sexually abusive behaviour, especially significant if the victim is part of the family.

Ideally, abusers who continue to make threats against the victim of abuse, who apportion blame to the victim, or who attempt to convince family members that the victim is lying, should not have contact with the victim. Some abusers can be quite subtle in their efforts to intimidate children, using eye contact and body posture to induce anxiety. The amount and quality of contact by telephone also needs to be considered. To avoid the possibility of the abuser harassing the victim it may be necessary to control use of the telephone; for example, adults may dial the number, make the connection, and only then pass the telephone to the young person. In extreme cases, visits and telephone contact with the family can be temporarily stopped altogether, using Section 34(6) of the Children Act 1989 (see Department of Health, 1991a).

It is important not to underestimate the damage that can be done by abusers through verbal interactions over the telephone.

One self-injurious 13-year-old girl seen in a children's home made disclosures that she had been sexually abused by both her teenage brothers over a number of years. During telephone calls her mother made constant demands that she should be allowed to return home, accused her of causing illness in the family due to the allegations, and insisted that she should 'pull herself together and get over the abuse'. The mother also colluded with both brothers in helping them to make telephone calls to the victim, when they would continue to verbally abuse and threaten her. Most incidents of self-injury occurred directly following visits and telephone contact, associated with considerable anxiety and emotional distress. Eventually, telephone contact was stopped and visits restricted to weekly supervised contact with the mother.

The provision of education can also cause difficulties. Although many children who have abused continue to attend their mainstream school, it is sometimes necessary to remove an abusive child due to the risks they present to other children. There is likely to be particular concern if there is evidence that the child has abused within the school setting, or shown some other form of sexually inappropriate behaviour, such as exposing his genitals or masturbating in public. Alternatively, the view may be reached that the risk of abuse within school is very low; there may be no evidence of behavioural problems, sexual or otherwise, and the victim(s) of abuse may be many years younger than the school peer group. For example, unless there is evidence to the contrary, there is no reason to believe that a 15-year-old boy who has sexually abused a 5-year-old girl will present a sexual risk to his all-male teenage peer group at school. However, it may nevertheless be prudent to arrange for the boy to be escorted to and from school, and to ensure that he is under adult supervision when there is a possibility of contact with younger children.

Finding suitable educational provision for abusive children who are removed from school can be problematic. Home tuition can sometimes be arranged, although this is often time-limited, with a restricted curriculum. In the longer term, attendance at a special school can sometimes be arranged. However, this may not be appropriate for the minority of abusive children who are particularly persistent and predatory in their abuse, as many schools do not have adequate resources to offer effective continuous supervision.

Andrew, a particularly abusive adolescent boy seen by the author, attended a special school for several years, during which time he managed to continue to abuse younger, vulnerable children, and engage peers in sexual activity. Andrew's stay at the school came to an end after he was found in the school toilets with his trousers round his ankles, anally raping another boy, whilst the adult providing 'constant' supervision waited outside with other children, unaware of what was taking place inside the toilet cubicle.

Longer-term goals: developing a framework for managing risk

Abusive behaviour does not occur in a vacuum. Rather, it takes place within a particular context, at a specific point in time, and involves a perpetrator and a victim who both possess specific characteristics. To arrive at an informed view of the extent to which an abuser is at risk of committing further acts of sexual abuse requires information to be collected about each of these factors.

The young abuser

Assessment of the young abuser is covered in detail in chapter 6. Attention here is given to information that is especially pertinent to the management of risk and the prevention of abuse. There is sometimes overwhelming evidence that other children are at risk yet, for some reason, the evidence is not acted upon.

> Several years ago the author was asked by a solicitor to undertake an assessment of Francis, a young boy, as part of care proceedings. One of the questions to be addressed in the assessment was the extent to which Francis was at risk of sexually abusing other children, in view of the fact that he had been sexually abused during childhood. This seemed like a challenge. Although there is no 'crystal ball' with which to make accurate predictions of future behaviour, the author nevertheless set about preparing an assessment agenda, expecting information relating to risk of abuse to be elusive and difficult to obtain. After all, not all abusive children are explicit in their intention or desire to abuse. However, upon receiving the usual bundle of background documentation the question of whether there 'may be a risk' became meaningless: Francis had been sexually abusing other children since the age of 5 and had continued abusing in every placement and school since that time. This information was well documented, yet no definitive action had been taken to keep other children safe or to try to address his abusive behaviour. Some of the professionals were unaware of the history of abusive behaviour, whilst others considered it to be an historical problem or had minimised its significance.

Although this case example is by no means exceptional, information about the young person and the extent to which he is predisposed to abuse is often harder to obtain. What little is known about individuals who sexually offend allows us to extract one useful 'rule of thumb': there is no one 'type' of person, no single personality 'profile', that is associated with sexual offending.

> Thus, in contrast to the example of Francis, David, a 15-year-old boy, was also seen by the author. He had been accused of anally raping two younger boys in a local park on several different occasions: extremely serious offences which, if proved and convicted, would result in a long sentence under Section 53 of the 1933 Children and Young Person's Act. David denied the offences, and there was no obvious background information suggesting that he had a propensity for this type of violent sexual behaviour. He came from an intact family with no criminal or psychiatric history, and no previous contact with social services; had no recorded history of offending or behavioural problems; was a 'model' school pupil; belonged to several local clubs and charities; regularly helped his elderly grandmother, doing her chores and shopping on a Saturday; and presented in interview as anxious and apprehensive. He said he had a girlfriend, whom he had kissed, but denied having any sexual experiences, abusive or otherwise, and limited sexual knowledge. Psychometric testing showed nothing unusual. However, although David did not seem like the 'type of person' who might commit acts of sexual violence against children, the absence of overt behavioural, family, and psychological problems did not make it safe to conclude that he could not have committed such acts. David was in fact subsequently convicted, partly on the basis of forensic evidence that later came to light, and sentenced, although he maintained his denial.

The examples of Francis and David are, fortunately, extreme. Not all abusers are so persistent in their abuse as Francis, and most of those that do come to the attention of child-care professionals present with less resistance and denial, and more overt sexual and behavioural problems, than David.

In the literature on adult sexual offending, a distinction has been made between sexually abusive men who have a strong predisposition (high motivation) to engage in sexually deviant behaviour ('preference' offenders) and those who are less predisposed (low motivation) but respond to specific situational triggers ('situational' offenders) (Laws and Marshall, 1990). To some extent, this is a false dichotomy: all sexual offences necessarily involve an interaction between extrinsic variables (those external to the offender, such as specific situational triggers) and intrinsic variables (those within the offender, such as thoughts and feelings). Nevertheless, there is some merit to the situational–preference distinction. It can help identify risk factors that are located within the offender ('preference' factors), those that are present in the environment in which the offender lives ('situational' factors), and those that result from an interaction between these two sets of factors.

Some offenders are clearly more risky than others, regardless of the situation: they possess personal characteristics that increase the risk of offending. In assessing risk it is especially important to gain a 'holistic' picture of the way in which the young person functions emotionally, cognitively and behaviourally in a range of situations. Especially important is the ability and motivation of the child to control, manage, and modify his behaviour. Abusive children who are impulsive, overactive, restless, agitated, emotionally volatile, and preoccupied with sexual fantasies and sexual activity, are more unpredictable and difficult to supervise, and certainly provoke a great deal more anxiety in their carers.

Various factors can diminish or undermine the ability and motivation to stop abusing (see Epps, 1997a, b). These include: established, habitual patterns of abusive behaviour; preoccupation with deviant sexual fantasies, especially when reinforced by exposure to pornography; entrenched beliefs and attitudes which support abusive behaviour, particularly when the same views are held by other members of the child's family; psychiatric disorders, such as Attention Deficit Hyperactivity Disorder (ADHD), or chronic substance abuse, which can impair the learning of behavioural and cognitive self-control strategies; cognitive difficulties, such as impaired intellectual functioning, which may restrict the ability to plan behaviour and to consider behavioural outcomes; emotional difficulties, such as an impaired ability to see things from the perspective of others or to empathise with others; and social and relationship problems, for example, an inability to trust adults, or to form attachments, or to make friends with peers. Some of these problems, especially in the emotional and behavioural domains, are more likely in children with disrupted care in early childhood, especially if this is compounded by abuse, neglect and inadequate attention to socialisation.

The need to tease out the relative contribution of preference and situational factors, especially the extent to which abusive patterns of thinking and behaviour are entrenched in the daily psychological functioning of the young person, reinforces the need for individualised problem-focused assessment.

Abuse behaviour

'Investigative Psychology', a branch of applied psychology (Canter, 1989, 1994), is concerned with using information from a crime scene about offence behaviour to make informed judgements about the likely characteristics of the individual who committed the offence. Unfortunately, information about offence behaviour is frequently neglected during the process of managing and treating sexually abusive children. Occasionally it is useful to be reminded what the abuser did and to reflect on the psychological characteristics that allowed the behaviour to occur: after all, exactly what is 'lacking' in a boy who ignores the distress of his child victim when he rapes? How and where did the abuser learn this type of sexual behaviour?

Collecting information about offences, especially about victim characteristics (age, gender, relationship to offender, physical characteristics, emotional and social functioning); the types of abusive behaviour perpetrated against the victim ('grooming' behaviours, sexual behaviours, verbal and physical threats, use of force and violence); and situational factors (location of offence, time of day, social context) contributes enormously to the estimation of risk and the development of strategies to reduce risk. Based on the principle that past behaviour is the best predictor of future behaviour, it is sometimes possible to describe consistent features of offence behaviour and to identify high-risk scenarios that should be avoided.

The context

The reciprocal relationship that exists between an abusive child and his immediate social environment (family home, foster placement, residential setting or school) has been alluded to earlier. Whatever the care context, there is an expectation that adults will be proactive in preventing abuse and will create a safe environment in which children are protected from abuse. Thus, regardless of the type of care environment, particular attention must be given to observation and supervision of the young abuser and the enforcement of behavioural boundaries. The setting and establishment of behavioural limits is an important function of caring for children, helping to promote healthy psychological and social adjustment. Children who lack boundaries are more likely to feel anxious and insecure, and to be exposed to inappropriate learning experiences. The backgrounds of sexually abusive children who also exhibit behavioural and conduct problems are often characterised by a lack of limit setting. These children are especially likely to create difficulties when entering residential or foster placements.

Family and foster care

Within family and foster care situations attention should be given to the quality of parental and family functioning, in addition to the quantity and quality of adult supervision. Various factors can undermine the ability of adults to supervise, such as illness, work commitments, or the need to devote attention to other children. Wilson (1998) suggests that the ability of some women to protect their children is diminished by the psychological consequences of their own victimisation within an abusive relationship. Women who have been victims of childhood sexual abuse, and who live in an abusive adult relationship, may be particularly vulnerable to feeling powerless or may 'overlook' evidence that abuse is taking place. Thus, various warning signs indicating that abuse is taking place are sometimes missed or not acted upon. For example, subtle changes in the abused child's behaviour may be ignored or viewed in isolation, and thinking processes that raise the possibility of abuse may be dismissed as over-anxious thinking and therefore not seriously entertained. In other instances, however, the decision not to intervene may be deliberate; some women are threatened by their abusive partner, or feel that they have too much to lose if they take action. Wilson recommends that child protection issues should be considered within the broader context of domestic violence.

However, concern has also been expressed in the child abuse literature that too much responsibility has been placed on women to protect children from abuse (Edleson, 1997; Wilson, 1998). In contrast, the role of non-abusive men in protecting children has received relatively scant attention (O'Hagan, 1997; Roberts, 1998). During child protection investigations the focus is usually on mothers, while fathers and other male carers are ignored. If such stereotypes remain unchallenged not only are women oppressed but men's rights are also ignored and opportunities to increase safety for children are lost.

Children's homes and secure units

Children living in children's homes are particularly vulnerable to sexual abuse. Farmer (1998) collected data on 250 'looked after' children. Of these, 96 (38 per cent) either had a history of sexual abuse and/or were sexually abusive, whilst 50 per cent of the adolescent girls in the study had been sexually abused. Several factors can either help or hinder effective management of abusive children in a residential setting. Particular attention should be given to the peer-group composition, with respect to age, gender and vulnerability.

The extent to which other children are similar to the abuser's victim(s) is an important consideration when placing an abusive child in a residential setting. Unless there is evidence to the contrary there is no reason, for example, why a female adolescent abuser who has targeted younger boys aged 7 and 8 years should necessarily present a risk to adolescent girls. In placing any child it is just as important to consider recent and current behaviour and attitudes as it is to consider historical information about abusive behaviour. It is not unusual to find children who have been 'labelled' as abusers, with no information about the specific nature of the abuse. The label becomes the predominant theme in placing the child, and all other children are considered to be at risk. In contrast, other children are not labelled as abusive, even though their recent behaviour suggests that they present considerable risks to other children. Consider, for example, an adolescent boy placed in a children's home because of his delinquent behaviour. He is observed to sexually threaten adolescent girls, and staff express concern about the risk of sexual assault. However, when he is later referred to a mixed-sex secure unit because of his violent, disruptive behaviour, information about his sexual threats is not included in the referral. It is always important to 'look behind' labels to examine the behaviour of the child and to consider risk in light of current behaviour.

Within residential settings, the concept of 'dynamic security' is useful. In recent years considerable attention has been given to the need for physical security in schools and children's homes, and the need for buildings to be designed in a way that facilitates supervision. However, it is equally important that staff have sufficient insight into peer-group dynamics to be able to predict and prevent abusive acts. For example, staff may overhear two young abusers planning an abusive act. Awareness of peer-group dynamics can also reduce the risk of older, more experienced abusers, using threats to coerce and intimidate potential victims, perhaps reinforced by their physical size and status within the peer group. In some instances, specialised care arrangements are necessary to reduce the risk of abuse to an acceptable level. For example, the young person may need to be looked after in isolation away from the peer group, with a dedicated staff team to provide constant care. Clearly, this is not a satisfactory long-term solution: apart from the obvious resource implications, social isolation can be a damaging experience, especially during childhood and adolescence. However, there may be no other option, especially if the child is persistent in his attempts to abuse other children.

It is advisable to have written policies informing young people, and carers, about the limits of acceptable behaviour, especially the degree of permissible physical contact. For example, should children be allowed to hug each other? Are older children allowed to form intimate relationships and, if so, what degree of physical contact is allowed? Should staff engage children in 'rough-and-tumble' play? Clearly, policy and practice in these areas will be determined by a variety of factors, such as the age of the children, their developmental needs, and their degree of vulnerability.

There is always a risk that some abusers will exploit opportunities for physical contact to gain sexual arousal or to groom potential victims. What may appear to be harmless play in the swimming pool, for example, could act as a source of sexual arousal for a young abuser. In making decisions about physical contact it is important to consider the extent to which the young abuser is deliberately planning and manipulating situations to gain sexual arousal, and the extent to which he is able to talk about his sexual feelings and fantasies in various situations. Sexual abusers who are persistent in their attempts to conceal their sexual behaviour, and who encourage other children to share 'secrets', are more difficult to manage and likely to arouse more anxiety in their carers.

Sexually abusive behaviour is less likely to occur in care settings which strive to develop an anti-oppressive culture, in which children are encouraged to be assertive, and open and honest in their attitudes and relationships. Part of the role of carers is to help children learn the boundaries of acceptable, healthy relationships, and to give children the confidence to assert their own personal boundaries (see Gilbert, 1988). In one of the few studies looking at the outcome of abuse-prevention education and training, boys who had received training perceived themselves as less likely to be abused (Dziuba-Leatherman and Finkelhor, 1994). Through social-learning processes, such as modelling, the behaviour of adults also has a significant influence on child behaviour. Children with learning difficulties, who are less able to regulate their own behaviour, may especially be sensitive to their social environment.

There is a need for carers to be especially mindful of potential 'hot-spots', where there is an increased risk of abuse. Hot spots include times of the day when children are in close proximity, such as in the classroom, at bedtime, or at mealtimes. For example, abusive children may ensure that they sit next to younger vulnerable victims at mealtimes and carry out abusive sexual acts under the table hidden from adult view. Other hot spots arise at unstructured times of the day, when adult supervision may be lax. For example, in the evening when children are engaged in individual recreational activities, or during the night, when children may be able to gain unsupervised access to the bedroom of another child. It is important that carers are aware of the need for vigilance and effective supervision, and to accept that abusive acts can be carried out in a matter of seconds.

Within any child-care environment, there is a risk that behavioural boundaries will gradually shift to the benefit of an abuser, with adults failing to recognise the long-term trend. For example, in a residential setting there may be a gradual increase in rough-and-tumble play between children, to which staff become accustomed. Boundary shifting can be a particular problem in residential settings, where the high level of contact between staff and children makes it difficult for staff to maintain an objective view of the social environment. The use of external managers and consultants who are able to provide independent overview can help to overcome this problem.

Reducing risk by helping the young abuser to stop abusing

Thus far, the focus of the present chapter has been on the prevention of sexual abuse through developing an understanding of the abuser and his abusive behaviour, and creating a safe care environment in which adult carers take stock of the young abuser's needs and the likely risks he presents. The onus has been on the adult carers to take preventive measures and, temporarily, to take control of the young abuser. However, this is not a long-term solution to preventing abuse. The *status quo* cannot be maintained indefinitely; sexually abusive children grow into young adults, and gain more freedom and access to situations in which they may be at risk of abusing.

Becker and Kaplan (1988) identified three developmental 'paths' taken by young abusers, one of which is the 'dead-end' path, in which the abuser stops abusing of his own accord with no intervention. Unfortunately, the current level of knowledge is insufficient to allow us to identify with any degree of confidence those child abusers who will follow the dead-end path, and those who will continue their abusive behaviour, perhaps into adulthood. However, as noted earlier, some child abusers seem to present a greater degree of risk than others, especially those who have experienced profoundly damaging and disrupting childhood trauma, and are persistent in their abuse, and preoccupied with sexually abusive behaviour.

The role of therapeutic intervention

Confidence in making predictions, and certainly in defending decisions about the care and management of an individual child, is generally made easier when there is information about the abusive child's inner world of thoughts and feelings. Insight into the psychological world of the abusive child is best achieved through active engagement of the child in a programme of intervention, with a view to helping the child to gain control of abusive behaviour. This is illustrated by the findings on the proportion of juvenile sex offenders who report a history of sexual abuse. Worling (1995) compared data on sexual abuse across different studies, with a combined total of 1,268 participants. The studies using pre-treatment data reported a mean abuse rate of only 22 per cent, compared to 52 per cent in the studies using post-treatment information. Worling notes that this finding 'corroborates the clinical experience of those who state that many adolescent sex offenders only acknowledge a sexual victimisation history after they have formed a trusting relationship with a therapist' (p. 610).

Recent years have seen an expansion in the number of treatment programmes for sexually abusive children. Most programmes use structured groupwork, employing a variety of cognitive-behavioural interventions (see chapters 8 and 11), although individual psychotherapy also has an important role to play (see chapter 7).

The benefits of formal intervention approaches will be maximised if complemented by appropriate carer attitudes and behaviours in the child's daily living environment. Unfortunately, even within some child-care agencies there is a chronic lack of confidence and skill in dealing with the problem of sexually abusive behaviour (Farmer, 1998). Some of the possible reasons for this are outlined in a manual for 'Residential workers caring for young people who have been sexually abused and those who abuse others', prepared for the Scottish Office by The Centre for Residential Child Care (1995). The authors suggest that the subject of sexual abuse arouses particular anxiety in care staff, leading to avoidance of the problem. Six factors are identified to explain this reaction:

1   Staff feel uncomfortable and awkward in responding to the sexually explicit and provocative behaviour displayed by some abused/abusive children;

2   It is difficult to listen to a child describing in detail the abuse he has experienced and/or inflicted;

3   Staff feel vulnerable, often fearing that they may become the subject of allegations that they have sexually abused the child;

4   Individual staff feel overwhelmed by the prospect of taking on responsibility for helping the child to stop abusing and providing a safe environment to prevent abuse, especially if unsupported by team members;

5   Some staff may have themselves been the victims of sexual abuse, and find the experience of working with the victims or perpetrators of sexual abuse too distressing;

6   Staff feel anxious about the uncertainty and unpredictability associated with working with abused and abusive children, where new disclosures can be made at any time which need to be handled sensitively according to policy and practice guidelines.

Despite these problems the authors of the Scottish Office report stress that staff in many children's homes already possess many of the skills required to undertake intervention work with sexually abused and abusive children, but that specialist training is required to develop confidence in this area of work and to facilitate productive collaboration with those providing formal treatment and therapy.

Arrangements for such collaborative working together must consider the boundaries of confidentiality and the need to establish effective systems for communication. Once established, the systems need to be sufficiently robust to deal with changes in care arrangements; for example, a move to another placement. A change in context will result in changes in behaviour and possibly a change in risk. New carers need adequate information to prepare for the arrival of the child, to ensure that the child can be safely looked after and that other children are protected. A sudden change in placement can result in a breakdown in communication, providing an opportunity for the abusive child to gain the trust of his new carers and to engage in abusive behaviour.

Issues concerning confidentiality can sometimes prove especially difficult to resolve, especially where different agencies have different policies. Much of the anxiety is carried by those looking after the abusive child, who may be concerned that other agencies are not sharing information which has a bearing on risk. Consider, for example, an abusive child who informs his therapist that he has strong and over-whelming sexual fantasies about another child with whom he has daily contact. From a child protection perspective, there is a strong argument for the therapist to communicate this information to the child's carers to enable them to plan effectively for the protection of the potential victim of abuse. Indeed, if the information is not disclosed and the child abuser acts on his fantasies and abuses the other child, the therapist could be accused of negligence. Nevertheless, some therapists continue to insist on complete client confidentiality, on the grounds that they need to foster a trusting relationship with the child. Clearly, issues surrounding communication and confidentiality should be resolved before commencing therapeutic work. The Ohio Teaching-Family Association (OT-FA) (Lee and Olender, 1992) insist that all children accepted onto their specialist fostering programme for sexually abusive children sign a waiver authorising the OT-FA to share information on a need-to-know basis.

Information about response to treatment should be made available to carers so that they can make adjustments to the care and supervision of the abuser. There may be times, for example, when there is a need for closer supervision, or a change in the amount of contact with certain family members. Some children who actively resist treatment, or lack the ability or motivation to change their behaviour, continue to present a serious risk to other children, with little prospect of change. At a minimum, educational and cognitive-behavioural interventions, such as the 'Stop and Think' model outlined in chapter 11, require the child to pay attention and to listen, and preferably to be sufficiently keen and motivated to practise and rehearse new behavioural and thinking skills. Psychotherapeutic interventions (see chapter 7) similarly require motivation, as well as the ability to explore with the therapist distressing thoughts, feelings and past experiences. Not all young abusers possess these qualities. Although some abusers are relieved to have an opportunity to talk about their experiences and feel secure in the knowledge that they are receiving help, others refuse to participate in individual or groupwork. Alternatively, some begin the work but are soon overwhelmed by anxiety, perhaps finding therapeutic work particularly threatening. This can result in 'acting-out' behaviours, such as aggression, which disrupt therapeutic progress. Therapeutic progress may also be slow in teaching disabled children, particularly if the treatment programme is not modified according to the degree of learning impairment (see Clare, 1993).

Where therapeutic efforts fail to produce changes in attitude and behaviour, and young abusers remain motivated to abuse, the role of adult carers in promoting change is particularly important. Various behavioural techniques can be used to encourage personal change. For example, behaviour modification programmes alter the environment around the individual abuser with a view to encouraging and rewarding desirable behaviours and attitudes. In residential child-care settings staff have more control over situational influences on behaviour, making this type of intervention particularly useful (see Cullen and Seddon, 1981; Milan, 1987). Rewards for achieving specific behavioural targets may take the form of staff approval, access to desired activities, or points or tokens which can be used to gain access to activities or to purchase material goods. Behavioural contracts may also be used, whereby the individual agrees to behave in certain ways and receives rewards for doing so (see DeRisi and Butz, 1975). For example, a child may be contracted to attend twice-weekly individual or group treatment sessions for which he will be rewarded. Once a regular pattern of attendance is achieved, the reward system is gradually withdrawn.

Sexually abusive children who are resistant to therapeutic intervention may also benefit from relapse-prevention techniques. Borrowed from behavioural medicine (Marlatt *et al.*, 1985), relapse prevention aims to prepare people to anticipate and cope with high-risk situations that may precipitate a relapse, and is now an important component of many sex offender programmes (Marshall, Hudson, and Ward, 1992; Pithers, 1990). The offender is encouraged to self-monitor his thoughts, feelings and behaviour ('internal management') in an effort to become aware of the sequence of events and decisions (the 'offence cycle') that culminates in offending behaviour. The onus is on the offender, or external agents such as family, friends, and therapists ('external management'), to prevent movement through the offence cycle ('relapsing'). The offender is also encouraged to learn coping strategies to prevent relapse. There are several advantages to using the relapse-prevention model to work with poorly motivated sexually abusive children: it emphasises the 'here-and-now', requiring little in the way of introspective analysis; has a clear focus on avoiding further offending and the associated negative consequences for the offender, which may include prosecution, removal from home, and being locked-up; and provides clear, concrete strategies for avoiding high-risk situations.

Monitoring, evaluating, and reviewing risk

In addition to the task of constantly monitoring and reviewing the response (or lack of) to treatment, it is also important to take a longer-term view: where will the child be living in a few months time? How will it be possible to demonstrate that there has been a reduction in risk? (see chapter 12 for treatment evaluation). One outcome of assessment and formulation should be the identification of 'clinically relevant behaviours' (CRBs). These are the behaviours (including 'internal' behaviours, such as thoughts and fantasies) that, in any one case, are considered to be central to the risk of re-offending, and therefore warrant particularly close monitoring and evaluation. In the case of a child who is particularly sexually disinhibited, the CRBs may be the frequency with which he engages in various observable sexual acts in a public setting. To assess the effectiveness of treatment on these CRBs requires detailed observations to be conducted pre-treatment ('baseline data') and post-treatment. A substantial reduction in the CRBs can be used as evidence of change, perhaps justifying a move to a less restrictive environment, or a return home.

Different types of CRBs will be required for different children. In another child, for example, sexually abusive behaviour may be closely tied to an inability to form satisfying peer relationships and to assert himself in his peer group. Lack of success in these areas may signal an imminent relapse, in which the child begins to consider engaging in further abusive behaviour. Information about the quality of peer relationships and assertiveness would therefore form an important element of risk evaluation. External agencies can sometimes be used as consultants to review and monitor progress, and to audit treatment and management programmes. Part of the consultancy role is to ensure that CRBs have been specified and to provide an independent, objective assessment of the extent to which risk may have been reduced.

Conclusions

This chapter has identified a number of areas that need to be considered if sexually abusive children are to be prevented from abusing, both in the short term and in the longer term. By acknowledging that a particular child is at risk of abusing it becomes possible to construct a framework for understanding the abuser and his abusive behaviour. The aim is to create a safe environment in which adult carers take account of the young abuser's care and treatment needs, the risks he presents to other children, and the extent to which risk changes over time and across care settings. Future development in this area of work must emphasise the need for closer integration of services, especially between residential services and fostering schemes, and the need for external agencies to monitor and evaluate the response of young abusers as they move between care and treatment settings.

6

ASSESSMENT ISSUES

David Will

Introduction

The assessment of children and young people who sexually abuse others requires a comprehensive approach, which addresses a wide range of potential predisposing, precipitating and perpetuating factors. As described in chapter 1, our knowledge of the causation of sexually abusive behaviour is at an early stage in its development (see also Vizard *et al.*, 1995). Many factors may be involved and it is therefore necessary to adopt an eclectic approach to assessment.

The vast majority of young people who are sexually abusive are male (Vizard *et al.*, 1995). Therefore, 'he' will be used to refer to the young abuser in this chapter. However, the same basic principles of assessment pertain when the young person is female (see also chapter 10).

Any adequate assessment must encompass different levels of possible predisposing factors. These include:

- individual factors such as biological vulnerability, impulsivity, and personal experience of sexual, physical or emotional abuse or other major traumas;
- family factors such as the exposure to a climate of violence in the home and discontinuity of care (Bentovim, 1996);
- social factors such as the effects of sexual socialisation on young people e.g. images of masculinity and male power; the impact of pornography.

In addition, an adequate assessment should also provide an understanding of the precipitating and perpetuating factors involved in the specific acts of sexually abusive behaviour. Most services for young abusers in the UK are based on cognitive-behavioural principles and it is important to try to obtain a detailed account of the abusive behaviour in order to develop a treatment plan.

Broadly, assessment has three main purposes:

- assessing risk – what is the likelihood that the young person will repeat his sexually abusive behaviour?
- developing a formulation on which an initial treatment plan can be based;
- assessing the young person's motivation to accept treatment designed to reduce the likelihood that he will repeat his sexually abusive behaviour.

Pre-requisites for assessment

Young people who behave in a sexually abusive way often create considerable anxiety and sometimes confusion in referrers. Any service offering specialised assessment services is therefore likely to receive referrals with requests for urgent assessment. It is important, however, to ensure that some basic pre-requisites are met before assessment occurs.

First, it is essential to have an initial discussion with the referrer about the case. It is essential to establish with referrers that child protection procedures are being followed. Has a child protection case conference been held on the alleged victim(s)? Is the alleged perpetrator still living in a situation in which other children are at risk of abuse? What steps are being taken to ensure that any risk of further abuse is being reduced? Usually, these procedures will have been followed, albeit sometimes with less than satisfactory outcomes such as the alleged perpetrator being placed in residential care where he is living with potentially vulnerable fellow residents. Issues relating to management of these situations are addressed in chapter 5.

Occasionally, child protection procedures will have been flagrantly ignored. For example, a specialist team may be contacted by a professional who wants an alleged perpetrator seen but has not informed the social work department about him and does not want to do so. In such circumstances, a referral cannot be accepted and every effort should be made to get the referrer to follow appropriate procedures.

Second, it is essential to obtain relevant information from the referrer and from other agencies involved. These include pre-sentence reports and information from the police. In England and Wales, but not in Scotland, victim statements can be obtained. These are of considerable value when assessing the perpetrator's account of his abusive behaviour, and their non-availability in Scotland is a major lack.

The assessment process

Assessment of sexually abusive adolescents should be a collaborative process involving his parents and his social worker. For young people in care, input from foster-carers or key workers is important. Information from school and any previous contacts with child guidance should be obtained (although in a health setting permission will have to be obtained from the parents and/or the young person for this). Such a collaborative approach is not simply a means of collecting information; it is also the start of building a collaborative team that will work together if intervention is offered to the young person.

Stage 1 – a general overall assessment of the young person and his family and/or carers

The first stage of assessment will usually start with one or more interviews with the young person and his parents or carers. Its purposes are to first make a general assessment of the young person and his family and, second, to assess the parents' attitude towards their child's abusive behaviour and the need for therapeutic intervention. Detailed discussion of the abusive behaviour and of the young person's sexuality is not a focus. (This will be discussed in subsequent individual sessions with the young person.)

These are often emotionally charged meetings. It is important to begin by providing the family with an explanation of the purpose of the meeting and by describing in general terms the help that can be provided. It is often reassuring for parents to be told that their child's problem is not an uncommon one and that many young people have been provided with help to reduce the likelihood that they will repeat this sort of behaviour.

It is helpful to establish next what the parents know about the abusive behaviour and what their reactions were when they first found out about it. These may range from intense feelings of anger and rejection of their child, to denial that their child could have behaved in this way and that he is being falsely accused of something he did not do. Many parents will be confused and uncertain and in a state of shock. Few will have discussed the allegations with their child in any detail and those that have tried will often have been unsuccessful in getting their child to talk openly about them. Some families will have experienced harassment from neighbours following the allegations and these may be a major source of current stress. It is important to allow parents an opportunity to ventilate any strong feelings about the allegations and their consequences for the family before proceeding with the first stage of the assessment, which is to obtain a good general developmental history of the young person.

Developmental history

This should encompass all the areas covered in any standard history of a young person's development such as a social background report or psychiatric history, but with special reference to factors that may be associated with sexually inappropriate behaviour. These include:

- birth injury or neo-natal distress and delayed developmental milestones;
- hyperactivity, distractibility and impulsivity from an early age;
- difficulties in relating with peers from nursery school/primary school onwards;
- learning difficulties;
- conduct disorder in childhood or developing in adolescence;
- social skills deficits;
- social isolation and poor peer relationships;
- depression or mood swings;
- poor anger control and/or generalised impulsivity;
- history of physically aggressive behaviour towards others;
- delinquency;
- drug or alcohol abuse;
- previous inappropriate sexual behaviour e.g. use of inappropriate sexual language in an abusive way;
- past history of sexual, emotional or physical abuse, including being bullied.

Parents are an invaluable source for much of this information. However, in some areas they may be unaware of important information. For example, a young person may have been sexually abused and not have disclosed this and such a disclosure may only occur once work with him is in progress. Similarly, parents may be unaware that their child is abusing drugs.

Family history and family assessment

Important aspects of family history which appear to be risk factors in the development of sexually abusive behaviour (Bentovim, 1996) include:

- discontinuity of care: experience of living with various parents, step-parents or being looked after by the local authority;
- exposure to a climate of violence in the home;
- experience of physical violence in the family;
- a feeling of being rejected;
- the mother having been sexually abused herself.

Other family factors, which may be relevant, include:

- the nature of behavioural controls within the family. For example, is the family an authoritarian one with a cowed young person or a laissez-faire family with a child who is out of control?
- the nature of parent/child relationships: Does the young person have close or distant relationships with his parents? What sort of role model does the father provide? Is he violent? Does the son identify with him or not? What is the quality of the mother/son relationship? Is the relationship over-indulgent or over-intrusive?
- gender role stereotypes within the family. For example, are gender roles rigidly defined? Are women in the family relegated to the role of skivvies?

In chapter 9 assessment and intervention issues with families are discussed more fully.

Ending the family meeting

At the end of the initial family meeting(s), it is important to explain to the young person and parents what the next stage of assessment will entail. There will be a number of individual meetings with the young person whose purpose is to build up a more detailed picture of him and in particular to assess his sexual knowledge, his attitudes and beliefs about sexual matters and his sexual experience. His sexually abusive behaviour will be discussed in detail and he will also complete a number of questionnaires about relevant issues. If the young person is under 16 it is important to have the parents' agreement for this. Usually this is given, but occasionally parents may express concerns, for example about sexual knowledge questionnaires. If this happens the question-naire should be shown to the parents and any reservations they have about it discussed with them. Permission should also be sought to contact other relevant professionals such as guidance staff at the young person's school.

It is also important to make clear to the parents that another meeting will be held with them to discuss the results of the individual assessment interviews and to make further plans, if appropriate, at that stage. Fostering a collaborative relationship with parents is of the utmost importance and they must be involved at every key stage in the assessment process.

Stage 2 – a detailed assessment of the young person's abusive behaviour, its antecedents and consequences

The second stage in the assessment process is to build up a detailed picture of the young person's sexual knowledge, attitudes and cognitions about sexuality and sexual experience and then to obtain as detailed as possible an account of his sexually abusive behaviour and its antecedents and consequences. This can usefully be achieved by the use of a semi-structured interview combined with the administration of psychometric tests. The number of sessions required will vary from individual to individual. If the young person is prepared to be open about his abusive behaviour and is of average intelligence, two to three sessions may suffice. On the other hand, young people who are initially defensive and less willing to talk about their abusive behaviour and young people with mild to moderate learning difficulties may require several more sessions.

It is important to establish a working relationship with the young person at the outset. A clear explanation of the purpose of the assessment combined with a shared understanding that the overall aim of the process is to help the young person learn to gain more control over his abusive behaviour provide a basic underpinning of a collaborative relationship. It should be stressed that the young person is not a monster, but someone who can be helped to learn to modify his behaviour. It is useful to demonstrate this by talking about general aspects of the young person's life, such as what has he been doing with his friends or at school, at the beginning of each session and by ending each session in a similar way (by, for example, asking what plans he has for the weekend).

By this stage, the majority of young people will acknowledge that they did something that was sexually inappropriate and agree to participate in the assessment. In one study (Will, 1994) about 80 per cent of young people referred to an NHS specialist team, which provides services for young abusers, did so. Only a minority of them fully acknowledged the extent of their abusive behaviour at this stage, but a partial acknowledgement was sufficient for assessment to proceed. It was often not until young people had been in treatment for some time that they were able to give a fuller account of their abusive behaviour.

The remaining 20 per cent completely denied that they had behaved in a sexually abusive way. The problems posed by such denial are considered below.

The semi-structured interview

The use of semi-structured interviews has been described by a number of authors (e.g. Steen and Monnette, 1989; Graham *et al.*, 1997). They are particularly useful in the assessment of young people, who are unaccustomed to talking about their sexuality and are often very embarrassed when asked to do so. Talking about the most intimate aspects of one's sexuality is a daunting prospect for most adults, let alone for an adolescent who has exhibited sexually abusive behaviour. A good semi-structured interview can provide a facilitating degree of distance between the interviewer and the young person, which makes the process less threatening. It is also important for the interviewer to stress that s/he has considerable experience of talking to young people about their sexual feelings and will not be embarrassed or shocked by anything the young person discloses. It should also be emphasised that it is important for the young person to be as open and honest as he can, because this will help the interviewer plan the most appropriate ways of helping him.

A good semi-structured interview gradually moves from relatively unthreatening areas to more difficult ones. Glasgow's (1988) 'Structured assessment of sexual offenders', which was originally developed for use with adults, has proved extremely useful, with some modifications, in the assessment of young people: As it is unpublished, its main features are described here:

1 ESTABLISHING A COMMON LANGUAGE FOR SEXUAL
   ORGANS AND FUNCTIONS

It is obviously essential to start by establishing whether the young person understands the meaning of basic sexual terms and what words he uses for them. A number of words such as 'intercourse', 'masturbation' and 'orgasm' are read out in turn and the young person is asked if he understands what they mean and what words he uses to describe them.

2 SEXUAL KNOWLEDGE

A number of very basic questions about sexual knowledge include 'Can you tell me what sexual intercourse is?' 'What is it for?' 'What does the man do to start sexual intercourse?' and 'When does sex finish?' While these basic questions will be supplemented by more detailed sexual knowledge questionnaires (see below), they provide a brief overview of the young person's sexual knowledge and can guide the subsequent progress of the interview. A significant proportion of young abusers have considerable gaps in their knowledge of even the most basic aspects of sex. The significance of this is unclear, since there are no norms for the sexual knowledge of non-abusing young people. However, a study by Kraft (1993) on a large sample of Norwegian adolescents suggests that there are considerable gaps in the sexual knowledge of young people in general.

3   SOURCES OF SEXUAL KNOWLEDGE

How did the young person obtain his sexual knowledge? From parents? From sex education at school? From friends? (The majority of young people will have received little if any sex education from their parents and will remember little of whatever sex education they received at school.) Has the young person read pornographic books or magazines or watched pornographic videos? (A minority will have done so, often having illicitly watched videos owned by their fathers.) Has he ever seen anyone masturbating or having sex?

4   SEXUAL EXPERIENCE AND BEHAVIOUR

How often does the young person masturbate? When did he start masturbating? Does he think masturbation is in any way bad, wrong or harmful? What thought and ideas go through his head when he is masturbating? It is particularly important to try to elicit deviant masturbatory fantasies, particularly fantasies related to the sexually abusive behaviour.

Has the young person ever had a girlfriend or a boyfriend? If so record a history of such relationships, including his age and the age of his partner, their typical activities, the duration of the relationship and the reasons for its termination.

What was the most sexually exciting thing that ever happened to the young person? Has he ever had any frightening or unpleasant sexual experiences? Has an adult or a friend or anyone in their family ever touched him sexually in a way he did not like? Is there anything to do with sex that really turns him off? It is rare for young people to acknowledge, at this stage, experiences of sexual abuse that have not previously been disclosed. Further disclosures may occur during treatment.

5   HISTORY OF SEXUALLY ABUSIVE BEHAVIOUR

The primary aim of this part of the interview is to build up a detailed description of all of the young person's acts of sexually abusive behaviour, including their antecedents and consequences. It is often possible to gain significant information about the important precipitants, risk factors and gratification which were involved. It is possible to consolidate a sense of collaborative inquiry by explaining why it is important to build up a full picture of the abusive behaviour. For example the interviewer might say:

> What we've got to do now is to build up as full a picture as we can of what happened when you behaved in a sexually inappropriate way. We have to see if we can figure out if there was anything about that day – or what happened that day – that made it more likely you would behave like that. If we can identify anything like that, it will help us plan what we have to do to help you learn to control your behaviour.

The history is structured into three stages. The first stage is to go through each act of sexually abusive behaviour in terms of the events and behaviours that occurred. What happened on the day the abusive behaviour occurred? Where did the behaviour occur? How did the young person meet his victim? What then happened? Was coercion or force used on the victim? Did the young person threaten the victim if s/he told anyone about what had happened? What did the young person do after the abusive behaviour?

Such questions may reveal significant precipitants to the offences.

> **For example Abel, aged 15, described how he had been bullied at school on the day he exposed himself to two young children while returning home. Brian, aged 17, had had an unusually successful day at work and had been lavishly praised by his supervisor on the day he attempted to rape a 15-year-old girl.**

Similarly, particular high-risk situations may become obvious. Young people may commit acts of sexually abusive behaviour when they are babysitting or in places like public parks where children are unattended.

At this stage, the young person's account of the abusive behaviour will commonly be a minimised one which significantly underplays the full extent of his abusive behaviour, the extent of coercion or physical force used and threats made to the victim. If the interviewer has access to police reports, witness information and other referral information about the abusive behaviour, these can be compared with the young person's account. Where appropriate such information can be used to question the young person's account and this may encourage him to disclose more details. It is however, rarely productive at this stage of assessment to directly confront the young person with a view to extracting a 'full confession'.

The second stage consists of the interviewer going through the account of the events and behaviours that occurred but this time focusing on the feelings and thoughts that the young person had at the time. This can first throw light on important emotional precipitants and gratifications.

> For example, Chris, aged 15, disclosed that indecently assaulting a 5-year-old girl made him 'feel big, like a real man'; whilst Daniel, aged 16, described that feelings of depression had preceded a number of his exhibitionistic offences.

Secondly, significant cognitive distortions may be revealed.

> For example, Evan, aged 14, who had sexually abused his 8-year-old niece, described her lying on a couch in the living room. 'She pulled her nightie back above her knees so I put my hand between her legs'. On further questioning, it became clear that Evan had thought the little girl was asking for sex.

The third stage of the history is concerned with the young person's appreciation of what his victim(s) experienced. He is asked to go through each act of sexually abusive behaviour, this time describing what he thinks his victims felt. This will often throw some light on his capacity for empathy or lack of it.

> For example, Frankie, aged 17, had seriously sexually abused a number of young boys. When asked what his victims might have felt, he became quite perplexed. 'How

can I imagine what they felt like?' he asked. 'I just don't know what you mean. It's stupid.'

The semi-structured interview and family interview are important parts of the assessment process. They are supplemented by additional tests.

Additional tests and investigations

Psychometric tests and standardised assessment measures

Many authors (e.g. Graham *et al.*, 1997; Mayer, 1988; and Salter, 1988) recommend the use of psychometric tests and standardised assessment measures. They can provide both an important adjunct to clinical assessment and can also be used as measures of change during treatment. There is no general consensus about which measures are the most useful and different authors make widely different recommendations. Chapter 12 discusses the role and use of such measures.

Penile plethysmography

In this procedure erectile response to a variety of sexual stimuli is measured by means of a flexible band placed round the subject's penis which is connected to a polygraph which records the expansion and contraction of the penis. It is rarely used in Britain with young people, in part because of the ethical problems inherent in exposing them to sexually explicit and pornographic material. It is more widely used with young people in North America (Becker and Kaplan, 1993).

Psychiatric assessment

Major psychiatric disorder is rare in sexually abusive young people, although about 50 per cent of them will show evidence of conduct disorder and 10 per cent will significantly abuse substances such as alcohol and marijuana (Kavoussi *et al.*, 1988; Will, 1994).

A small minority may suffer from significant psychiatric disorders and if this is suspected, a psychiatric assessment is indicated. These disorders include:

*   Attention Deficit and Hyperactivity Disorder (ADHD) which is characterised by problems in attention and concentration, overactivity and impulsivity (Taylor, 1994). The vast majority of children

and young people suffering from this disorder do not exhibit sexually abusive behaviour, however it may be a contributing factor in a small number of cases. Treatment with stimulant medication may improve the symptoms of ADHD and may also improve the young person's ability to use treatment.

- Depression of clinical significance occurs in about 4 per cent of the general adolescent population (Whitaker *et al.*, 1990). It is characterised by low mood, social withdrawal, lack of interest and enjoyment in usual activities, deterioration in school performance, poor concentration and somatic symptoms such as sleep and appetite disturbance.

- Hypomania is rare in adolescents but can result in acts of seriously disinhibited and inappropriate sexual activity. It is characterised by euphoric mood, often with associated irritability, grandiosity, reckless over-spending, pressure of speech with flight of ideas and greatly reduced sleep (Harrington, 1994).

- Post-traumatic stress disorder, which is characterised by flashbacks and/or nightmares of traumatic experiences, associated with anxiety and hyper-arousal (van der Kolk, 1987), may sometimes be present, particularly in young people who themselves have been victims of abuse.

Stage 3 – developing a formulation

The next stage in assessment is to develop a provisional formulation of the young person's problems. This describes the different factors that may have contributed to his sexually abusive behaviour and those that may be maintaining it. It should include:

- a description of the abusive behaviour, if possible identifying its precipitants and gratifications;
- a summary of his psychosexual functioning, with particular reference to any deviant fantasies;
- a summary of individual vulnerabilities or weaknesses in relevant areas e.g. sexual knowledge and cognitions, social skills, anger and impulse control, use of drugs/alcohol and general adolescent maturation;
- relevant family or psychosocial factors currently influencing him;
- a summary of any developmental or historical factors that may be relevant.

An example of a formulation

Glen, aged 17, was referred after pleading guilty to

having behaved in a lewd and libidinous way with four boys, aged between 7 and 9, on several occasions over the previous year.

The offending behaviour

All the offences took a similar form. Glen, who was unemployed throughout this period, would stay at home on his own during the day while his parents were at work. All his victims were friends of his younger brother. If one of them came round to the house when Glen was feeling 'bored' or 'lonely', he would ask him in. He would bribe him with sweets and persuade the boy to let him undress him. He would fondle the boy's genitals and then fellate him. He would not have an orgasm. He would let the boy leave, telling him that what had happened would be their 'secret'. He would then masturbate to orgasm, fantasising about what he had just done. His sexual offences provided him with sexual gratification, a release from feeling bored and lonely and a sense of power.

Psychosexual functioning

He repeatedly masturbates to fantasies of his offences. The frequency of masturbation has increased over the last few months and he is currently masturbating five or six times a day. He has never masturbated to fantasies involving age-appropriate partners of either sex. He is anxious because he has started to go to a local playground to look at little boys. While he denies ever having actively sought out a victim in this way, he is worried that he might. He has never had a girlfriend and is not interested in girls. He has sometimes felt sexually attracted to boys of his own age, but feels very guilty about such feelings.

Individual vulnerabilities or weaknesses

- sexual knowledge: patchy. Good on the mechanics, very poor on the emotional aspects of sexual relationships.

- distorted cognitions: 'The little boys didn't mind what I did to them because they did what I asked them', 'I'm weak sexually, there must be something wrong with my body.'
- social skills: can enjoy being in an all-male group, particularly in the pub. Feels self-conscious and embarrassed in the company of girls.
- assertiveness: cannot assert himself at all with his peers. Feels he is 'a sheep'.
- adolescent maturation: unemployed for last year, with no qualifications. Has tried to live away from home once since he was 17 but only lasted a couple of weeks. No hobbies or interests apart from playing pool in the pub and listening to music.

Family factors

Describes life at home as 'miserable'. Father is very authoritarian, always going on at him to get a job. His parents have refused to attend after an initial family meeting.

Historical factors

- born with a cleft palate, which was repaired. Was teased a lot about his slight speech defect.
- was a loner for most of his primary and secondary schooling.
- attended numerous schools because his father was in the forces until he was 13.
- father physically abused him regularly during his childhood. He is still terrified of him.

Developing a treatment plan from the formulation

A treatment plan is developed on the basis of the formulation. It should outline the types of treatment that the young person requires and their priority. It is important to tailor a treatment plan for each individual, rather than assume that a single treatment package will meet everyone's needs.

Glen's treatment plan will be used as an example:

1 *Control techniques* are required as a matter of urgency, given the frequency and intensity of his deviant fantasies and the obvious risk of his seeking new victims. He should be taught strategies to avoid high-risk situations such as being alone at home and helped to develop strategies to deal with feeling lonely or bored. He should be told in the strongest possible terms never to go unaccompanied to public parks or other places where there are unattended children. He should be taught covert sensitisation as soon as possible and may well require to use verbal (Becker and Kaplan, 1993) or masturbatory satiation (Steen and Monnette, 1989). These and other behavioural methods (including sexual re-conditioning, which is mentioned below) should only be undertaken by suitably trained practitioners.

2 *Group therapy* is indicated. In particular this should address his poor sexual knowledge, his cognitive distortions and his problems with assertiveness (Will *et al.* 1995). If group therapy is not available, these areas should be addressed in individual treatment.

3 *Environmental change* – liaison with his probation officer is necessary about the possibilities of his obtaining employment or obtaining accommodation outside the home.

4 *Sexual re-conditioning* – he has a strong sexual attraction towards children, but has shown some evidence of being sexually attracted to age-appropriate males. He should be helped to develop an orientation towards age-appropriate partners by techniques such as masturbatory re-conditioning (Maletzky, 1991).

5 *Individual psychotherapy* may be useful in providing him an opportunity of working through his feelings about past issues particularly the physical abuse he received from his father.

Risk assessment

Assessing the risk of recidivism or dangerousness is one important purpose of assessment. Commonly, the question that referrers most want answered is 'Will he do it again?' Unfortunately, there is little research evidence or empirical data to permit a confident answer. Chapters 5 and 12 discuss these issues in more detail.

Assessing the young person's motivation and suitability for treatment

Abel *et al.* (1984) describe their assessment of motivation of adult sexual offenders as follows: 'Our own criterion for motivation is whether the patient walks into the treatment room' (p. 9). A minimalist approach to motivation should similarly be adopted with young people who have been sexually abusive. While it is important to endeavour to establish rapport and a collaborative working relationship with young people, it is also important to recognise the ambivalent feelings that young people will inevitably have about treatment. While young people are less likely to have developed the massively cognitively distorted rationalisations shown by adult sexual offenders (Salter, 1988), their motivation for treatment is often affected by adolescent ambivalence towards the idea that they need help (Evans, 1993).

A similarly minimalist approach should be adopted when considering suitability for treatment. The major criteria of suitability for treatment in a non-custodial setting are:

- The young person admits that he has behaved in a sexually abusive way, even if he minimises its seriousness and even if he denies committing other acts of sexually abusive behaviour that he is known to have committed;
- He is prepared to come for treatment or can be legally compelled to do so;
- He is cognitively equipped to cope with the treatment programme available. (Young people with moderate to severe learning difficulties should be referred to appropriate services.)

Conversely, the major criteria of unsuitability for treatment in a non-custodial setting are:

- The young person maintains a stance of total denial about his sexually abusive behaviour;
- He appears to be so dangerous that he requires a secure or custodial setting;
- He refuses to attend and cannot be legally compelled to do so.

DAVID WILL

Minimisation and denial in the assessment process

Minimisation is almost inevitable during assessment. Young people are often embarrassed, ashamed and guilty about their sexually abusive behaviour and as a result will give cosmeticised accounts of what they actually did. It is unrealistic to expect a young person to give a full and frank account of his behaviour from the start. Indeed, this may only occur as treatment progresses and rather than being an aim of assessment should be seen as an aim of treatment. However, as long as the young person is able to admit that he did something that was sexually abusive, this is sufficient to allow treatment to start.

Total denial on the part of the young person about his sexually abusive behaviour must be considered contextually and not simply attributed to the young person's refusal to acknowledge what he did. Contextual factors that should be considered are:

- The alleged sexually abusive behaviour is *sub judice*. If a young person is facing pending legal proceedings he may well not wish to discuss his alleged offences. In these circumstances his right not to discuss his offences must be respected;
- The young person's parents are colluding with him in denying that he behaved in a sexually abusive way. As discussed above, it is important to change parents' perceptions of the seriousness of their child's behaviour.

Total denial on the part of the young person can be difficult to change. If the interviewer is driven by a desire to make him 'confess' in the shortest possible time, he is likely to reinforce denial. It is essential to strike a balance between appropriate confrontation and over-zealous inquisition. Adolescents are often oppositional and excessively confrontational questioning will usually have the effect of making the young person adopt an entrenched position of denial.

It may be helpful to discuss the options available with the young person. He has behaved in a sexually abusive way and if he does not want to acknowledge what he has done, then there is a risk that he will do the same thing again and get involved in further trouble. Alternatively, if he is able to acknowledge what he has done, help can be provided to increase his ability to control his behaviour. If the young person appears to be denying what he did because he is ashamed about it, he can be told that other people are going to regard him as a sexual abuser regardless of whether or not he denies what he did. He has nothing to lose by acknowledging it.

While most young people will at least partially acknowledge their sexually abusive behaviour, during assessment, most will maintain that they will never repeat it. This might appear to be a major obstacle to their working effectively in treatment, particularly if it is based on a relapse prevention model (Pithers *et al.*, 1983). In practice, however, such an acknowledgement is more usefully seen as an aim of treatment rather than of assessment.

There will always be some young people whose denial remains entrenched at the end of assessment. There is some evidence to suggest that they may be more liable to re-offend than those who do not persist in their denial (Will, 1994). They therefore represent a worrying group. It may be possible to provide them with some therapeutic input on areas of difficulty that have emerged in the assessment process e.g. sex education, social skills training or anger control. It is uncommon, however, for such work to lead to the young person's abandoning a stance of denial about his sexually abusive behaviour. Sometimes, such young people will only abandon their denial after they have committed further sexually abusive acts for which they have been apprehended.

The role of legal compulsion in increasing motivation for treatment

Some authors (e.g. Abel *et al.*, 1984; Becker and Kaplan, 1993) do not use legal compulsion as a means of increasing motivation to attend for treatment. It can however, play a useful role. Thus a recommendation can be made for a probation order to have as a condition that the young person attend for treatment. (In Scotland, a supervision order from a Children's Hearing can have a similar condition). This serves two main purposes. First, it underlines the significance of the treatment being offered. Second, there is evidence to suggest that legal compulsion facilitates attendance and reduces drop-out from treatment (Will, 1994).

Conclusion

An adequate assessment takes time, but it is time well spent. Sexually abusive behaviour is a complex phenomenon, which may be influenced by a wide range of factors. In order to develop a strategy for the treatment of a particular individual, it is essential to have an adequate understanding of what particular factors are of relevance to *his* inappropriate behaviour. An adequate assessment allows treatment to be tailored to the needs of the individual.

7

PROVIDING INDIVIDUAL PSYCHOTHERAPY FOR YOUNG SEXUAL ABUSERS OF CHILDREN

Eileen Vizard and Judith Usiskin

Introduction

This chapter is based on the work of the Young Abusers Project set up in 1992 to provide an outpatient assessment and treatment service for children and young people who sexually abuse other children. The Project is part of Camden and Islington Community Health Services NHS Trust and is supported by the NSPCC.

Literature review

A literature review in relation to the psychoanalytic aspects of young sexual abusers is inevitably brief given the present dearth of writing on the subject. By contrast there is discussion about the origins and meaning of adult sexually abusive behaviours, albeit that this is described in the early literature in rather old-fashioned and pejorative terms such as 'perversions', or 'aberrations' (see, for example, Freud, 1905; Glasser, 1979). More recently concepts relating to child abuse and trauma have introduced a more up-to-date psychoanalytical under-standing of the inner worlds of child abuse victims (Scharff and Scharff, 1994; Miller,1984); offenders with learning difficulties (Sinason,1997a); and abusing families (Bentovim, 1992). However it is not surprising that little has yet been written about the inner world of the young sexual abuser since it is only recently that there has been acknowledgment of the prevalence of the problem, with definitional problems apparent, and concerns about the early naming or identification of this young client group without the use of potentially stigmatising labels (NCH, 1992; Vizard *et al.*, 1995 and 1996).

In discussing any abnormal pattern of sexual behaviour it is clearly necessary to describe the current norms for sexual behaviour and yet nearly one hundred years after Freud's papers on sexual aberrations and infantile sexuality (1905) there are few normative studies in relation to childhood sexuality. Indeed within the field of psychoanalysis even the concept of normal infantile sexuality without a traumatic basis has been questioned (Miller, 1984).

Freud's own concept of normality in relation to adult sexuality was extremely conservative as might have been expected in Victorian times. He states that 'the normal sexual aim is regarded as being the union of the genitals in the act known as copulation' although he goes on to acknowledge that 'even in the most normal sexual process we may detect rudiments which, if they had developed, would have led to the deviations described as "perversions"' (Freud, 1905, p. 149). However, Freud says little about the origins of sexually abusive behaviour in children, partly because he appears to have had certain difficulties himself in accepting the abusive nature of sexual contact between children and adults (Masson, 1992) and partly because, as a clinician working with adult patients, he was not clear about the limits of sexual behaviour and experimentation in normal young children. Freud's final formulation that childhood 'sexuality' (that is, sexualised behaviour) was the result of attempts by the child to come to terms with Oedipal conflicts (that is, a wish to have sex with the parent of the opposite sex) remains highly unsatisfactory and limited. It ignores the sexualising role of an experience of child sexual abuse and there is no compelling evidence to suggest that normal children do want to have sex with their parents. Nevertheless, it is fair to say that Freud's work on sexuality points out the early origins of many adult sexual disturbances and the homeostatic function of perverse behaviour in maintaining a psychic equilibrium in a patient with the avoidance of serious emotional conflicts.

This is to some extent echoed by Glasser's view (1979) that the resistance to treatment of perverse sexual interests in adult life is connected with a fear of annihilation, known as the 'core complex' in which 'closeness and intimacy [are envisaged] as annihilating, or separateness and independence [are envisaged] as desolation-isolation' (p. 280). McDougall (1990) postulates a somewhat similar self-preservative solution to these early fears of disintegration by the adult sexual deviant when she states that 'perversions demonstrate that their creator is using sexual capacity to deal with deeper narcissistic dangers' (p. 179). However, even in this more recent writing there is little or no mention of the possible role of early trauma (abuse) in the origins of later deviance or abusing.

Limentani (1989) appeared to be struggling towards an integrated understanding of the origins of perverse behaviour which could relate both to a fear of psychic disintegration and also to early trauma when he stated that, 'I suddenly felt that I was reaching the overriding conclusion that a perversion, after all, is not an illness but only a symptom' (p. 237). He goes on:

> This [symptom] forms the core of a syndrome which has its roots in disturbed object relations in early life, eventually surfacing as perverted acts. It should be noted that in general the original traumatic experience is subject to disavowal. The fantasies associated with the primary excitation [the traumatic experience] seldom reach consciousness but their derivatives [perversion/abusing] will be found in later life.
>
> (p. 238)

Stoller's *Perversion. The Erotic Form of Hatred* (1975), does openly acknowledge the key role of sadism and hostility towards the object or victim of the perversion without specifically naming child abuse as the hostile basis for paedophilia.

A more informed and up-to-date psychoanalytic text (Scharff and Scharff, 1994) discusses the 'Traumatic Continuum' of child abuse within an overall object relational view of trauma. The authors are at pains to acknowledge the 'transmission of trauma to the next generation' (pp. 284–5) but there is no mention of the abused to abuser links which characterise much of the mainstream child abuse literature.

Clear links between childhood trauma and later sexualised disturbance in vulnerable children and adults with learning difficulties have been described from a psychoanalytical perspective (Sinason, 1997b). In therapeutic work with abused children the need to use therapy as an emotional space in which the abusive experience can be 'forgotten', worked through via play, drawings and containment in therapy and then carefully 'remembered' with the help of interpretation from the therapist has been described (Alvarez, 1990). A brief, focused psychoanalytical approach was taken within the Great Ormond Street research programme on young sexual abusers (Hodges *et al.*, 1994) where extended psychotherapeutic assessments over twelve sessions with a therapist allowed conscious remembering and/or discussion of a boy's own abusing behaviour to open up the possibility of later therapy needing to address both abused and abusing experiences. The roots of sexual violence in children and adolescents have been explored in the light of more recent literature from the fields of traumatic stress, brain chemistry and emotion (Le Doux, 1994; Perry, 1994). The possibility is then discussed (Hawkes *et al.*, 1997) that aspects of early sexualised behaviour which may have been induced by child sexual abuse can become imprinted on the brain chemistry hence leading to a persistent state of arousal in the young person which can then result in a tendency towards sexually abusive behaviour.

Clinical descriptions of psychotherapy with sexually abusive young people are now emerging in the literature (Hodges *et al.*, 1994; Vizard, 1997; Woods, 1997). The therapeutic themes described include the sexualisation of violence, traumatic experiences resulting in psychic retreat; sexualisation of the therapeutic relationship, re-enactment of trauma, testing of the therapeutic boundaries; sexualised transferences; the implications for safe practice and working with issues of attachment and loss.

In conclusion, although the literature from a psychoanalytical perspective discussing young sexual abusers is limited at present, interest in the physically and emotionally traumatic origins of abuse and abusing is increasing steadily. Important research looking at links between sexual victimisation and later abusing behaviour has been undertaken by the Great Ormond Street Team (Bentovim, 1998), and has indicated that certain risk factors for later perpetration can be identified including experiences of physical abuse; witnessing of physical violence; discontinuity of care and rejection by the family. These research findings are clearly relevant information for prospective therapists of such young sexual abusers and highlight the role of early trauma of all types in the genesis of abusive behaviour.

Setting a safe child protection context for psychotherapy with dangerous children

The Young Abusers Project tries to provide a secure base for outpatient psychotherapy with a disturbed child population using the support and resources of a specialist multi-disciplinary team in collaboration with referring agencies. Such a secure base is difficult to achieve since the behaviour of these dangerous but vulnerable children causes great professional anxiety and there is confusion about how best to meet their needs. Some of this confusion is reflected in uncertainty about how to describe these children and young people with understandable concerns about labelling younger children as 'abusers', or 'offenders' when their presenting behaviours may be more akin to those of over-sexualised child victims of abuse and apparently less comparable to the behaviours of older adolescent and adult abusers (see also chapter 3).

From a dynamic perspective, however, it appears that many colleagues are 'identified' with the victimised aspects of their young clients to such an extent that they may become relatively blind to the developing dangers posed to others by these sad, vulnerable but dangerous children. Such dynamics are part of everyday work with many child abuse cases but it becomes particularly important to clarify, name and resolve these dynamics in an open and co-operative manner with colleagues before psychotherapy is started, to avoid communication problems and the possible breakdown of therapy with resultant further emotional damage to the child or young person concerned. It follows that the clinical criteria for accepting a young sexual abuser into individual psychotherapy must accept wider systemic issues including the creation of a safe child protection context, the pragmatics of funding, setting up and supporting treatment as well as the more subtle intrapsychic and dynamic issues involved in each case.

More specifically, certain key issues have emerged from the work of the Young Abusers Project in relation to safe psychotherapeutic practice with this client group:

The dangers of treating young abusers in isolation from colleagues

At the outset it is important to stress that, for several reasons, no individual from any discipline should undertake psychotherapy (of any type) with a young abuser on their own without a supportive, professional framework being in place. Firstly, therapy with this client group involves child protection issues at every step of the process from assessment, during therapy, in holiday breaks and at termination of therapy. It needs to be remembered by prospective therapists of known or suspected young sexual abusers that 'acting out' with this type of client may well include further abuse of children who can be seriously damaged both physically and emotionally. Should re-offending occur during therapy or other past abusing emerge, the therapist needs to have a previously established, functioning and positively supportive professional network with whom to share concerns and any relevant information.

Therapists should remember that only local authority social workers and NSPCC social workers are authorised and expected to take child protection action when disclosures of abuse are made, either during therapy or at other times. The therapist cannot act alone to protect child victims on information given during therapy and, conversely, the therapist is not entitled to keep secret such child protection information which may have very serious consequences for prospective victims (DHSS, 1988; GMC, 1997). On a more positive note, adequate communication between the therapist and the wider professional network will usually pre-empt serious child protection issues, will greatly assist local management of the case and will, as a consequence, ensure the gratitude and continued support of colleagues in relation to therapy.

The second reason for not working alone with these cases is that there will be serious transference and counter-transference issues to be expected in relation to sexuality, sexual abuse, perversion and violence. Sexual overtures, both overt and covert, from such clients are commonplace and must be managed as a matter of course without panic or paralysis in the session. Although the likelihood of a rapacious assault is low in an appropriately assessed case, there is no doubt that some young sexual abusers do pose a serious risk of physical or sexual assault to professionals who may challenge their distorted belief systems. Clinical accounts (Woods, 1997) of the persecuted, aggressive and sexualised behaviour of patients give a clear picture of some of the technical difficulties surrounding individual work with this client group. It is essential that a supportive systemic context exists around the therapist, not only to provide safe physical structures for the therapy and much needed emotional support for the therapist, but also to make clear to the patient that the therapist is in touch with colleagues and is not an isolated and vulnerable individual over whom he may gain power.

Linking external and internal realities: the key systemic role of the specialist social worker

Given the unusual forensic demands of outpatient work with this client group, it is important that there is one individual within the team who can maintain an awareness of all the external world complexities mentioned above and links these to the main task of providing therapy for the inner world of the child concerned. In the Young Abusers Project, the NSPCC specialist social worker has a key role in arranging psychiatric, psychological and psychotherapeutic assessments, liaising constantly with local agencies on both practical and therapeutic issues and providing a conduit for relevant child protection information from the network to the therapist and vice versa. The specialist social worker is responsible (in consultation with other colleagues) for reports and correspondence; for telephone liaison on cases, which is often extensive; for making, confirming and then checking local arrangements for the young person to be brought to therapy regularly, and for providing support and consultation to the carer or key worker with responsibility for the young person. Clinical experience suggests that it would be unwise to attempt to set up individual therapy with such a disturbed client group without this support and the cases seen in the Young Abusers Project make clear the pivotal role of the specialist social worker in discussing issues with foster carers, key workers, local clinicians and managers who are responsible for funding.

In relation to funding it is clearly essential that there is an undertaking at the outset from the funding agency to make a commitment to long-term treatment. Uncertainty about this issue is easily conveyed to the young person and the therapist, with the possibility that the patient may try to end the treatment destructively before the money runs out, thereby trying to take back at least some control over the situation.

The issue of open confidentiality in therapy with young sexual abusers

Traditionally, medical consultations including interviews with psychiatrists, psychotherapists, psychoanalysts and counsellors are contexts in which absolute confidentiality is usually expected. However, in recent years, the difficulties surrounding confidentiality in child abuse cases have been raised for debate and it has become clear that such cases cannot be seen within the traditional framework of confidentiality, which might prevent the reporting of appropriate concerns about past or present child abuse. The issue still remains controversial, particularly with dynamically trained psychotherapists and analysts who may feel that the transference/counter-transference relationship will be irreparably damaged if the therapist is seen as a leaky 'container' with whom confidences cannot be trusted. Such therapists may feel that child or adult clients experiencing or inflicting child abuse will not bring their disclosures of abuse or their most perverse fantasies or behaviours to the session if they know that the information will be passed to the local authority. The argument then goes that it is better to hear the disclosures, fantasies and behaviours and to work in confidence with the client to heal abuse sequelae or to stop abusing behaviour.

The other side of this argument, however, is that by maintaining confidentiality in abuse cases in therapy, the therapist is consciously or unconsciously colluding with the original dynamics of denial and secrecy which allowed the abuse to occur and that such collusion gives a message to the patient that the therapist is also untrustworthy and corrupt. Furthermore there is a real possibility of abuse continuing throughout the course of therapy, a situation bound to be damaging to the victim if he or she is also attending regular therapy and returning home to be abused, perhaps frequently, before the next session. A clear message is then given, by not intervening, that all the adults are in it together, as it were, and that no amount of meaningful drawings, comments or play by the child in therapy will be understood by the therapist as indicative of current abuse.

This is also true for abusers when their own disclosures of re-abusing a child or children are made in therapy. If no action is taken by the therapist to report the abuse or early attempts to target, isolate and groom other children, then the abuser will assume that the therapist does not really take the problem seriously and that, like previous authority figures, no consequences for their actions will follow. In other words it will be assumed that the abuser can do what he likes to the victim(s). In the mind of the abuser, it will seem that the wool can well and truly be pulled over the therapist's eyes and that the therapist can be 'groomed' (just like the victim) into acquiescence and silence.

The need for safe practice by trained and supervised psychotherapists

Another consideration in relation to open confidentiality in work with juvenile sexual abusers relates to the need to protect the young person from an inept or possibly abusive therapist. It is important to stress that sexual, emotional and physical abuse of patients by therapists is a sad reality (Scharff and Scharff, 1994) and that a traditional confidentiality model is the perfect context in which such abuse can occur. Furthermore, when the patient is an extremely vulnerable and sexually provocative young abuser who may project all of his most deviant, exciting and destructive impulses into the therapist and when the same young person may present as sexually aroused in the session, possibly making physical or verbal overtures towards the psychotherapist, then it becomes clear that much of this behaviour may be a re-enactment in the session of the problem of sexual arousal outside the session over which the young abuser has no control. A knowingly corrupt therapist may readily take advantage of such dynamics to sexually abuse the patient.

However, even the most experienced and responsible therapist may become caught up in the sexually charged atmosphere which pervades individual work with sex offenders and juvenile abusers. It is before this situation arises, when the therapist is overwhelmed by excited and omnipotent feelings about controlling the patient through his or her interpretations, that open communication and open confidentiality should be established. Such a transparent and non-ambiguous context should make it clear to the therapist, patient and professionals that no inappropriate secrets will be kept in this therapy and that the therapist and the professional network are safe and incorruptible, in contrast to the adults previously known to the patient. For these and other reasons, it is now good practice for professional work with the victims and perpetrators of sexual abuse to occur in a context of open confidentiality where all relevant information about known or suspected child abuse is shared.

Providing a safe clinical context and physical environment for young sexual abusers in therapy

Appropriate preparation of the young person by referring professionals for visits to the clinic is absolutely essential if therapy is to succeed. If the young person arrives for a psychiatric, psychological or psychotherapeutic assessment then he should have been fully prepared for the format and the length of the interview; where applicable, that assessment interviews will be videotaped (for child protection reasons) and that a consent form will need to be signed; whether the interview will be live supervised by other members of the team through the video system and that very specific enquiry will be made about the nature of the offences known or suspected to have been committed (Vizard *et al.*, 1996). Carers should also be prepared in advance for the possibility of 'acting out' i.e. risk-taking behaviour by the young person before or after therapy sessions and there should be continued discussion with the young abuser about the mixed feelings which may be stirred up in the sessions.

The waiting area or waiting arrangements and the therapy rooms, toilets and refreshment areas in any clinic offering assessment and treatment for young sexual abusers of children are clearly important aspects which require careful thought and planning before children start to arrive at the clinic. First, arrangements need to be made to ensure that young sexual abusers are escorted to and from interviews and therapy rooms by their professional carers who need to be available for this task during the sessions. This is because the children and young people who are the subject of this book are both vulnerable to approaches from unscrupulous adults and also dangerous to other young children to whom they are sexually attracted. The clinical experience in the Young Abusers Project shows that certain boys in this client group will approach other young children in the toilets of clinics to which they are taken in the hope of targeting and isolating the child for sexual abuse.

More impulsive abusers may simply try to reach out and grab the clothing of another child to pull down their trousers, for instance, or they may expose themselves to other children causing great distress. Long absences in the toilet whilst the carer or therapist waits in the corridor may indicate anxiety or resistance to therapy but may also indicate masturbation to sexual images stirred up in assessment or therapy which the young person does not wish to disclose. Apart from risk to other children, the young sexual abuser may put himself at risk by making inappropriately friendly or sexualised comments to adults in or around the toilet.

A 13-year-old boy, Jimmy, who came for a psychotherapy assessment, asked to visit the toilet. Since the boy's carer was engaged on the telephone, one of the Project's male workers accompanied Jimmy to the toilet and stood inside the door, facing away from the boy and waiting to take him back to the session. Whilst standing at the urinal Jimmy called over to the Project worker in a chatty way saying what a long, tiring journey he had today coming to the clinic and asking how the worker felt today? The boy had never met this worker before. Despite the worker making it clear that it was now time to leave the toilet, Jimmy continued to stand at the urinal, holding his penis, wanting to make animated conversation and quite unworried about talking so freely to a strange man.

Arrangements therefore need to be made to ensure that the children attending the clinic for help with sexual arousal to other children do not inadvertently mix with victim children and that such young sexual abusers are not allowed to wander unsupervised around clinics where there are also victimised children. When in place such supervision arrangements are perfectly well understood (and appreciated at some level) by the young abusers who feel contained, as well as providing peace of mind for the accompanying carer, therapist and home-based professionals.

The assessment and therapy rooms should be comfortable and the child or young person orientated with plenty of paper and drawing materials, traditional child psychotherapy assessment toys, a flip chart for drawing diagrams or writing messages, a box of tissues and some neutral pictures or decorations on the walls. The toy shop scenario with every known stuffed toy, doll, car and game, together with posters of sad, vulnerable children being exhorted to ring ChildLine or the NSPCC often seen in some children's homes or therapeutic institutions for victimised children would be wholly inappropriate for work with this client group of young sexual abusers. Many young abusers are turned on and excited by pictures of sad, vulnerable children and some clients of the Young Abusers Project (and adult sex offenders too) have been known to use ChildLine for heavy breathing phone calls in which their graphic sexual fantasies about the children in the posters are shared.

Care is therefore needed in furnishing and decorating the clinical rooms in which these abusing children are seen, although the psychotherapy setting (even for teenagers and certainly for learning disabled young people) should always include the drawing and basic play materials mentioned above. This is because the psychological processes of splitting, projection and denial, which have, in a way, helped to keep the young person functioning at some level may be very challenged by a rigidly traditional psychoanalytic approach. 'Splitting' has been described as a process leading to 'feelings and relations (and later on, thought processes) being in fact cut off from one another' (Klein, 1946, p. 6). Subsequently these 'split off' disavowed feelings may be 'projected' or pushed into another person (the victim or possibly the therapist) in such a way that the original owner of the unwanted feelings can more readily 'deny' their origins. Denial is a key mental mechanism in most sexual abusers, including young people, and there will be the strongest possible resistance by the abuser towards any discussion or verbal exchange which attempts to challenge this denial. Hence, the provision of drawing and play materials emphasises the importance of play (Alvarez and Phillips, 1998), and gives a message that the therapist is sensitive to his resistance to open up and communicate and has provided additional methods for doing so where words are not needed.

In some cases children act out during their assessment. There may be many reasons for this behaviour. For instance, unwillingness to attend, often because of extreme anxiety, is common, though in some cases children are not adequately prepared by their carers. Examples of the kinds of destructive behaviour which have damaged clinic furnishings include:

- a boy who sat viciously and angrily digging chunks out of the wooden arm of a chair whilst discussing his abusive behaviour;
- another boy who sat silently getting red in the face with anger at interpretations and deliberately crushed his empty coke can with one hand after which he bit into the can leaving teeth marks;
- a boy who set fire to paper in the (group) therapy room and threw it out of the window on to cars in the car park below (this boy was subsequently convicted of an arson offence).

The level of persecutory anxiety in some young sexual abusers is so high that they may easily feel 'trapped' in a confined therapy room. It is usually sensible to arrange the seating such that the young person can, if absolutely necessary, make a quick exit without tripping over the therapist. However, developmental considerations may be important here since much younger sexualised children, for instance, may need encouragement to stay in the room and not to charge up and down the corridors.

> An 8-year-old boy, Michael, resident in a children's home for severely disturbed children, was referred for an assessment of his psychotherapeutic needs. Michael refused to sit down in the room, threw the toys up in the air, and prevented the therapist from speaking by placing his hand over her mouth. Unable to acknowledge her comments relating to his extremely high level of anxiety, he attempted to climb out of the window. Eventually the therapist suggested opening the door to the therapy room and Michael managed to settle down long enough to look around him and verbalise his fear of finding monsters in the room. The door remained open for several more sessions until Michael's persecutory anxiety gradually diminished and he began to feel safe.

In some cases young sexual abusers may be brought for a risk assessment or an assessment for psychotherapy directly from secure accommodation or from a Youth Offender Institution either in handcuffs or accompanied by one or more prison officers. Arrangements will then need to be made for the young person to be seen by the assessment team whilst the prison officers keep him in view either through the video system or sitting next to him in the room. It does not follow that because a young person requires supervision and an escort of this sort that he is necessarily unsuitable for psychotherapy on release into the community. Obviously the exact nature of the offending, the degree of physical violence and the level of assessed dangerousness will be critical in determining suitability for outpatient treatment (see chapter 6).

Recurrent themes in therapeutic work with young abusers

Fear of contamination

There is often a great fear in the minds of professionals and the public alike about any contact with sex offenders of whatever age. Serious over-reactions are reported in the press when vigilante groups get together to hound out sex offenders in the local community. However, less extreme reactions in otherwise balanced and well-educated professionals are still common and the fact is that very few professionals are interested in working therapeutically with this client group whether child or adult perpetrators (Sinason, 1997b).

When asked, colleagues will maintain that there are good reasons for not being able to take on the work such as a lack of resources, training or facilities. However, further enquiry usually reveals that there is considerable fear and resistance from colleagues about sitting in the room with young sexual abusers discussing their sex offending behaviour. Male and female colleagues may fear sexual overtures and female colleagues may fear rape and/or physical attack whilst colleagues of both genders may fear the erotic counter-transference and sexual feelings stirred up in them by this work. In some cases psychotherapists who become consciously aware of these sexual feelings may then unconsciously convert these into feelings of parental concern, which, although less threatening, are equally inappropriate and disturbing to the therapist/patient relationship.

These reactions may not be expressed at a conscious level and colleagues may be unaware of their own behaviour in relation to the work. For instance, some colleagues may show an exaggerated fear or hesitation about entering the clinic premises or they may appear to be very shocked, angered or mesmerised by the information which they see emerging in the assessment session through the video system. Others may feel physically sick whilst watching assessment videos, whilst more vulnerable trainees may experience 'frozen' moments in the assessment interview when the reality of the type of client they are speaking to suddenly becomes clear. Some reactions to the work can be more idiosyncratic as in the case of the young, pregnant psychologist who watched assessment tapes calmly and with professional disinterest, but became very distressed, felt rather sick, held her stomach with both hands and could not share her feelings in the debrief session after watching a group of young sexual abusers discussing their fantasies about young children. Only subsequently could this young woman admit that it was the sight of 'all of them together somehow' which had made her feel sick and intensely protective towards her unborn child.

Such reactions are commonplace and are probably a perfectly normal reaction to working with unpleasant material which comes, confusingly, from a vulnerable but dangerous group of young clients. Supervision and support from senior colleagues and from other team members is essential to allow the person concerned to understand and deal with their feelings in a constructive manner. Difficulties arise if these reactions are noted in colleagues who are not part of the specialist team and who may be going back to an unsupported context after having brought the young person to the session. The need for supervision cannot be over-emphasised for experienced and for novice practitioners alike and this is something for which preparations should be made before any therapy for the client is started (see also chapters 2 and 13).

Trivialisation and minimising of abusing behaviour

It is not uncommon in work with adult sexual abusers to encounter trivialisation of the index offence not only by the offender but also by professionals involved in the case. The typical defence plea that this was a 'one-off' offence in a man of previously good character has been argued vigorously in criminal courts for many years. Such a defence is easier to pursue when the criminal laws of evidence do not allow for admission of evidence of earlier offending or of patterns of behaviour which suggest an interest in children. However, in the civil courts, where known or alleged sex offenders are dealt with in the context of proceedings under the Children Act 1989, the whole evidential 'jigsaw of sexual abuse' (Hobbs and Wynne, 1993) can be considered, including past histories and patterns of behaviour of both victim and alleged abuser. This wider evidential remit in the civil courts has allowed for a more systemic assessment of risk of significant harm to children based on the balance of probabilities. Having said this, trivialisation of abusive behaviour persists in all professions and at all levels.

A 13-year-old adolescent boy, Roy, confessed to the police and to social services to the long-term sexual abuse of three of his younger sisters all under 11 years old. The young person, Roy, was seen in the Young Abusers Project for an assessment of risk and to look at the possibility of treatment. Roy's social worker and his team leader viewed the interview through the video system and again heard their client state quite casually and without embarrassment or remorse that he had been having regular sexual intercourse with all the sisters for three years since he was 10 years old. None of this was new information to the local authority but after the interview the Team Leader's response to the interviewers was that there had, after all, been no medical findings on any of the sisters so perhaps Roy was exaggerating or over-stating the sexual contact which may have been occurring as a sort of mutual comforting experience between very deprived children? This Team Leader could see no problem for Roy in being returned home to live with his siblings as long as he, Roy was in treatment and as long as his sisters were being watched closely by his parents.

Other examples include the use of trivialising language by profes-sionals who may refer to abuse between older and younger children as 'inappropriate sexual relationships', 'sexual play' or 'experimentation' rather than recognising the components of coercion, bribery and abuse involved. The key issue which is often trivialised is the intent by the young person (whether conscious or unconscious) to abuse and to inflict pain on the other child (the victim).

At the root of this trivialisation is professional resistance to accepting that children can be cruel and sadistic to others and that this cruelty can be highly sexualised and compulsive. There appears to be a determination in some of us to perceive children and childhood as a passive, pure state of being in which children can only be the recipients of actions such as abuse and never the agents of actions such as abuse, particularly sexualised abuse. Sexual abuse of children by other children and young people is particularly likely to be dismissed or trivialised simply because children are not perceived as sexual beings and are not expected to have sexual feelings or show sexual behaviours until puberty.

This denial of the premature sexualisation of abusing children is exactly what most paedophiles would want and seems to play into society's collusion with the secret sexual exploitation of children.

Victim or abuser

In the case of a learning disabled girl victim of sexual assault by a group of four boys in a playground, the local authority refused to attend a professionals' meeting in relation to a pre-trial psychiatric assessment of one of the 11-year-old defendants, Shaun. The reason given for this refusal was that the local authority was acting on behalf of the girl as an alleged victim and that they could not be involved on behalf of Shaun since he was the alleged abuser and was facing a criminal trial. This situation was clearly unjust and wrongly denied Shaun his rights to services as a child in need in terms of the Children Act 1989. However, the local authority made it clear that it was either to be aligned with the child victim or with the boy defendant and that it simply could not hold in mind the needs of both vulnerable children.

A similar situation arises with young sexual abusers who are both victims of child abuse and also perpetrators against other children. Many professional colleagues can only envisage one view of the young sexual abuser, either as a sad, sexualised victim or as a dangerous young perpetrator. Either perception is usually inaccurate and incomplete since both victim and abuser identities (Hodges *et al.*, 1994) exist together with more healthy functioning identities within the mind of the abusing child.

In many ways this tendency to polarise views reflects society's impatience with complexity or with situations where there is no one simple unambiguous answer to a problem. Unfortunately, if psychotherapy with abusing children is to succeed it is essential that the professionals supporting the process are able to bear in mind all aspects (however contradictory) of the young person's identity if there is to be any hope of future healing and integration.

'Acting out' by patients and professionals

Many patients in therapy will 'act out' with disturbed behaviours outside the therapy setting, often at weekends, over holiday periods or shortly before termination of the therapy. Such acting out seems to represent issues which have been too difficult to mention or too complex to resolve in the therapy sessions and not infrequently the acting out may be self-harming or risk-taking and apparently intended to raise the therapist's anxiety levels. This often succeeds particularly if the acting out behaviour involves targeting or abusing children whilst in psychotherapy. If the patient's provocative behaviour succeeds in raising the therapist's anxiety, then the therapist will need to be particularly careful that he or she does not fall into the trap of also acting out in response.

A young boy, Troy, was seen once a week in psychotherapy and in his sessions played a game which involved him having been hurt in a car crash, writhing in pain on the floor and getting the therapist to act as the doctor who had to physically examine him. Troy's need to be touched was paramount, and he continually created situations that might provoke physical contact.

Given the potential dangers of the erotic counter-transference mentioned above, the therapist must be vigilant about professional standards including physical contact with the patient. It is often easy to feel very sorry indeed for certain young sexual abusers who are deprived and neglected and who may stir up strongly protective as well as disgusted feelings in professionals. Limentani (1989) has described the special features of transference and counter-transference in sexual deviations and makes it clear that psychotherapy sessions may be highly eroticised, the analyst may be dehumanised and treated as an object by the patient; the analyst may be forced into the role of a voyeur to the patient's repeated sexual fantasies and that very primitive, psychotic anxieties may be stirred up by treatment. Glasser (1979) has described the primitive anxieties stirred up by therapy with perverted individuals as follows: 'the patient conceives the state of oneness with the object he desires and fears as a passive merging with; being engulfed by it; getting into and being invaded by it' (p. 280). Limentani (1989) concludes that, 'The one-to-one situation, therefore, seems to play havoc with long standing defences' (p. 247) and this is clearly a warning to therapists considering work with 'perversions', including sexually abusive behaviour, to proceed with caution in terms of technique.

More up-to-date approaches to therapy with young sexual abusers have recently been described (Woods, 1997) in which the potential dangers of the transference/counter-transference relationship are described and psychotherapeutic techniques appropriate for work with this client group are described within an overall child protection framework. Given the vulnerability to abuse of this group of children and young people, it is not, for instance, a good idea to start to give the patient friendly pats on the back or encouraging hand squeezes, let alone hugs, no matter how needy he may seem. Like many victims of abuse, the young sexual abuser may ascribe very different and erotically charged meanings to physical contact from the meaning ascribed by an ordinary child who may not even notice a pat on the back.

In relation to professional acting out, when funding is a key issue in arranging long-term psychotherapy, strange excuses can be found to avoid the commencement of therapy for a suitably assessed young person or to call a halt to current therapy.

A 10-year-old abusing boy, Wayne, was progressing well in individual psychotherapy, was attached to his therapist and was starting to acknowledge his potential to abuse children without continued help. As a result, Wayne's sexualised and aggressive behaviour towards other children had greatly improved and he was far less of a management problem in foster care. The local authority's interpretation of this happy state of affairs was that since Wayne was better, he obviously did not need therapy any more and his sessions should therefore cease. The fact that Wayne had only been able to improve during therapy, that he had asked for his therapy to continue and that the therapist had predicted that there would be an adverse result from stopping the therapy was all to no avail since the local authority had decided that this particular boy had been given 'enough' therapy and that money would be better used on children who had so far been given no treatment.

There are complex psychoanalytical reasons why professionals may 'act out' in these ways in relation to work with young abusers. However three common reasons include the professional being strongly identified with the abusive aspects of the young person; the professional being identified with the helpless victimised aspects of the client and the professional having intense unresolved personal feelings about sexual abuse, possibly having been an abuser or victim themselves in childhood. Other examples of such acting out have included:

- letting the therapist know that the professional, perhaps the social worker or key worker, is leaving their job very soon, possibly, that very afternoon, and that the young person will not therefore be seeing them again;

- having agreed that therapy can start with the specialist project, the worker going ahead and arranging for more assessments in other projects and accepting a place for the young person in therapy to start two days before the agreed date in the specialist project;

- forgetting that a carefully planned and discussed first or last therapy session was to occur on such and such day and just not arriving with the young person; the professional bringing his or her own child along during the escorting of the young sex offender to his therapy session and being baffled and angry when the safety of their own child is queried and

- acting out jealousy/rivalry with the therapist. This may include cancelling a therapy session in favour of an outing to a theme park, for instance.

Such attacks on the therapeutic process are not uncommon and cause a great deal of distress to young people who have managed to engage in treatment with many reservations.

Conclusions

Psychotherapy with young sexual abusers is an essential part of the recovery process for the abuser as well as being a vital part of child protection practice designed to protect victims. This chapter has described some of the relevant clinical issues and therapeutic dilemmas arising from this work which have been experienced in the Young Abusers Project. It is hoped that other colleagues will be encouraged to undertake therapy or to support others to undertake therapy with this client group to prevent them from becoming the adult abusers of the future.

Acknowledgements

All case vignettes have been altered to ensure confidentiality. We are very grateful to the NSPCC for their unstinting support of the Project's work over many years. Thanks are also due to the dedicated members of the Young Abusers Project Team who have contributed their considerable expertise and care to this therapeutic work. Particular thanks are due to Jane Dutton who has acted as consultant to the team and helped us to make sense of the intense and distressing feelings arising from the work. Most importantly, thanks are due to the young people who are the subjects of this chapter and from whom we have learnt so much about trauma and recovery.

8

WORKING IN GROUPS WITH YOUNG MEN WHO HAVE SEXUALLY ABUSED OTHERS

Bobbie Print and David O'Callaghan

Introduction

Groupwork has emerged as the predominant treatment method for those who display sexually aggressive behaviours. In a survey of North American treatment providers by Knopp and colleagues (1992), 98 per cent of programmes identified peer groups as the preferred treatment model in work with adults and adolescents who had sexually abused. In the UK, Allam and Browne (1998) found cognitive based sex-offender groups to be operating in 97 per cent of probation services.

Although in the UK the number of groupwork programmes for adult sex offenders has increased dramatically throughout the 1990s, groupwork programmes for young people who abuse are confined predominantly to specialist projects (HM Inspectorate of Probation, 1998).

The rationale for groupwork becoming the preferred mode of treatment is not entirely clear and it is an approach not without its critics. Lab *et al.* (1993) have questioned the rapid development of such programmes for adolescents in North America and suggest there has been insufficient analysis of their effectiveness to justify their predominance. Such caution is also reflected in the Monck and New study (1995) of services for child victims and young abusers in the UK. They commented that more focused assessment processes, systematic record keeping and integrated evaluation procedures should be consistently incorporated into therapeutic programmes for young people.

Outcome studies of groupwork for people who have sexually abused are relatively few and most have sample sizes too small to allow significant conclusions to be drawn (Becker, 1990; Craissati and McClurg, 1997; McClune, 1995; Will *et al.*, 1995). Allam and Browne (1998) suggest that whilst in-house evaluation systems are of value it is only large-scale, independent research that will provide reliable evidence about the impact of groupwork. Whilst there is a current initiative under way to develop an evaluation base using data from several UK adolescent programmes (Beckett and Brown, in process) we must, in the meantime, rely on the evaluations of smaller studies which provide tentative support for group-work as a potentially effective component of intervention with sexually aggressive males (Hall, 1995; Hedderman and Sugg, 1997; Craissati and McClurg, 1997).

This chapter explores the value of groupwork with young people who have sexually abused and highlights some of the principles and approaches that appear to be the most effective. Also discussed is the importance of incorporating groupwork into an overall therapeutic response to young people. Finally, a groupwork programme developed by the authors at G-MAP is outlined.

The benefits of groupwork for young people

Not all young people benefit from inclusion in a groupwork programme (see pre-group assessment below), but there is a significant body of opinion that advocates groupwork for young people who sexually abuse as a particularly effective method of therapeutic intervention. This support arises from acknowledgement of adolescence as a developmental stage, experience of groupwork with young people more generally and theories relating specifically to sexual aggressive behaviours.

The developmental context

Most authors on groupwork with young people stress that particular developmental tasks of adolescence can be positively influenced and supported in appropriately led and focused groups (Evans, 1998; Malekoff, 1997; Carrell, 1993). These tasks can be summarised as follows:

1 *Separation from family.* The striving for practical and emotional independence from parents/adult; increasing autonomy and greater intimacy with peers.
2 *Developing a consistent identity.* Young people's cultural, social and personal reference points may be highly volatile during adolescence. Groups may provide another setting in which 'trying on' identities may occur.
3 *Developing a peer group identity.* Carrell (1993) suggests this is the 'hub of the developmental wheel for adolescents'. For those young

people who are isolated from peers a group provides an important opportunity to begin this process.

4   *Forging a healthy sexual identity.* When working with young people whose sexual behaviour is problematic it is essential to recognise that developing sexuality is a complex and important transitional stage in adolescent development.

5   *Development of a personal value system.* It is a natural process for adolescents to begin to question the values and beliefs of their parents and other strong influences. For many of the young people considered in this chapter this is vital not solely for personal growth but to progress to a non-abusive lifestyle.

6   *Preparing for the future.* Developing skills, career goals, and aspiring to more mature relationships.

Groupwork with troubled young people

As a therapeutic medium for young people several advantages have been cited for groupwork techniques (Malekoff, 1997; Carrell, 1993; Dwivedi, 1993; Duboust and Knight, 1995). A summary of their findings includes:

- The group offers a potential to learn from others whilst developing competency in self-disclosure for young people who have difficulties in expressing emotions and experiences;
- Groups can reduce a sense of isolation, particularly for young people whose problem has a degree of social stigma;
- The group environment can become a safe psychological space in which to explore difficult or anxiety-provoking issues;
- Important interpersonal and social skills can be effectively rehearsed in a group setting;
- Groups allow a range of experiential activities that actively engage children and young people but are not practical within an adult–child interaction;
- Peer education and reinforcement is seen as particularly effective for adolescents.

Groupwork with males who sexually abuse

In respect of work with adolescents who have sexually abused, there is significant support for groupwork as a therapeutic approach. For example, Steen and Monnette (1989) state:

Group therapy is unquestionably the modality of choice when working with adolescent sex offenders. It provides the offender with a safe milieu in which to explore his functioning, his sex offences, and his own victimisation with others who share similar experiences. Self-esteem is restored through group support and mirroring. ... Peer pressure breaks down denial and minimisation, and the techniques that will put him at low risk to re-offend are learned and practised.

(p. 29)

Further support for groupwork was offered by the STEP Report (Beckett *et al.*, 1994) which evaluated community-based groupwork with adult sex offenders and identified that 'group-work, as opposed to one-to-one therapy reduces the likelihood that therapists offering treatment will enter collusive relationships with clients' (p. 174).

Despite such positive comments evidence for the effectiveness of groupwork as a treatment modality with sex offenders remains scarce.

What makes an effective group?

Therapeutic interventions with sexually abusive young people are most often described as 'cognitive-behavioural' in approach (Richardson *et al.*, 1997). Cohen (1997) commented that effective change occurs as a result of the integration of emotions, cognitions and behaviour. The group experience can offer a context within which to achieve this integration if the group process functions effectively.

Malekoff (1997) suggests cognitive-behavioural approaches do not preclude an understanding of effective group process. Evans (1998) cautions therapists not to neglect the contribution other group members have to make, in order to avoid allowing them to become spectators in leader–member interaction. Attention to process issues is therefore vital.

There has been little research on the perspectives of adolescents in rating therapeutic factors of group experience. Corder *et al.* (1981) found adolescent group members placed the ventilation of emotions (catharsis) most highly, as did members of adult groups. Adolescents, however, differed from adult group members in placing little value on insights generated through contemplation of historical experience. Evans (1998) suggests adolescents are too concerned with gaining distance from childhood and moving towards adulthood to find reflection on childhood comfortable or of interest.

Whilst analytically oriented groupwork theory identifies a number

127

of features associated with therapeutic effectiveness we would wish to highlight three factors from our experience of running groups: clarity of purpose, group cohesion and emotional engagement.

Clarity of purpose

Malekoff (1997) proposes four aspects of group functioning to measure this:

- when the purpose of the group can be stated clearly and concisely by the workers and the group members;
- when the purpose has the same meaning for both the group members and workers;
- when the purpose is specific enough that both the client and worker will know when it has been achieved;
- when the purpose is specific enough to provide direct implications for the group content.

Group cohesion

Douglas (1995) reflects that it is difficult to isolate the factors which contribute to a sense of group cohesion but the degree to which it is present tends to be instantly recognisable for members and leaders by its consequences for group functioning. Influencing factors include: a sense of common purpose; open communication; skilled leadership; and a positive view of group efficacy. As part of their evaluation of group-work programmes with adult sex offenders the STEP study (Beckett *et al.*, 1994) examined the therapeutic environment within which treatment was conducted and identified particular elements which they considered characteristic of effective treatment:

- high levels of group cohesiveness, where all participants felt involved in the group;
- high levels of task orientation, placing emphasis upon practical tasks and decision-making;
- clear structures and explicit rules;
- an atmosphere where members felt encouraged and respected as individuals and did not feel that they were viewed solely as 'sex offenders'.

Experiencing and expressing emotions within groups for adolescents

Garland (1992) identified five stages of 'collective competency' relevant to groups for young people in developing a genuine emotional content:

1   In the *pre-affiliation* stage young people explore their perceptions of other group members. The facilitators need to set boundaries, agendas and establish opportunities for developing trust;
2   As the distance between group members closes *power and control* issues dominate with a need to re-state purpose and boundaries;
3   Once the group has progressed through these challenges to meaning and authority it can enter a more *intimate* stage in which it is characterised by greater emotional depth and increased self-disclosure;
4   Successful and longer-term groups can develop a sense of identity, culture and values which survive membership and facilitator turnover. New members progress through these personal stages of group integration more rapidly. Garland (1992) refers to the process as '*differentiation-cohesion*', thereby denoting how an individual can enter and participate in the group fully without threat to their personal identity;
5   The final stage is *separation/termination*, which can relate either to the group as an entity or to an individual in the group.

Experienced groupworkers are likely to recognise that these stages are not linear and that in long-standing open groups there can be regressive stages, either of individual group members or of the group as a whole.

Without some degree of emotional engagement, groups for young people can be a meaningless ritual, leading to distraction and loss of focus. For young males the sharing of emotionally significant events and supporting others may be a unique experience (Russell, 1995) and will only occur if the group is considered a safe setting. Respect amongst group members is therefore a fundamental requirement for a group that aims to address abusive behaviour. Group mores must be established that take account of victims' experiences and promote respectful behaviour towards others in the group setting.

Differences between groups for young people who have abused and other therapeutic groups

It has been shown that a number of features of therapeutic engagement with young people who have sexually abused others are distinct from traditional counselling relationships (Ryan, 1996). In particular:

- It is likely that young people's participation in a therapeutic programme results from some form of external mandate. The mandate may be formalised through legal processes or arise out of a family's wish for the young person to obtain help. Successful progress in work on abusive behaviours may be linked to increased community access and decisions about returning home or extending family contact. The implications of such mandates can often mean that a young person regards his involvement in a programme as involuntary and possibly coerced;
- The primary focus of concern is not the young person but previous or potential victims;
- There are limits to the level of confidentiality that can be offered in therapeutic work with young people who have abused others. It is important that information that could impact on the risk or safety of the young person and/or others is shared with those who 'need to know' in order to reduce risk and promote protection;
- The concept of a 'non-judgemental attitude' (Rogers, 1951) must be applied differentially. It is important for group members to receive clear statements (judgements) as to the unacceptable and harmful nature of their abusive behaviours;
- The therapeutic relationship cannot be based on mutual trust. A young person who has abused others has abused power, manipulated or coerced others, probably denied or minimised his behaviour and developed distorted cognitions regarding his behaviour and its impact. Hence the level of trust offered to these young people must be firmly limited and increased only at a level commensurate to their demonstrable progress towards reduced risk through the therapeutic work.

In order to develop a positive and constructive therapeutic relationship, within these constraints, it is important for group leaders to:

- *Develop a young person's self-motivation as part of the programme of work.* Adolescents entering a programme often feel depressed, pessimistic and have low self-esteem. In order to enhance motivation for change they have, first of all, to develop a sense of their potential to achieve change. This requires a climate of respect within the group together with regular and constructive feedback from group members and leaders. A young person who is helped to recognise his attainments and his potential to achieve further realistic targets will become more motivated to succeed than someone who feels they are being punished, disempowered or failing;

- *Recognise that the primary objective of a groupwork programme is to prevent further victimisation* and consequently that the needs of victims and potential victims must be the first consideration. However, other aims should be identified to provide group members with targets designed to improve the quality of their lives and help their needs to be met in non-abusive ways. These targets should be relevant to the circumstances and abilities of the adolescent concerned and they should be realistic and achievable. As Steen (1989) observes:

> Protection of society does not require changing the adolescent offender into someone who is just like the therapist. Rather, it is to enable the youth to develop skills within his own social, emotional and intellectual milieu, skills that will put him at the lowest possible risk to re-offend. If some of his values, such as derogatory attitudes toward girls, hurt or hinder progress toward the program goal, then they must be addressed in those terms.
>
> (p. 126)

- *Ensure that rules regarding confidentiality are clearly outlined* from the beginning and regularly reviewed within the group. Each group member must fully understand what the limits of confidentiality are and what information may be shared, in what circumstances and with whom. Whilst this may in some cases inhibit the sharing of some information, it offers the young person an informed choice regarding disclosures and reduces the risk that he will view the professional sharing of such information as a breach of trust. Additionally, emphasis on responsibility rather than blame is important not only within the group but with carers and external professionals in order to promote incentives for honesty and disclosure. For example, if a young man who is working well in a group, discloses previously unknown abusive behaviour, it is important that others can be helped to see this as evidence of progress and not simply an indication of increased risk;
- *Offering positive regard to each group member* and ensuring that their strengths and positive attributes are recognised and acknowledged.

This is not to say that there should be any collusion with abusive behaviours. It is important, however, to recognise that a set of behaviours does not define the person and that group members are 'young people' who have abused not 'abusers' who happen to be young people;

- *Recognise that the nature of the experiences, thoughts and behaviours which young people are expected to share in the group can give rise to particular difficulties.* To promote openness it is important for the group environment to be considered a safe place, where vulnerability and honesty are not abused or misused. Whilst relevant group rules can contribute to the establishment of a positive environment, it is the group leaders' modelling of sensitivity and respect that most profoundly sets the tone for group interactions.

Group leaders play an important role in modelling desired behaviours which extend not only to the attitudes they express, the methods of control they exert and the behaviour they demonstrate but includes the style of leadership they employ. A confident, assertive group leader who adopts a relaxed approach to running a group is more likely to engender an atmosphere of security than someone who appears anxious, passive or rigid.

A further example of the importance of effective modelling is concerned with challenging participants' denial or inappropriate behaviours and beliefs. A strongly confrontational style is likely to produce resistance from young people, many of whom will already be at a rebellious stage of their development. The form of their resistance may vary from 'shutting out' the views of others, falling back on distorted but well-rehearsed arguments, to aggressive counter-challenge. The overall result, however, is only likely to reinforce defensive distortions, amplify pre-existing low levels of self-esteem and heighten feelings of shame. Skilled group leaders can model more sensitive and supportive methods of challenge such as asking a young person to 'try to remember events more accurately' rather than accuse him of being untruthful. They can also help group participants in appropriately challenging each other, particularly since challenges from peers can often be more meaningful than those expressed by group leaders.

The role of other methodologies

An increasing consensus has been emerging that treatment interventions with young abusers need to be multi-systemic (Bourke and Donohue, 1996). Relapse prevention (Laws, 1989; Pithers, 1990) has become a primary treatment model for sex-offenders programmes across the UK and North America and is predicated on the individual being able to transfer knowledge and skills from the therapeutic setting to external community situations. Barber (1992), writing more generally on relapse prevention, has suggested that the quality of an individual's social network is the primary factor affecting whether any skills and know-ledge are maintained post-treatment. Practitioners working with young abusers should be particularly sensitive to the need to establish a supportive framework around the individual to monitor and reinforce key messages.

Rich (1998) proposes a developmental framework in which the constellation of possible services is tailored to the needs of the young person and co-ordinated and cross-referenced, such that evaluation is based on the young person's overall global functioning. In order to support such a holistic approach we have found it vital to establish a coherent case management strategy in which the young person and key individuals meet to review progress and ensure a consistent approach. This process is essential in determining whether young people are inte-grating therapeutic messages and demonstrating behavioural change.

The role of carers is central to such an approach, both to monitor progress, reinforce key messages and assist the young person to identify areas of risk. Most group members therefore have concurrent individual work undertaken jointly with their supervising officer or residential key-worker and regular progress review sessions with their carers.

When a young man is not currently resident at home, family partici-pation can prove an invaluable motivator and source of support, supervision and information. An evaluation of the Dublin-based Northside Inter-Agency Project (Sheridan et al., 1998) found a corre-lation between positive treatment outcomes and the degree of familial support and participation. We have found the involvement of families to be an important factor, particularly when young people are able to share with parents issues from the treatment context (Hackett et al., 1998). Families usually find it empowering to learn more of the nature of the work being undertaken and respond positively to being approached as allies. Not all young people or their families, however, can function in such an open, positive or supportive way and many will need help to do so. As Bentovim (1998) has addressed in his work on family systemic approaches, many families need intensive concurrent therapy if they are to make changes to develop safe environments for victims or abusers.

An example of a groupwork programme

G-MAP has been running groups for young people who have sexually abused others for over ten years. We have benefited from the involvement of a multi-disciplinary staff team in the programme, including child protection and youth justice workers, forensic psychiatry staff, forensic psychologists and an art therapist. Whilst the following outline of the processes, methods and programme content is offered as an example of current practice it should be recognised that outcomes have not yet been thoroughly evaluated and further programme development will undoubtedly be required as knowledge and experience in this work increases.

The programme described operates for young men aged 15-17 years who have sexually abused others. Potential group members are referred by professionals and then involved in a process of assessment and pre-group preparation before engaging in the groupwork programme.

Pre-group assessment

There is always a risk when establishing a groupwork service that it will be seen as a universal panacea for all young people who have problems with their sexual behaviour. Groupwork is not, however, an appropriate method of intervention in all cases. For example, Craissati and McClurg (1997) found poor treatment outcomes associated with more severe offence patterns and childhood experiences of abuse. In such cases individual work has proved more effective in achieving change and progress which may then allow the young person to benefit from inclusion in a groupwork programme at a later stage.

The value and potential benefits of inclusion in a groupwork programme must be assessed in each individual case. Such an assessment should not only identify individual treatment objectives but also consider the group's needs and how the individual may impact on the functioning of the group and its other members. An example would be where a young person's behaviour is too disruptive to enable the group to function effectively. Additionally, the role of a groupwork programme within a network of responses should be identified and potential problems in terms of boundaries, responsibilities and methods of communication should be examined.

Thus when considering the value of inclusion in a groupwork programme consideration should also be given to the suitability of groupwork for that individual; the role of groupwork in a comprehensive therapeutic package and the suitability of the individual for the group.

The suitability of groupwork for the individual

A comprehensive assessment of the young person is normally required prior to consideration for group inclusion (see chapter 6). The assessment not only provides a baseline for measuring and evaluating the young person's progress in the group but also allows an individual's specific therapeutic needs to be matched to the groupwork programme being considered. The comparison of individual need and groupwork provision, in most cases, is likely to identify areas of work that will need an additional service provision. It is important, therefore, to consider whether the gap between need and provision would be better addressed by alternative services. For example, a programme designed to work with young people of average ability may use techniques and methods unsuitable for a young person with learning disabilities.

The role of groupwork in a comprehensive therapeutic package

Groupwork, in most cases, is seen as only part of a required response to a young person and his family. It is important to identify how any additional needs are to be met and to establish very clear boundaries and effective methods of communication between the group leaders, the young person, those involved in other services or therapeutic work, the case manager and the carers. Without such considerations the potential for unrealistic expectations, dangerous misunderstandings and poor outcomes is greatly increased.

It should be made clear, for example, that the role of group leaders does not include making case management decisions. Whilst the information provided by them may influence such decisions, their therapeutic role should be clearly recognised as different from those responsible for case management. To minimise the possibility of such conflicts or confusions occurring, G-MAP only accept young people for group admission when:

- a comprehensive assessment of risks and need has been completed;
- child protection issues have been addressed;
- a young person referred for intra-familial abuse is not living with his victim(s);
- a young person is not otherwise placed in a situation that promotes continuance of the inappropriate behaviours (see chapter 5);
- professional case management responsibility remains with an external agency, such as social services, probation or the health authority.

Furthermore, in order to avoid confusion and to promote a positive, consistent and comprehensive response to a young person and their family, it is important to ensure that clear and structured communication networks are established. This requires an effective feedback system with the active participation of all concerned. G-MAP groups provide:

- immediate telephone contact with professional case managers and/or carers in the event that significant concerns are raised about an individual in a group;
- regular written feedback on a young person's performance and progress;
- periodic review meetings;
- requests for feedback on significant behaviours, events and other relevant issues that may have been noted by others in the young person's network.

This feedback loop is a crucial part of making a young person's involvement in the groupwork programme relevant to their wider life experiences and enhances the monitoring of progress and risk outside the therapeutic sessions.

When considering the possibility of group membership for an individual it is important therefore to determine the extent to which others in the young person's network are motivated and willing to engage in a systematic communication and feedback process.

The suitability of the individual for the proposed or existing group

This is frequently a particularly difficult issue. It is often considered that those young people with a variety of problem behaviours are the individuals who would draw particular benefits from a supportive group that encourages and models more positive behaviour. Whilst this may be true, it is necessary to balance the needs of the individual against the possible negative impact of their behaviour on the group and on the other group members.

Regrettably such decisions regarding which young people are suitable for a group can lead to a service that excludes some of the most difficult and high-risk young people. Although a significant number of less problematic individuals may receive a more effective service it is none the less important to ensure that alternative resources and responses are available to those not accepted into group. G-MAP will, in many cases, undertake individual work with a young person, with a secondary aim of modifying behaviours sufficiently to allow later group entry.

Preparing young people for entry into a group

Most young people will be anxious about joining a group. Many believe they will somehow be different from other group members or that they will not be accepted by the others. They may also have fears about the way the group will operate and what will be expected of them. A further problem for new group members is feeling 'lost' since they lack knowledge of some of the basic concepts, terminology and processes that are routinely employed in the group. Whilst the provision of information to the young person can help alleviate these problems to some extent, we have found that it helps to involve prospective group members in a pre-group, two-day 'education block'. This provides new starters with an introduction to key concepts involved in working in a group as well as offering a further opportunity to evaluate their suitability for group.

The 'Education Block' allows two or three prospective group members to work alongside others in a safe and somewhat less challenging setting than the group and enables staff, the young person and their key worker to make a more informed assessment of the applicability of a group setting for that individual.

The aims of the two-day block are to:

- provide the young people with information about the problem of sexually abusive behaviour and acceptable terminology;
- further assess an individual's competence in a group setting;
- provide a supportive, safe environment for young people to begin to talk openly about their abusive behaviour;
- introduce concepts such as Finkelhor's pre-conditions (Finkelhor, 1984), Lane's cycle of sexually abusive behaviour (Lane, 1991) and relapse prevention (Pithers, 1990);
- provide the participants with information regarding the aims, rules and format of the therapeutic group.

Contracting

Each young person entering a group, together with their case manager, parents and/or carers should have a clear understanding of what is to be offered to them and what will be expected of them. It is useful to detail these expectations in the form of a written agreement. Such a document might outline in appropriate language:

- the programme aims;
- principles and commitment of the group leaders;
- issues and rules regarding confidentiality;
- rules regarding attendance;
- rules regarding behaviour in group;
- rules regarding behaviour outside the group, including specific conditions, for example regarding contact with victims or potential victims;
- timescales;
- personal goals – these are usually identified by the group leaders but can include issues identified by the young person or others;
- methods for evaluating progress including review meetings;
- expectations of case managers, carers, parents and relevant others;
- contingency arrangements and consequences if the contract is breached by any of those involved.

The groupwork curriculum

G-MAP operates a rolling groupwork programme with entry and exit points at the end of 'blocks' of work. Each group session runs for two hours. The first part (approximately thirty minutes) consists of group members' news items and other relevant matters. The second part follows a set plan of work on topics identified within the overall programme. The potential of the group setting is enhanced by involving the group members in varied and experiential activities.

The programme is divided into three 'blocks' of work (see figure 8.1) each of which has specific objectives and is designed to help group members address their thoughts, feelings and behaviours in relation to the topics covered.

The work undertaken in sessions is complemented by use of homework assignments and often requires the involvement for monitoring and feedback purposes of carers, case managers and others in the young person's network. Free weeks are included within each block to allow attention to additional points or matters raised during the blocks of work. These can be group process issues, additional time on a topic or an individual in group or any other matter the group members and group leaders consider necessary and relevant. In this way it is possible to give attention to issues raised without losing sight of the programme schedule and timetabling.

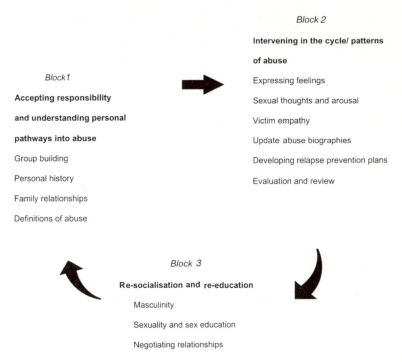

Figure 8.1 G-MAP group programme blocks of work

Each young person enters the programme with specific targets and goals, which are regularly reviewed at the end of each programme block and at formal six-monthly reviews. He will remain in the programme until these goals are deemed to have been achieved by the programme workers, the young person, other group members and those involved in the young person's network. This usually means that an individual will cover the complete programme at least twice.

The group programme is divided into three distinct blocks of two–three months' duration. The main elements of the programme curriculum are shown in figure 8.1.

Programme content

The following describes in more detail the topics covered in each block. (See table 8.1 for summary.) The methods and techniques used to address each topic are varied so that an individual undertaking a block of work for a second or subsequent time is offered a fresh opportunity to explore each topic.

Table 8.1a G-MAP groupwork programme. Block 1: Accepting responsibility and understanding personal pathways into abuse.

Group building	Group and personal roles and responsibilities
My past	My family experience – strengths and deficits of family, roles and boundaries
	What I learnt from my own experiences (positive and negative)
	The impact of my abusive behaviour on me and my family (gains and losses)
Current life situation	Risks and responsibilities
	Agenda for change
What is sexual abuse	Power, coercion and the meaning of consent
Pathways into abusing	Models of sexually abusive behaviour
	The impact of personal experiences and consequent thoughts, feelings and behaviours
	Understanding thinking errors and their role; identifying individuals' distorted thinking
	Developing a personalised cycle
	The implications of individual's cycle for risk, current and future
Abuse biography	Developing an individual abuse biography: a chronology of the abusive behaviour exhibited by an individual
	What has changed and how can further abusive behaviour be prevented
Young person's self-evaluation and evaluation of others in group	Group members' evaluation of group functioning
	Group members' views of the group workers
	Young person's self-evaluation of progress in this block
	Young person's view of the achievements and difficulties of other group members
	Feedback from group workers on evaluations of group members
	Individual review meetings with young person, group leaders, other key professionals, family and carers

Table 8.1b Block 2: Intervening in the cycle/patterns of abuse.

Relapse prevention	The cognitive behavioural model of relapse prevention
	Identification of risk/dangerous situations
	Risk escape and avoidance
	Development of relapse prevention plan
Expressing feelings	Feelings and their link to behaviours
	Distinguishing between types of feelings, blocks

	to healthy expression of feelings
	Responding to anger
	Coping with negative feelings
	Relaxation, coping with stress
Sexual thoughts and feelings	Appropriate and non-appropriate fantasy/sexual thoughts (with specific reference to risk and relapse)
	Coping with dangerous sexual thoughts (*N.B. Details of sexual thoughts are not shared in group. Intensive work on sexual thoughts is undertaken only in individual work*)
Empathy	Developing general empathic skills
	Respect; what does it mean, who do we respect?
	Sexual abuse as disrespect
	Developing empathy towards victims
	Use of apology or responsibility acceptance letters/ revision of apology letters where they exist
Revision of abuse biography	As in block 1
Evaluations and reviews	As in block 1

Table 8.1c G-MAP groupwork programme. Block 3: Re-socialisation and re-education – fitting the pieces together.

Masculinity	What does it mean to be male?
	Reviewing male and female models that have been learnt
	The unacceptability of male violence and oppression
	Development of pro-social attitudes and thoughts
Sexuality and sex education	The development of sexuality
	Sexual orientation – attitudes and beliefs
	Sex education ~ terminology and basic facts
	Defining a healthy personal sexuality
Self-image	How do others see me?
	My view of myself, strengths and relative weaknesses
	'The impact of abusive behaviour upon self-perception'
	Grief and loss work
	Hopes and ambitions for the future
Negotiating relationships	Developing social networks
	Negotiating non-abusive relationships in the future/present
	Reviewing family relationships
Relapse review	Skills inventory
	The challenges of maintaining change
	Developing, updating and renewing plans

Revision of abuse biography   As in block 1
Evaluations and reviews   As in block 1

Objectives and progress evaluation

Each block in the programme has specific objectives. An individual's progress is evaluated at the end of each block with reference to a set of specific goals and targets.[1] Individuals are re-assessed by themselves, other group members and the group leaders. Feedback from others in an individual's network is also considered so that overall progress, within and outside of the group, in their cognitive and behavioural functioning can be evaluated and reported.

The objectives of each block are listed below.

BLOCK 1   ACCEPTING RESPONSIBILITY AND
           UNDERSTANDING PERSONAL PATHWAYS INTO
           ABUSE

The overall aims for this block of work are for the young person to understand the context of his abusive behaviour and to learn to accept responsibility for his behaviour. Work on personal history and family dynamics is designed to help the young person understand and accept what has influenced his behaviour and to evaluate his own personal strengths and deficits. The use of models such as Finkelhor's four preconditions to sexually abusive behaviour (Finkelhor, 1984) and Lane's cycle of offending (Lane, 1991) are used to assist the young person's comprehension of his abusive behaviour and he is helped to consider the consequences of his abusive behaviour for himself and for others.

Each individual is assessed on the following specific block objectives:

1   contribution to developing group cohesiveness, rules and processes;
2   understanding the effects of his own experiences;

---

1   Copies of standard goals and targets which can be amended for an individual are available by sending s.a.e. to G-MAP, Suite 10, 1 Roebuck Lane, Sale, Cheshire M33 7SY.

3   recognising and owning responsibilities, risks and the need for
    change;
4   demonstrating an accurate basic sexual knowledge and use of
    appropriate terminology;
5   understanding and demonstrating what is acceptable and unaccept-
    able sexual behaviour, language and attitudes;
6   understanding the thoughts, feelings, circumstances and behaviours
    that make up the individual's cycle of offending;
7   understanding of personal cycle;
8   recognising risk situations;
9   recognising and admitting to any sexually abusive behaviour.

BLOCK 2   INTERVENING IN THE CYCLE/PATTERNS OF
          ABUSE

In the second block the young person explores how to intervene in his
pattern of abusive behaviour. He is encouraged to recognise situations
which may be identified as involving risk and to recognise how he
would, at the earliest opportunity, intervene to minimise any risk. It is
also expected that a young person will be able to demonstrate skills and
techniques for managing, controlling and suppressing behaviours that
lead to offending.
    Each individual is assessed on the following specific block objectives:

1   understanding the model of relapse prevention;
2   identifying and demonstrating how he would intervene to minimise
    risks;
3   developing appropriate methods of coping with negative feelings;
4   recognising the role of inappropriate fantasies and arousal and how
    to manage them;
5   understanding the consequences for his victims of his abusive
    behaviour.
6   demonstrating skills and techniques for managing, controlling and
    suppressing behaviours that lead to offending.

BLOCK 3   RE-SOCIALISATION AND RE-EDUCATION

The third distinct treatment block aims to engage the young person in
gaining more appropriate thoughts and behaviour patterns to replace
antisocial thoughts and behaviours. Time is spent on helping the young
person acquire a positive and appropriate self-image and new expectations of himself. There is a focus upon the acquisition of new and

modified social and relationship skills to enable each young person to develop positive, satisfying and non-abusive behaviours.

Each individual is assessed on the following specific block objectives:

1 recognising oppressive and abusive attitudes and their role in abusive behaviour;
2 replacing antisocial thoughts and behaviour with more positive ones;
3 acquiring a positive self image and new expectations of self;
4 acquiring new social and relationship skills to enable him to develop positive, satisfying and non-abusive behaviours;
5 developing understanding of sexual knowledge, relationships and sexuality;
6 reviewing and amending relapse prevention plan.

Conclusions

Whilst there is little empirical evidence of the effectiveness of group-work as a methodology with adolescents who sexually abuse there is a widespread clinical consensus that therapeutic groups can provide a helpful forum for many troubled young people. Adolescents are at a complex and demanding developmental stage and often find it difficult to deal with issues of separation/independence, authority and emotional sharing. Groupwork can offer young people support, safety and oppor-tunity to explore thoughts, feelings and behaviours together with the chance to develop and rehearse skills and coping strategies. Peer pres-sure and challenge are powerful influences that groups can utilise positively to influence change and a sense of group cohesion and achievement can enhance an individual's self-esteem and confidence.

These features of groupwork are of particular importance to young people who have experienced problems in their sexual behaviour. The thoughts, feelings and behaviours they need to examine are complex, intimate and often based on strongly held distorted thoughts, inappro-priate coping strategies and powerfully gratifying behaviours. The support, challenge and modelling of openness from peers can be a most effective mechanism to help young people address these issues. Recognition by group members that they are not alone, are worthy of respect and have positive attributes that are valued by others can provide young people with a positive motivation to succeed. Additionally, seeing progress in others can also provide a potent message to the young person that change is possible and beneficial.

To be effective, however, groupwork has to be managed in ways that promote aims and potential benefits. This requires considerable group leadership skills, planning, programming, reviewing and evaluation. The resource requirements to establish a useful group should not be under-estimated. Group workers should be trained, supported and provided with sufficient time to plan, run and debrief group sessions. Groupwork with young people who have sexually abused others can raise intense feelings and challenges for group workers and good quality supervision and consultancy should be available on a frequent and regular basis.

Groupwork, however well it is managed, is rarely a sufficient inter-vention for young people who have sexually abused. Individual and family work are likely to be additional essential components in any ther-apeutic programme and a close and communicative network, involving professionals and carers, is important in order to extend support and monitor the changes that therapeutic intervention can bring about.

9

WORKING WITH FAMILIES OF YOUNG SEXUAL ABUSERS

Assessment and intervention issues

John Burnham, Julia Moss, Jeff deBelle and Ros Jamieson

Introduction

In 1986 a group of colleagues formally established a child sexual abuse project in a regional child and adolescent psychiatry unit in Birmingham. Work at that time focused mainly on children who had been abused and their non-abusive carers. The decision in 1990 to extend the project to include work with young abusers resulted from a confluence of factors:

- working only with children who had been abused placed the responsibility for recovery and future safety solely on the victims, thereby recreating the abusive system in which they had often experienced feeling responsible for the abuse itself;
- an increase in referrals to the project of young men who had been sexually abusive;
- the professional community freeing itself from anachronisms such as 'boys will be boys';
- working effectively with abusers to interrupt their pattern of abuse before it became established as a lifestyle was seen as protecting, not only the 'victims so far', but potential victims too.

Since then a half day per week clinical project has been developing specific ways of working with adolescents who have sexually abused other young people and this chapter will explore the possibilities and problems of working with their families as part of an overall treatment package.

The group of professionals involved in the project has included psychiatrists, a community paediatrician, a social worker from the juvenile justice bureau and a family therapist. So far the project has seen eighty young people, between the ages of 10–18;, mainly male, white British and from a range of social classes. Most of their abuse was intra-familial and in most cases the abuser had moved out of the family home. Usually there is no legal mandate meaning that more emphasis has to be placed on creating a collaborative relationship, which the young person and his family experience as offering them something as well as requiring things from them. The full range of family forms have been involved in our work including intact nuclear families; single parent and step-families; foster families and adoptive families.

Primary, secondary and tertiary protection

The literature relating to adolescents who have sexually abused relates mainly to *primary protection*, working towards the person who has abused taking responsibility for and working on changing their own behaviour rather than other people's. This includes individual and groupwork, sometimes in residential programmes. (See, for example, Madanes, 1990; Bremer, 1991; O'Callaghan and Print, 1994; Hawkes *et al.*, 1997; and Hoghughi *et al.*, 1997, as well as other chapters in this book.)

Secondary protection relates to how significant others – family, friends and closely involved professionals – can be a resource and/or a restraint in assisting an adolescent abuser in working towards the goal of *primary protection*.

A network of people including extended family, family doctor, school personnel, social services and other professionals involved who have contact with the young person and family but who are not living with them can offer a valuable *tertiary protection*. These people would need to be aware of what has happened, be alert to signs of abuse, be available to the victim children and be ready to take action on their behalf when and if necessary. It is less effective than *primary and secondary* since there is less direct contact with the young person concerned, and because it often depends on the child victim(s) taking the responsibility for disclosing further concerns or episodes about abuse.

We have developed a questionnaire, 'Changes', which addresses each of the levels to some extent. It asks significant others to focus on areas, including sexual activity, in which signs of change can be noticed. This can be completed by any person who may be able to contribute to the evaluation of the young person's progress while attending the programme. Involving these significant others can help assessments become more co-ordinated and avoid the work at the clinic becoming too central. This chapter focuses on our work with families in particular, while remembering that primary and tertiary levels are also important. It is also worth noting here that our work with the families of the young men may involve the family members being present and/or included hypothetically.

Why work with families?

Including the family in the process of assessment and therapy is regarded as an important aspect of work with young sexual abusers, yet literature on how to do this work is limited (Madanes, 1990; Byrne and McCarthy, 1995). These authors and our own experience indicate that there are a number of reasons why working with the families of young people who have sexually abused other young people is important:

The advantages for the victim include

- seeing that the professionals are working to change the ideas and behaviour of the person who abused them;
- releasing the victim from a feeling of self-blame;
- creating a more positive view of the future in which relationships can be rehabilitated, even if living together may not be possible;
- resolving dilemmas of loyalty that may hinder relationships between the victim and other family members.

The advantages for the abuser include

- facilitating the abuser himself and other family members to accept that the abuse has happened;
- creating a context of responsibility that offers a way forward in relationships;
- reconstructing how others see the abuser and in so doing reconstruct relationships;
- constructing a context of relational empathy.

The advantages for the other family members include

- feeling they can contribute to the process of change;
- demonstrating to all members of the family that they are all taking what happened seriously;
- gaining an understanding that makes re-offending less likely.

Working with the family – voices of caution

Dobash *et al.* (1993) offer a useful cautionary note, quoting feminist scholars (for example, Avis and Myers, 1988 and Lamb, 1991), to show how therapies based on 'family systems theory remove responsibility from the offender and locate it, at least partially, in the behaviours of the women and children' (p. 128).

This message from work with adult abusers indicates that professionals working with a family must avoid shifting responsibility for the abuse from the abuser to the victims. Resolving this dilemma involves achieving a both-and position (Bateson 1972): *both* including family members in the work *and* maintaining clear definitions of responsibility for the abuse, and this we attempt to do.

Frameworks

Systemic, social constructionist ideas

A systemic, social constructionist approach (for example Boscolo *et al.*, 1987; Cecchin, 1987; White and Epston, 1991; Frugerri, 1992; McNamee and Gergen, 1992; Boscolo and Bertrando, 1993; Cecchin *et al.*, 1994) guides our approach. All the methods and techniques generated by the systemic family therapy movement are potentially useful in this area of work and some will be outlined in the practical examples in this chapter.

Approach–Method–Technique

The framework of Approach–Method–Technique (AMT) (Burnham, 1992 and 1993) provides a means for distinguishing and analysing relationships between *why* professionals work in a particular way (A), *how* they organise the way they work (M) and the *practical skills* they use in their work (T). These distinctions can help practitioners to analyse the interrelationships between their actions in therapy and the values and theories that guide those actions. For example the personal and professional values of professionals (A) are often 'stretched' and challenged in a variety of ways when working with young sexual abusers (see chapters 4 and 13). AMT allows professionals to explore and develop new ways of working whilst still maintaining a coherence with personal values and preferred theories. Similarly AMT enables workers to evaluate how changing values and evolving theories can open space for new ways of working to emerge. When working in teams it is useful to explore one another's practice using the framework of AMT. This can help to avoid 'taken for granted' assumptions about one another becoming enmeshed in the work and inhibiting progress.

Two important aspects of our approach include knowing which domain we are foregrounding in our practice at any particular time and how to co-ordinate different contexts towards a therapeutic outcome.

Domains of practice

The relationships between the legal, therapeutic and moral aspects of a professional's practice are often experienced as restrictive either/or dichotomies in this area of work. Practitioners need to be able to incorporate the obligations of each aspect and maximise the therapeutic potential of each. The concept of domains from Maturana and Varela (1987) offers a way of thinking about this kind of issue and their work is imaginatively interpreted for professional practice by Lang *et al.* (1990), and Herington (1990). Lang *et al.* (1990) propose that using the domains of *aesthetics, production* and *explanation* helps practitioners to 'know how to go on' in a piece of work. The domain of *aesthetics* overarches the domains of production and explanation. It refers to a moral framework generated by, and for, those people living in communities, and foregrounds a concern for such features as desirability, justice, ethics, beauty, harmony and elegance. The domain of *production* requires professionals to adopt a position of *investigative curiosity* toward the production of a judgement, related to objective criteria of guilt and innocence within an established truth that exists within a monocultural uni-verse (*sic*). The domain of *explanation* creates space for *exploratory curiosity* which embraces the idea of a cosmopolitan multi-verse in which there are many versions of reality, all of which are equally valid though not all considered to be equally desirable by the members of a community at any particular point in time. Professionals exist in all three domains simultaneously yet we may be more aware of, or wish to foreground a particular domain at any stage in the work.

For example, in work with young sexual abusers it is easy to be drawn towards feelings of blame and punishment towards those who have been violent to others. A 'visit' to the domain of aesthetics can remind us, for example, of the ethical obligations to the adolescent offender as a young person who is situated in a complex network of relationships of meanings. This can help practitioners to *both* maintain clear goals for treatment (domain of production) *and* maintain a curiosity about the particular ideas, personal stories and family narratives that give meaning to the abusive acts (domain of explanation).

Co-ordinating and managing multiple contexts of action and meaning

Over time, young people create their ways of thinking and living in a variety of *significant contexts*, which are important to consider when understanding the abuse and in helping the young person achieve a non-abusive lifestyle. A young person's *life script* is not likely to be a 'singular' internal entity and 'self-stories' may emerge in the co-ordination between these different contextual demands/resources. We find it helpful to explore in detail how *episodes* of abusing or caring, construct and define different kinds of *interpersonal relationship* (abusive/loving; bully/bullied) in which a person develops different *stories about self* (what kind of person am I/do I want to be?) relating to *family narratives* (what does this mean about us as a family, what do people think about us?); *social mores* (the laws, regulations and social prescriptions about this kind of behaviour) and *cultural patterns* (beliefs, values and practices about, for example, sexual behaviour and male–female relationships).

Within their model known as 'the Co-ordinated Management of Meaning' (CMM), Pearce and Cronen (1980) and Cronen and Pearce (1985) arrange these contexts into a relational hierarchy that can crystallise the current situation as well as changing over time. Figure 9.1 shows how it can be useful to map a particular aspect or aspects of the work, in this example *abuse* and *empathy*, alongside the levels to achieve a richer sense of the meaning of these aspects through asking about them in each context and considering the relationship between the contexts.

Cronen in Cronen and Lang (1994) stresses the circular and reflexive relationship (heterarchy) (Scaife 1993) between 'levels'. For example, how his *family thinks about and acts* towards a young person who has abused will have a 'downwards' contextual influence on his *self-story*. If a young person can begin to enact a new *self-story* this can have an 'upwards' implicative influence on the *family narrative*. If the family, and significant others, respond by changing their contextual influence then this may further strengthen the young person's determination to adopt a preferred, non-abusive self-story, and so on. This hierarchical 'ladder' is relatively clear and easy to understand. However the map in figure 9.2 conveys that these experiential contexts are not separate and distinct but are more likely to be lived as a 'tapestry'

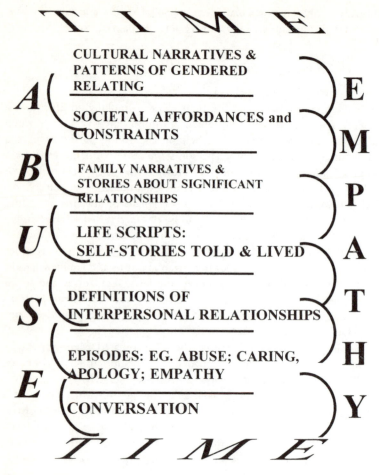

Figure 9.1 Abuse and empathy as understood through multiple levels of experience

Source: Adapted from W.B. Pearce (1994) *Interpersonal Communication: The Making of Social Worlds*, New York: HarperCollins.

(Lang, 1993), 'kaleidoscope' (Pearce, 1992) or 'seascape', Shotter (1993). Figure 9.2 is a difficult text to read indicating that 'lived experience' can only be 'read' in conversation with the persons concerned.

Both maps can be useful in practice. A therapist can imagine and foreground each person's experience in a family/network, as visualised in figure 9.2 and can interview so as to co-construct a clearer map of the significant, contextual and implicative, relationships between aspects

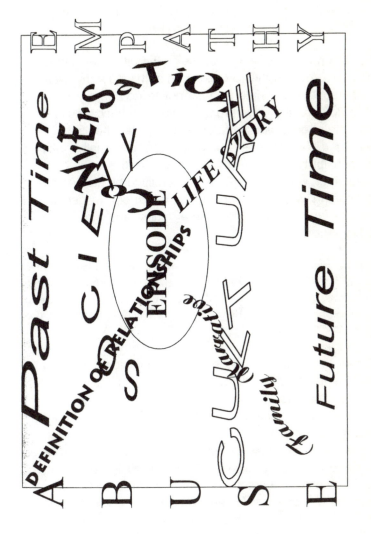

Figure 9.2 Abuse and empathy as understood in the 'seascape' of experience
Source: Adapted by Burnham (1994), inspired by Pearce (1994)

of their life as organised in figure 9.1. Wittgenstein's concept of 'centres of variation' as interpreted by Cronen and Lang (1994, p. 13) is useful here. Conversations begin (are centred) using the language, descriptions and organisation that the client thinks are important. This engages with the personal, family and cultural 'grammar' (Cronen and Lang, 1994) of the young person and their family.

> For example, in a family discussion the difficulties about 'taking responsibility' were explored at the different levels of personal life scripts ('what I got to do'); family story ('we do/don't that', 'we are/aren't like that'); local culture ('on the street'), and broader culture (what 'they' say). It emerged that for the young man to personally 'take responsibility' for the sexual abuse to the next door neighbour, would open the whole family to be blamed for everything else that happened in the street. In general people who 'took the rap' were 'mugs' and 'got taken advantage of'.

As work proceeds, novelty and difference (variation) can be introduced within this 'grammar' and between the levels, with the intention of facilitating the young person and their family/network to challenge those values, beliefs and practices which they have, up until now, used as a moral code.

> For example, as the above family discussion continued the therapist began to ask reflexive questions (Tomm, 1987a) such as: 'If you were to make your new goal of being a "responsible person" (preferred self-story) more important than what people thought on "the street" (cultural story) what would you do?' ... 'If you were to "take a stand for, instead of against, responsibility" (episode) and become a person in your family/the street who accepts responsibility for the sexual abuse, would you see your self (self-story) more as a "mug" or a "leader"? ... 'You said before that you hoped that your family would begin to think about you as a person who had abused not as an abuser (family narrative), how might taking responsibility help them to see you (self-story) in that

light?' To other family members: 'How might you encourage your son to feel that it was to his advantage to take responsibility, rather than he would be taken advantage of?'

We are emphasising CMM's potential for helping practitioners to be constantly aware of the complexity of experience; to have a way of visually mapping experience; of organising and re-organising the coherence of different aspects of experience; and exploring the 'seascape' of consciousness and action (after Bruner, 1986). Using this structure effectively in assessment and therapy requires the abilities to explore *within* each level; to understand the local arrangement of the levels; to elicit the patterned connections *between* the levels; to bring forth which levels are most influential and how in relation to the reason(s) the family is meeting with the professional. These abilities are coherent with and are facilitated by the postures and practices known as circular interviewing (Selvini *et al.*, 1980; Burnham, 1986; Penn, 1983, 1985; Tomm, 1987a, 1987b, 1988; Cecchin, 1987).

What follows is an account of our work divided into beginning, continuing and ending. This neat literary device should not be read as an indication that the work can be so easily divided. In reality the work is usually experienced as difficult for the young people, their families and the professionals involved.

Beginning work: assessment 1

Initial consultation meetings for young people and one or more members of their significant network, family and/or professional(s) involved are held every fifth week to enable a prompt response to referrals. Our preference is to become part of the significant professional contexts in furthering the work that has already taken place. Referral requests include requests for direct work, groupwork, evaluating the safety of someone returning home and consulting to other professionals' work. Our undertaking not to discuss the details of the *episodes of abuse* at this meeting are usually appreciated and seems to enhance the creation of a collaborative meeting. The referred person and their family meet a member of staff and experience our working methods including team working, one-way screen and videotaping facilities. Staff can orient themselves towards the people who attend, the nature of the request and how they work best. We have developed a flexible format which covers important questions including:

- What are their *reason(s) for attending* (voluntary or involuntary)?
- Where do they see the *responsibility for the abuse* lying (themselves or the victim)?
- Which *experience of the abuse* are they more conscious of: action (what happened); meaning (stories told about what happened); emotion (what they and others feel about what happened)?
- Which aspect do they think they need to work on first – *action, meaning or emotion*?
- What sense do they have of *the effect of the abuse on the victim* and themselves (relational empathy)?
- Which people are significant to them in their lives (*relationship networks*)?
- Are they more focused on the past, present or future (*time*) and when to do what kind of work (*timing*)?
- How would they describe their *relationships with professionals*?

Not all of the issues will be discussed and some selection will be made depending on a number of factors. At this stage with the family we are treading the line between expecting the person to accept responsibility whilst not appearing punitive, which might provoke the family to rescue. It is not uncommon for participants in these interviews to say things like 'I have said more than I thought I would' (young person), 'This is the first time I have seen him accept that he needs to do some work' (father), 'I didn't realise that he relied on my opinion so much' (older brother). Thus the meeting would have an implicative effect on the family's ideas about what therapy meant and how important the opinions of family members were to their son who had sexually abused his cousin.

In another case an initial consultation meeting comprised a 14-year-old boy (who had abused his 8-year-old step-sister), his mother and his maternal grandmother. The son said he found it difficult to take responsibility openly for what he had done to his mother since she had taken several overdoses since the abuse had been disclosed. He was worried that if she 'broke down in tears' when he talked about the abuse it would prompt another overdose. During the session maternal grandmother agreed to provide support for mother during and after sessions. This created a 'safety net' and enabled the conversations to proceed in future sessions.

If the interview is conducted *aesthetically* then at the end of the initial consultation the young person and his family (if present) should have the impression of talking to professionals who are clear about their own purposes in the work (domain of production) and who are able to help him and his family navigate his way through his own thoughts, feelings and emotions towards a more preferred lifestyle (domain of explanation) which does not include abusive behaviour or thoughts.

The decision about how and when to include the family in work begins in the initial consultation and continues throughout the work. Families respond differently and so we find it useful in our initial meetings to create and clarify a range of different explanatory rationales for why we meet and work with families during the process of the work. These rationales include:

- risk assessments: the importance of eliciting family views in this process;
- progress in therapeutic work: keeping the family up-to-date;
- monitoring the effects of the work with the young person on the feelings of each family member in relation to feelings of personal responsibility, the family's responsibility, parenting abilities and safety for re-integration;
- co-ordinating meetings with the family in relation to individual work;
- making the decision to end: co-creating contexts of evaluation;
- exploring particular themes such as empathy in relation to family relationships and narratives;
- mapping out the restraints and resources for the young person and the family.

Therapists can also express their preferences in arriving at initial decisions about how to proceed and the formats and composition of interviews can anyway evolve over time. Some families wish to be involved from the beginning, others want their son to be seen on his own first and do not want to be involved until much later, if at all. Such wishes have to be understood within the context of the relationship between the abuser and his family which is itself influenced by various factors: the context of the abuse, whether it occurred inside or outside the family or both; the current living arrangements as the abuser may be living in the family home, be in residential care or have left home and be in lodgings; and current relationships, family members may have severed all contact with the abuser, or may be very committed to helping the abuser. The response from families is seldom 'uniform' and is also likely to be related to culture and ethnicity which must be considered at this point and throughout the work (Burnham and Harris, 1996).

Continuing work

In relation to the criteria outlined above, work rarely proceeds in a straightforward and smooth fashion. Initially, young people often relate to us as investigators and only gradually begin to experience the work as having some benefit to them. Some young people do not seem to move very far along the continuum from a position simplified as: 'I won't do it again, because I don't want to get caught and mess my life up' (self-story in relation to secondary and tertiary protection) to 'I don't want to do it again because I realise how it messes other people's lives up' (self-re-storied in relation to primary protection). These are often people who feel they have been 'abandoned by their families' and left to take all the blame unsupported. The work with families during this stage is of particular importance.

Present family members

When family members are physically available to attend sessions we are looking at such issues as their abilities to explore issues their son is working on, in the context of *family narratives* about how this came to happen, and *self-stories* about the adults as parents. This is both to 'centre' the understanding of the sexual abuse in the particular situation of the cultural, family and personal contexts and introduce 'variation' through creating and living new stories as families. Thus the overall programme is intended to create multiple 'centres of variation' of which the family work is an important one.

Multiple levels of complexity

Some difficulties are dealt with through patience, persistent education, listening and questioning. For example, the abuse by the young person may have been part of some situation which has ended and he may now be determined to create a different pattern of relating.

A young man, living in a children's home, had abused his step-sister out of 'revenge' against his step-father who had raped his mother. In individual and groupwork he had worked on the ability to 'make your own mind up' (life script/personal agency) rather than: 'get your own back' (step-father's motto); or 'following the crowd' (cultural prescriptions). The young man was able to discuss openly with his mother that he wanted to continue living at a children's home because he was getting professional help to help him to develop non-abusive ways of relating. He had been concerned that she would feel hurt and rejected if he said this, because her two younger children had also been removed from her. To his surprise the mother said that she was relieved because she didn't feel she could cope with the responsibility of him coming home full time. This opened space for a different relationship between mother and son, based on what was best for them rather than conforming to some 'family ideal'. They continued to see one another and enjoyed the relationship they could have rather than being disappointed by the relationship they couldn't.

As the work progresses the different levels of context become clearer, and opens space for therapeutic possibilities:

A young man, Mark, who had sexually abused his younger sister whilst the family were in a family refuge, was referred. The family had gone to the refuge following the revelation that Mark had been sexually abused by an uncle. Mark was now in a residential home and the request was to work towards his return home if appropriate. As the work progressed we undertook individual sessions with Mark, individual sessions with his mother, sessions between him and his mother and then sessions which included both his sisters in the sessions.

The abuse was contextualised by the information that Mark was the product of an incestuous relationship between his mother and her father, thus his father was also his grandfather, and his mother was also his half-sister. Most of the women in the family had been sexually abused by their father or by their brothers. The mother/sister was trying to act from two positions simultaneously in creating a family narrative that was a discontinuous change from her own experience. As can be imagined, a singular focus on the young abuser would have been inadequate to understand the complexity of this situation.

An important change came from reworking Mark's ideas. In the moment his mother told him that his grandfather was his father, he said I 'lost both my father and my grandfather'. Mark was therefore in a position of also trying to discontinue the family line of how to be male. As the mother became more confident in her own abilities to be a mother to her son, rather than an older sibling, she was able to be more forthright in her demands about how he should be in the work. Our first full family session (mother and three children) involved discussing Mark's return home. As part of the session he was to apologise openly to his sister. He declined to do this in the session, saying he had done it already some time ago. This was explored in terms of the meaning of an apology at different stages in the work, and how his sister felt guilty that she was responsible for keeping her brother away from home. The therapist talked with the sister with her brother as 'audience'. She said that she was frightened to talk about the abuse because she did not want to get her brother into further trouble or stop him from coming home. As the therapist talked to the sister with Mark as audience, about how she felt, Mark listened. Although he was not able to apologise during the session, this episode in the family session had implicative potential and became a useful experience to: evaluate the progress of the individual sessions; indicate what further work needed to be done and provide Mark with a deeper understanding of his sister's experience that could be used to enhance his abilities in developing empathy.

Dilemmas for families

As the work continues there are common dilemmas which emerge for families and professionals:

'Who to blame?/To blame or not to blame?'

The concept of blame sits more easily in the domain of production (Lang *et al.*, 1990) than in the domain of therapy. Yet in this area of practice the issue has to be addressed aesthetically so as to further the process of change. In individual and groupwork young men are encouraged and coached to accept responsibility. In family meetings these issues may become more complex. For example in families where a brother has abused his sister then the parents may experience a dilemma of wanting to support both their children, but supporting one may be seen by the other as betrayal or desertion.

A mother expressed this dilemma and said she was scared to blame her son, in case he felt abandoned, yet if she did not blame him she felt her daughter would think she was condoning what he did and feel betrayed. This dilemma emerged in a family meeting. The therapist asked the son/brother (who was also engaged in individual and groupwork), in the mother and daughter/sister's presence, 'You've said that one of your aims in working here is to create an "abuse-free lifestyle". Which is more useful to you in pursuing this aim: if your mother blames you or doesn't blame you?' He replied 'It's more useful if she blames me, 'cos then it's easier for me to keep taking responsibility'. This interchange seemed to move people on and for the son/brother to 'sanction' his mother to blame him (say he was responsible) as a useful contribution to his work on developing an 'abuse-free lifestyle'.

This is the kind of dilemma which Pearce and Cronen (1980) refer to as a 'strange loop', which is 'escaped' from when the apparently irresolvable either/or dichotomy (*either* blame *or* support) is dissolved through co-constructing a both-and position (*both* blame *and* support) which allows the two positions which seemed mutually exclusive to be adopted simultaneously.

'To return or not to return?'

In many families the issue of whether a young person who has abused another member of the family should return or not return to live in the home, is an important decision. If an abuser has been excluded from the family for a period of time, how is the decision made to return, who makes this decision and how is the situation monitored if a return is achieved? This decision will involve the voices and opinions of the network of people (professionals and family members) involved in the work so far.

When discussing with a family the possibility of a brother returning home after a period of time out, the criteria that members of the significant network were using included: how hard the young man had worked in the individual programme (and therefore if he didn't return he would feel this work had been wasted); if he didn't return his mother would feel a failure and become depressed (and unavailable to the other children, including the victim); 'I don't want my mum to be depressed because she is missing my brother (and so I should not think about my own concerns about him coming home)'; 'that you have to try it sometime (otherwise you won't know if the individual/groupwork has worked or not)'; 'He has been punished enough (and therefore has the right to come home)'.

Each of these reasons was expressed by a different member and each could be taken into account. However, how are they then prioritised? How can a victim express her own thoughts without feeling she is making the whole decision and might end up being blamed because she still does not feel safe, even though everyone else says her brother has changed? Work in this area does not involve simple linear progression. Success at one stage does not necessarily lead on to the next stage. Success at one stage may elicit difficulties in other areas.

'What is the difference between adolescent experimentation and sexual abuse?'

This question was asked by a social worker and echoed by the mother, in a meeting held which included the young abuser, his mother and the referring social worker. The family/professional meeting was held after young man had completed a course of groupwork. Resisting the attempt to answer the question himself the therapist turned to the young man and asked him if he would explain. He went on to give a clear and full description of the difference between what he had done and what could be regarded as consensual experimentation, and showed his learning from the group.

The implicative effect of this episode was marked in relation to how the boy saw himself as someone who could make the case for responsibility; and how he was seen by significant adults as able to consider the feelings of others in making clear distinctions between abusive and non-abusive behaviour. The family members began to support him in making this distinction rather than protecting him from professionals who they saw as making their son go through unnecessary work.

Absent family members

In those instances where the family is not physically available to attend sessions then the current significant relationships such as foster carers, residential workers, social workers, and probation officers can be involved in the work with the family members through the use of 'hypothetical interviewing'.

> A young Indian man whose father had died some time ago and was living with his sister and brother-in-law following sexual abuse outside the family, was brought to the sessions by a probation assistant who shared the same religious faith. This cultural/religious connection was used to good effect during the work. The father was 'involved' through hypothetical questioning such as 'If your father were here today, what kind of things would he be saying to you, about what you did?', 'If we asked your father to guide us in our work with you when would he tell us to be "firmer" with you and when would he tell us to be more "gentle" with you?' In this way the 'absent' family members can be used as a resource in the sessions.

This can work similarly when absent family members are seen as a restraint to progress.

> A young man in foster care had not seen his father for many years. He had constructed a legend that his father was a good man, which contradicted the social services records that his father had been abusive. The legend and the records became mutually exclusive and the more the social services tried to convince him that his father was

not someone to emulate the more the young man would not listen to any advice they proposed. The young man 'lived out' a message he remembered his father's telling him 'never let people push you around'. He lived this by pushing other people around, including being sexually abusive at school. We took the approach of engaging in his legend of his father as a good man who would want the best for his son. We developed discussions around questions such as 'Do you think your father would want you to have a good education, and become successful?' 'If you were in a position where you could do something that got you into trouble, or do something that would lead you towards being seen as sensitive towards others, what would your father advise you to do?' In this way we acted within his definition of his father as a good man and allowed him to *both* change *and* remain loyal to his father.

When family members are not present it is possible to use a process referred to as 'internalised other' interviewing (see Nylund and Corsiglia, 1993; Burnham, 1999) originally developed by David Epston and Karl Tomm. This kind of work involves interviewing the young abuser as the person he has abused and/or other members of his family. This gives the young man the opportunity to 'put himself in the shoes' of the other person and is a valuable part of the process towards increasing relational empathy. On occasions we have shown the videotape of such an interview to the person who was abused for them to evaluate how close the person has come to appreciating their experience.

Endings: assessment 2

This is one of the most difficult areas to discuss since it is difficult to achieve a position of 'safe certainty' and perhaps the most that can be achieved is 'safe uncertainty' (Mason, 1993).

The issues that were considered to be important in assessment 1 when we began the work will form the basis for assessment 2 at the end of our contact with the young abuser and his family. We use the phrase 'end of our contact' rather than end of the work as there is a sense in which this work never comes to an 'end' since this form of abuse continues to be a source of concern for family and professionals long after any formal work has been completed. There seems to be a societal belief (including amongst professionals) that 'once an abuser, always an abuser', and so a position of permanent vigilance is advised for the abuser, families and professionals.

> A young man with whom we had completed work in our programme some 5 years earlier had now married and his wife was pregnant. The social services wrote to us asking if we thought he posed a risk to the child in his family of procreation, rather than his family of origin. He had done well in terms of the programme, but it seemed the question was based on an idea that professionals such as ourselves could arrive at an objective assessment that was 'timeless'.

We do not see ourselves as ever being able to say 'this young person now poses no risk at all'.

Ending our contact may come about in several ways:

> A young man who had abused his sister and was still living at home was referred to our programme. The social services department who had referred the family had not been able to obtain a legal mandate to remove him from home. The parents were seen as responsible, middle-class people who would be sufficiently vigilant to protect their daughter from further abuse. In the initial meeting he was seen with his parents, who had decided not to bring their daughter. The young man seemed reluctant to talk and his parents spoke from very different positions during the session. The mother was very uncertain about whether her son realised what he had done and was in favour of her son entering therapy and was willing to participate, 'if my daughter had been abused by someone outside the family I would want that person to have therapy and so I want my son to as well'. The father spoke of his certainty that this was now in the past and he did not want his daughter to be dragged through any more sessions and the issue was best forgotten now.

> The family chose not to return and attempts to create a legal context for further therapeutic sessions met with failure. Social services continued to monitor as best they could.

Ending contact can therefore be precipitous and before work has even begun, or at some point during the work, the assessment 1 and 2 can be completed simultaneously.

When the end of contact is co-constructed between ourselves and significant others the criteria for ending will be related to:

- the way the work began and the specificity of the initial remit;
- issues which emerged during the work and whether we were able to take these on;
- the changing nature of the relationship between family members;
- the opinions of other professionals.

Increasingly we are looking at convening the significant relationship system, including family members, to evaluate the emergence and strengthening of change in relation to significant themes such as responsibility and empathy. In relation to family members we are looking to see if the changes the young person has made are supported by the family members.

> A young man who had been sexually abused by his father (who spent time in jail for this offence) had lived for four years with foster parents and he began to behave in a sexually abusive manner. After a period of work within our programme and at a particular age he chose to go back to live with his father and family. Social services were powerless to prevent this due to his age. The work we had done and the changes he had made were likely to be undermined by his family who continued to express abusive values and no regret for the abuse of the past. This ending of contact is not an optimistic one and might be called 'unsafe uncertainty' (Mason, 1993).

Alternatively, in the situation outlined above where the young man explained to his mother what the difference was between adolescent experimentation and sexual abuse, this led the mother to begin questioning her own values and eventually the step-father came to sessions and was prepared to reshape some of the ways that the family talked about sexual matters, especially the different gender expectations of boys and girls in the family; what they considered was 'natural', and what could be changed. By the end the family were clearly expressing support for the change in their son's values and behaviours and saying how their own thinking and attitudes had changed also. This seemed a much more optimistic ending where the responsibility for maintaining change was not the sole responsibility of the young man.

Endings continue to be a difficult area in this aspect of our work. Some young men have expressed frustration that: 'It doesn't matter how hard we work, it seems like we can never change enough for people to believe that we won't do it again'. This sentiment may well continue while there remains a high expectation on the part of the public and other agencies regarding our responsibilities as therapists if an abuser re-offends sexually after a therapeutic programme has come to an end.

The future

With longitudinal studies not yet available the future of this kind of work is uncertain. Nevertheless we feel encouraged that the project continues and that this book collects the work of professionals who are, in different ways, developing services in this difficult area of practice. In 1994 we joined the York Project, a multi-centre research project from which more specific data is due. Hopefully with further research we will come to have a better idea about which ways of working are making 'a difference that makes a difference' (Bateson, 1972).

10

WORK WITH ADOLESCENT FEMALES WHO SEXUALLY ABUSE

Similarities and differences

Anne Blues, Carole Moffat and Paula Telford

Introduction

> The seriousness of sexual assaults by females needs to be addressed
> with Social Services providers, Police, Probation and the Courts.
> Specific treatment programmes need to be developed for female
> offenders and made available in every community.
>
> (Cavanagh-Johnson, 1989, p. 584)

Those working in this area know only too well that this scenario is far
removed from the current position in the UK where services for young
female abusers are few and far between. The authors work at Kaleidoscope,
a community resource for children and young people up to the age of
17 years and their families, and for several years have been working
with children who have sexually abused other children. These young
abusers are primarily boys and young men but relatively recently young
females have also been referred. On the basis of this albeit small clinical
sample this chapter will consider the significance of gender issues in
working with child-on-child abuse and will compare similarities and
differences in the characteristics of young male and female sexual
abusers.

Until the late 1980s, it was taken as fact that all child sex abusers
were adult males and the majority of victims female. More recently, it
has become clear that a large percentage of boys are also the victims of
sexual abuse and understanding of the links between victim experiences
and victimiser behaviour has developed in the UK (Bolton *et al.*, 1989;
Morrison *et al.*, 1994). However, whilst there has been a developing

awareness of women as sexual abusers of children in the USA from around 1984 (Finkelhor and Russell, 1984) it was only some eight years later that this knowledge base crystallised into a national UK conference (Kidscape, The Last Taboo, 1992).

The more general context for this growing understanding is one where women committing any kind of offence are not dealt with consistently by criminal justice systems. Gelsthorpe and Morris (1990) suggest that because criminology has been crime led: 'Criminology in all its guises has ignored women to a large extent. The construction, production and dissemination of knowledge has been dominated by men and men's discourse' (p. 7).

The issue of gender therefore has been largely overlooked and the idea of women behaving in a sexually abusive way has remained a difficult one to accept.

The prevalence of sexual abuse by women is also a matter of debate. Partly because of the varying definitions used (Matthews *et al.*, 1989) research is not conclusive, with some disagreement about the numbers of female child sexual abusers as a proportion of all sexual abusers. Females are generally viewed as recipients rather than instigators of sexual behaviour, and the ideology of women as essentially passive, as mothers, nurturers, carers and moral arbiters within the family, combined with the notion that sexual abuse is a male activity, makes acceptance of the fact that women sexually abuse children painful and perplexing. Given the struggles to accept that children sexually abuse children and that women sexually abuse children, acceptance that female children sexually abuse other children requires an enormous shift in thinking and perception.

A review of the literature on the prevalence and circumstances of sexual offending by females, however, highlights the need for a service for girls. Approximately 10 per cent of victims of child sexual abuse are molested by women and girls (Matthews *et al.*, 1989; Saradjian, 1996; Finkelhor, 1984; Mayer, 1992; Scavo, 1989; Elliott, 1993). In the UK, records from ChildLine indicate that of the 8,663 children and young people who rang and disclosed sexual abuse during one twelve-month period, 780 (9 per cent) identified the perpetrator as female (Harrison, 1993). It is reasonable, therefore, to extrapolate that there is a sizeable number of young women who abuse who potentially require a service.

Saradjian's *schema* theory (1996) provides one explanation as to why there will always be fewer female than male sex abusers as women and girls themselves have to make a bigger leap to overcome internalised views about stereotypes of acceptable behaviour and rules. Girls behaving in sexually abusive ways have often been perceived of as acting out their own abuse rather than as behaving abusively to other children (Ryan and Lane, 1991). Other psychological research suggests that: 'female victims often internalise their control-seeking behaviours [self-harm, eating disorders, depression] whereas male victims externalise them with aggressive behaviours' (Bannister and Gallagher, 1996, p. 93).

Notwithstanding the relatively small numbers of female abusers, service providers must address the seriousness of sexual assault by females in order to protect victims (Cavanagh-Johnson, 1989). Familial and societal gender stereotypes and attitudes may compound the experience of their victims as it is more difficult for them to disclose abuse by females and clinicians may be less likely to probe this area. This may mean that appropriate services are difficult to access and inappropriate services may compound the problem. Sgroi and Sargent (1993) suggest that victims may be inhibited about even regarding such behaviour as abusive in the first place: 'because female sexual abuse arouses such strong reactions, particularly in other women, survivors fear being ostracised, receiving anger and criticism or being gossiped about' (p. 52). As a result direct disclosure is less frequent because of concern about a negative or dismissive response. Thus victims feel additional shame and stigma.

In the authors' experience, appropriate services are not readily available and victims/survivors have indicated anxiety about being involved in group therapy with those who have been abused by males. Similarly many projects providing services for young people who sexually abuse will only accept males, and of those whose service is open to females many report an absence of referrals or, even when proactive in seeking girls, have referral rates of significantly less than 5 per cent.

Theoretical perspectives

Major theories relating to sexually abusing behaviour in adolescents are outlined in chapter 1. The authors have found combinations of cognitive-behavioural work (Ryan and Lane, 1991), Lane and Zamora's (1978) cycle of abusing behaviour and Finkelhor's four preconditions (1984) applicable to work with girls who sexually abuse. Some of these theories are used as tools with the young people and others are used to inform analysis of the work undertaken with them. In general significant differences in the use or applicability of these theories in relation to young male or female sexual abusers have not been found.

An additional approach the authors have used which is not described elsewhere in this book is solution-focused brief therapy

(Insoo Kim Berg, 1991; Selekman, 1993), which has been applied with equal degrees of success with girls and boys. Solution-focused ideas are used to gather information, to build on young people's strengths, to look at exceptions to their abusing behaviour and also to elicit information regarding risk. Stereotypical assumptions might suggest that boys are less likely to engage in exercises which might require them to describe visual imagery but this has not been borne out in practice.

Scaling questions, either by using numbers or visual images, are introduced to measure young people's perceptions of their own dangerousness, what needs to be done to reduce that dangerousness, how supportive parents and carers are and for predicting risky situations. Using 'the miracle question' (of waking up one morning and finding that the problem of their sexual abusing behaviour has gone away) encourages thinking in terms of hope and change as well as eliciting valuable information about interactions with others in their lives and how these may impact on their problem behaviour. It can also elicit valuable information about risk.

> A 14-year-old girl who was gravitating towards an unstructured environment was experiencing a 'push-pull' between that and therapy. When asked to imagine going to bed that night and a miracle happening so that the next day her abusing behaviour had gone, she was encouraged to describe the first difference that she would notice. She answered that she would be able to go babysitting with a friend without having sexual feelings about the children in their charge.

None of the professionals had known that she was babysitting and it transpired that she had been very worried about the situation but did not know how to explain her reluctance to her friend. She was then helped and supported in not putting the children and herself in dangerous situations.

Discovering exceptions to a young person's abusing behaviour helps workers to identify what to build on in the future and to plant young people firmly in a future 'possibility land' (O'Hanlon and Beadle, 1997). Self-esteem can be raised when young people are able to appreciate that there have been times when they have felt bad but have managed to control that behaviour.

Similarities and differences

A legitimate concern for those considering extending their work to include services for young women is that of similarities and differences with young males. What follows is a consideration of areas which have emerged as central in work with young female sexual abusers, some aspects of which are in contrast to current understanding of and work with young males who sexually abuse. It should be noted however, that these differences are greatly outweighed by issues which are similar to males.

Sexual abuse

First it would appear that girls who sexually abuse are much more likely to have experienced sexual abuse themselves. Matthews *et al.* (1997), for example, suggests that approximately 77 per cent of girls and women who sexually abuse are also sexual abuse victims. In contrast Cavanagh-Johnson (1989) and O'Callaghan and Print (1994) suggest respectively that 30 and 50 per cent of boys are themselves victims of sexual abuse. Furthermore, it is suggested that girls are more likely to have been abused by a perpetrator with whom they had sustained a close ongoing relationship (Matthews *et al.*, 1989; Thomas, 1996). All of the girls who have attended Kaleidoscope to date are known to be victims of sexual abuse. In all but one case, the alleged perpetrator was known and named and in the majority of cases this was a male co-parent.

Despite this strong correlation in young females between prior sexual abuse and sexually abusing behaviour, to use this factor as a precondition to abusing must be considered inappropriate as only a few of the many tens of thousands of female victims of child sexual abuse become perpetrators. As discussed above it has been suggested that the way girls are socialised encourages them to internalise trauma and because of this girls may be less likely than boys to show the effects of hurt and harm in the form of aggression or violence to others. It would therefore follow that girls who develop such patterns of abusing behaviour would be more likely to be those who had experienced a greater degree of hurt and harm themselves. Matthews *et al.* (1997) conclude:

'in comparison to their male counterparts, the developmental histories of the juvenile female perpetrators reflected even more extensive and severe maltreatment' (p.187).

Whilst this has not been our clinical experience this may be connected to the fact that we are a community-based resource who become involved with boys and girls at a young age and give importance to helping them tell of victim experiences.

Emotional abuse

Emotional abuse is a significant phenomenon for boys and girls who sexually abuse, often perpetrated by distant, inaccessible parents, with experiences of degradation, humiliation and 'put downs' commonplace. Saradjian (1996) found, in her research of women who sexually abuse children: 'One of the most compelling differences between the women in the comparison group and the offender groups was the degree of emotional deprivation and abuse experienced by the women offenders as children' (p. 59).

Parents and caregivers are clearly not directly responsible for their child's sexually abusing behaviour unless they have directly perpetrated sexual abuse themselves. However, they are responsible for the emotional climate in which the young people are raised. All of our service users have suffered emotional harm with all of the girls the least popular, most scapegoated, child in the family. More recently the significance of unstable attachments to their caregivers has become apparent in ongoing relationships, undermining their position and security in the family. This appears to have been an extremely significant feature for the young people, boys and girls alike, in their pattern of abusing behaviour.

Physical abuse

Physical abuse has been a significant feature in the lives of the young people, both boys and girls, with whom the authors have worked. For most of the girls, the physical abuse has been directly related to their levels of compliance or otherwise within their own experiences of sexual abuse. This is in contrast to the boys whose experiences of physical abuse tend to be responses to non-compliance to male caregivers or older brothers although not necessarily in a sexually abusive relationship. Cavanagh-Johnson (1989) identifies physical abuse as a significant feature for the girls in her study.

Domestic violence

To view domestic violence as a child protection issue is a very recent development in the UK (Brandon and Lewis, 1996). O'Callaghan and Print (1994) identify spouse abuse as a significant feature for 38 per cent of the young people with whom they work. Bannister and Gallagher (1996) also documented this experience as present in the families of the very young children with whom they worked.

A striking similarity in the backgrounds of all the children and young people the authors have worked with has emerged over the last eighteen months to two years. For almost all of our service users, domestic violence has been or is a very significant feature in their lives. It is perhaps, on consideration, not surprising that this would be so. They have a model of behaviour which teaches that strength is desirable and that stronger partners (men in particular) can take what they want by either being bigger or stronger or over-powering those more vulnerable than themselves. When these young people are faced with their own feelings of lack of control and disempowerment, they have been given an example of unacceptable ways in which to make themselves feel powerful. In addition, it has been observed that girls who have experienced their mother's abuse by a male caregiver, often actively struggle against images of women as victims and have used abusing behaviours against other children in order to avoid repeating the pattern experienced in their own families.

Use of force and coercion

Although the use of force and coercion when abusing is well documented there is some evidence to suggest that boys are more likely to use force and girls coercion in order to keep the abuse secret. Early studies (Mavasti, 1986) suggested that female sexual abuse of children was non-violent. However, later research (Cavanagh-Johnson and Gill, 1989; Thomas, 1996) has suggested that sexual abuse by children of both genders is often accompanied by verbal and physical violence. Gail Ryan (Ryan and Lane, 1997) argues that girls who sexually abuse are less likely to use threats to maintain the silence but instead use coercion, hidden in the realms of special secrets to be kept because of the sanctity of the relationship.

The possibility of violence should not, however, be overlooked because of gendered expectations of boys and girls. Matthews *et al.* (1997), Elliott (1993) and Weldon (1988) also document violent acts as part of the repertoire of women who abuse. It is also important not to underestimate the significance of violence, when present, as a predictive risk factor. Thus in relation to adolescent male sex offenders at least, Ross and Loss (1991) identify the use of force and coercion as a high tariff risk within the twenty-one areas they list as needing to be explored: 'in order to most fully understand the presence, nature, extent and seriousness of sexually aggressive behaviour problems' (p. 199).

All of the children with whom the authors have worked, whether boys or girls, have used force, aggression or coercion as part of their abusing behaviour. This has occurred whether in terms of preventing their victim shouting for help or in singly or jointly holding down their victim. For some of the older boys this aggression has become part of the sexual gratification, but this has not been identified as a feature with the girls.

Responsibility Taking

Matthews *et al.* (1989) have suggested that females were more likely to take responsibility for the abuse and are less likely to place blame on the victim. In all likelihood this is connected to societal expectations of women's roles. Weldon (1988) also suggests that girls who re-enact trauma via abusing are less likely to want power and control and therefore are more amenable to stop abusing if their own issues are addressed. However, Cavanagh-Johnson (Cavanagh-Johnson and Gill, 1993) argues that there appear to be few gender differences in relation to taking responsibility and victim blame. Denial and minimisation are also a feature for both girls and boys in therapeutic intervention. This is felt to be related to previous experiences of denial as a coping mechanism and connected to restraints about lack of trust and fear of consequences.

In relation to responsibility taking, however, there may be an interesting difference between young male and female sexual abusers. Evidence of, and work on, girls' abusing behaviour may be most easily accessed in settings where feelings and emotional responses are discussed in relation to the young person's own abuse, whereas boys are engaged more easily when they are able to intellectualise and externalise about their abusing behaviour. Matthews (1993) suggests that the socialisation of boys leaves them more focused on cognitive issues which enable to them to intellectualise and therefore distance themselves from the abuse and their abusing behaviour. She suggests this is why they tend to focus on their offending more easily than on victim experiences. Girls appear to access feelings more easily, including those connected with their own victim experiences, and can also use this ability to address their abusing behaviour.

Cavanagh-Johnson and Gill (1993) suggest that girls are more likely to disclose their own abuse and abusing behaviour when in therapy for other presenting problems, whereas boys' abusing behaviour has often come to the attention of professionals via disclosure by their victims. In our own experience the process would seem to be that young people initially acknowledge responsibility when first involved with professionals (usually within a child protection investigation) and then as they become aware of the consequences of this admission, they become restrained in acknowledging responsibility during therapeutic intervention. Our experience is also that both girls and boys have been more amenable to a programme which explores the restraints to their responsibility taking (Jenkins, 1990) and these restraints are similar for both boys and girls, for example: If I tell ... will I be sent away? Will my parents want me? Will the police become involved? Will the child's parents retaliate against me or my family? Will the worker be disgusted, shocked, punitive and unable to cope?

In addition to these restraints, experience also indicates that very often the young people are still close to their own experiences of hurt and harm, many of which are of a more serious and protracted nature than the abuse they have inflicted on other children. In the case of boys who have not disclosed sexual abuse, but where this is suspected, being unable to disclose their own victim experiences, and therefore being unable to deal with them, acts as a barrier to dealing with how they have harmed others. However, in the case of all the girls worked with at Kaleidescope, as stated earlier, there has been clear information about their having previously been sexually abused. One outcome of this is that it has been easier to access the girls' abusing behaviours by working with their own victim experiences. This has not resulted in their excusing their abusing behaviour and we have found that they can access a range of feelings more readily than do boys. Boys appear to be able to be in touch with anger, although unable to express it constructively and they are most often unable to acknowledge or deal with sadness. For example one 10-year-old boy said if he allowed himself to look at the sadness in his life it would kill him.

One of the greatest restraints to responsibility taking for both girls and boys is the attitude of family to the allegations made against their child. Ranges of responses from disbelief to outright rejection clearly impinge on young people's ability to talk about their abusing behaviour. One other factor more likely to affect girls' ability to engage in treatment relates to the types of service they have previously been offered. In the authors' experience many of the girls had been offered services exclusively for their victim experiences, even when their abusing behaviour was known. Those services would, of course, be less likely to focus on the girls being asked to take responsibility. In the case of one young woman, for example, whose sexualised behaviour had been known since she was 4 when she was at nursery, she received months and years of recurrent therapy focused on her own hurt and harm but this had not addressed how she had coped with this by abusing others.

Other offending behaviour

There is some debate about whether young sexual abusers are also likely to exhibit other non-sexual offending behaviours and whether boys are more likely than girls to do so. Some research suggests that this is a significant feature for adolescent boys and it is an important consideration in the twenty-one high-risk factors outlined by Ross and Loss (1991). O'Callaghan and Print (1994), however, suggest that the boys in their study show significantly less examples of other offending behaviours, that is, only some shop-lifting and petty crime.

Issues pertaining to alcohol and drug misuse may be significant, particularly for older children. Thomas (1996) suggests that 50 per cent of girls had substance misuse history which appeared to be linked to their response to their own abuse. However although alcohol misuse has been a feature for two boys in our sample, one aged 16 and one 9 years, alcohol or drug misuse has not been a significant feature for any of the girls. Indeed it has been the authors' experience that the vast majority of the young people referred have had no previous involvement in criminal activity that is known to the police. Only one girl had had any involvement with the police and this was in response to one of her many manifestations of troubled behaviour whilst being looked after by the local authority. Two service users, one a very young girl and one an older boy, had set fires but these had not come to the attention of the police.

Age of onset

Both boys and girls are known to be capable of behaving in a sexually aggressive way from approximately 6–7 years of age, if not younger. The age at which this behaviour is deemed worrying enough for intervention would appear to be still slightly later for girls. In respect of boys who sexually abuse, Ryan and Lane (1997) and O'Callaghan and Print (1994) have reported that young people have been approximately 14–16 years of age when they were referred, although their histories have often revealed that their abusive behaviours had begun earlier than this, but without attracting concern.

Matthews et al. (1989), Elliott (1993) and Mayer (1992) suggest that girls begin abusing at a slightly older age than boys, approximately 16–17 years and that this onset coincides with their move into caregiving roles, for example babysitting. However, as with research into age of onset of boys who sexually abuse, this estimate is a matter of some debate. For example girls worked with so far at Kaleidoscope have been between the ages of 6 and 14 years. It follows then that the girls seen in our project began abusing from about 3 years through to 14 years which would not be in keeping with this earlier research but would be in line with the work of Thomas (1996) and Cavanagh-Johnson (1993) who identify 7.5 years and 4–12 years respectively as more probable ages of onset. For most of these girls in our sample the time of referral was close to the time of their disclosure. However one very notable exception was the girl mentioned earlier whose sexualised behaviour had caused concern in nursery to the extent that she had been excluded because of complaints from other parents. Approximately ten years later she was referred to our service for assessment and treatment because of her abusing behaviour.

Victim selection

Why and how a victim is chosen is important in determining future risk and protection and strategies for avoiding rehearsed abusive behaviour. Most samples of children reported in research findings (for example, Matthews *et al.*, 1997) and those in Kaleidoscope's experience have abused more than one child of either gender. Cavanagh-Johnson (1993) and Elliott (1993) suggest that girls are most likely to be the victim of abuse by girls whereas Thomas (1996) suggests that the selection of victims by younger children is more likely to depend on circumstance and availability than gender. Information from ChildLine (Harrison, 1993) has recently suggested that their referrals indicate boys to be the most frequent victims of sexual abuse by girls and women. It may be, however, that it is easier for boys to disclose this type of abuse by telephone rather than face to face, with the result that this finding may be based on a skewed sample.

The authors have found that the younger the child at the age of onset of their sexually abusive behaviour, the less likely it is that the activity is gender specific. Usually children abuse those to whom they have legitimate access, either as siblings, younger children in the neighbourhood who trust them, children of their parents' friends and with whom they spend a considerable time, children of their extended family or members of their peer group. Whilst all of the children worked with could be described as the least favoured child of the family, and would often describe their anger towards the most favoured child of the family, none of the girl abusers had abused this child, whereas this was a prevalent abuser/victim relationship in the families of the boys. It is a matter of speculation that this may be connected to prescribed and expected gender roles within the abuser's family.

Progression and escalation of abusing behaviour

Cavanagh-Johnson and Gill (1989) suggest that female children who sexually abuse are initially reacting to abusive experiences and that the abusive behaviour progresses from non-contact to contact abuse. The Spark programme (Cavanagh-Johnson, 1989) provided information that girls perpetrated a range of sexually abusive behaviours including oral and digital penetration, anal penetration, fondling and genital contact. Information from O'Callaghan and Print (1994) and Ryan and Lane (1991) identify a similar range of behaviours for boys who abuse.

In helping young people at Kaleidoscope to understand their cycle of abusing behaviour, workers have looked for evidence of a progression or escalation of the abusive activity. In only one case could the progression from non-contact to contact abuse be clearly seen. This was in the case of the girl who had been sexualised since nursery school. The clearer identification of escalation in this case might owe itself to the availability of documents chronicling her earlier behaviour. So often this information is not available as less intrusive sexual behaviours, particularly those of a non-contact type, are not often documented.

A proportion of the girls (and boys) worked with have had family histories of intergenerational sexual abuse. For these young people a hypothesis about the difficulty in tracing a clear pattern of escalation is that when children's daily lives are so punctuated by a climate of ongoing abuse it is difficult for them to think in terms of isolated incidents and sequences.

Whilst for almost all of the girls engaged in treatment work it was not easy to see a clear progression, whereby unchecked this behaviour was unlikely to disappear of its own accord, there was evidence for all of the girls that it continued at a static rate for considerable lengths of time and perhaps, without intervention, there would subsequently be a progression in adulthood to abusing their own children.

Educational ability and achievement

Whilst many of the children and young people who display sexually aggressive behaviour do not have any organic form of limited ability, their circumstances have almost inevitably led to poor attendance and poor functioning in the school setting, leaving them with less ability and limited education.

Ryan and Lane (1991) suggest that a large number of the young men with whom they have worked had a history of behaviour problems, including truancy, which led to a labelling of below average ability. Matthews *et al.* (1989) described the women and girls in their study as 'less able', possibly due to their emotional experiences. Cavanagh-Johnson (1989) described the girls in the Spark project as all having been in trouble in school academically or socially.

In terms of learning disability, the majority of girls we have worked with at Kaleidoscope have been considered at some point to have had learning difficulties. These difficulties were not thought to be organic but to be emotionally based. Similarly, a significant number of boys had been subject to educational statements and some were already in special educational placements. There was no evidence that the learning difficulties related to the sexually abusing impulses and it has been a salutary lesson for staff that perceived learning difficulties in no way preclude children from taking responsibility. Indeed, one boy in particular, whose learning disability had led to his being treated leniently by police on each occasion of his abusing, came to Kaleidoscope desperate to acknowledge his behaviour as abusive and to learn to control it.

Social skills and self-esteem

Poor self-esteem is a very significant factor for children who sexually abuse other children and again, gender is not significant here. Thus Cavanagh-Johnson (1989) described girls in the Spark programme as having no peer-age friends and living as isolates, whilst Ryan and Lane (1991) evidence the same in respect of the adolescent boys with whom they worked. O'Callaghan and Print (1994) and Cavanagh-Johnson (1989) describe depression and suicidal ideas as featuring in both boys and girls, rather than only in girls as is often assumed.

Given the levels of emotional, physical and sexual abuse and difficulties with belonging and attachment experienced by the children seen in the project, it is clear why all of them struggled with low self-esteem which would appear to have pre-dated the onset of their abusing behaviour. Mental health issues have been considered in relation to some of these young people, in particular where there has been evidence of depression. Issues of self-harm, eating disorders or other internalising manifestations have not been in evidence although one girl needed to work in a modified treatment environment which she felt befitted her vision of herself, that is made messy and dirty with paint spatters, graffiti and spit.

The importance of early identification and intervention

Early identification and intervention is a key factor in positive outcomes for both girls and boys. Matthews *et al.* (1989) suggest that the ability of females who sexually abuse to acknowledge responsibility and have their issues dealt with indicates a better prognosis for girls than for boys. However, Saradjian (1996) and Weldon (1988) suggest that this is less likely because consequences in terms of familial, societal and professional responses to their abusing behaviour are likely to be harsher for girls than for boys.

Not surprisingly it has been suggested (Ryan and Lane, 1991) that more intact family lifestyles and circumstances for both boys and girls, where parents and carers are willing to consider change in the emotional climate of the family home and who are supportive and engaging in the therapeutic process, will also predict more hopeful outcomes. Where parents are either not believing that their child has abused or where they believe and reject the child, these children would appear to have the poorest prognosis for change and safety.

Lorna (7 years) who abused her little sister (3 years) at times when she was extremely irritated by her, was only able to learn alternative strategies for her behaviour to the limit of a 7-year-old's ability. However, when Lorna's mother came to understand the dynamic and when Lorna was able to access her mother's help and support to deal with her feelings and avoid abusing, the younger sibling was clearly safer.

Flexibility of approach to address the issues most at the forefront of the young person's mind when they enter treatment would seem also to increase the likelihood of positive change.

Conclusion

In conclusion it would appear that there are more similarities than differences between boys and girls who sexually abuse in terms of factors contributing to their abusing behaviour, how they abuse and their amenability to treatment. The biggest difference would seem to be in how both society and professionals view and respond to them.

In the same way as there has been a raising of awareness about children and young people abusing other children in the last ten years, we would hope that there would be the same journey in awareness of the issues of girls abusing as it is clear that there is a need for this problem to be taken seriously. The impact of their actions on their victims is every bit as harmful as abuse by young males and increased awareness may make it easier for victims to tell their story and receive appropriate services, and for young female abusers to be given the opportunity to change their behaviour.

11

STOP AND THINK

Changing sexually aggressive behaviour in young children

Linda Butler and Colin Elliott

Introduction

This chapter will discuss a framework for working with young children of 10 years and under who are sexually aggressive. It describes the use of a 'Stop and Think' model, an inter-personal problem-solving approach based on cognitive-behavioural theories, which can be used with individual children or with groups. Strategies for simplifying complex, abstract concepts into concrete forms that can be understood and used by young children will be described and illustrated with brief case examples. Issues of particular relevance to this population will be discussed such as the importance of working with the non-abusing carer; safety and protection issues; developmental aspects of the work; the dilemmas of working with children who are both victimisers of other children and victims themselves, and the importance of working within statutory and professional networks.

Throughout, examples will be provided to illustrate particular points, based largely on work with one particular child, Billy, a boy aged 8 whose serious sexually aggressive behaviour towards a number of smaller children extended back three years. Billy came from a chaotic background, where he had been rejected emotionally by his mother such that the local authority had accommodated him on several occasions. He had been physically and sexually abused by several of his mother's partners. Sexualised behaviour and sexual aggression at home had not been seen by his mother as a reason to seek help but, following referral to the Child and Adolescent Mental Health Service for generally aggressive and disturbed behaviour, it was discovered that many incidents of sexual aggression had occurred at home and in school over the previous three years. These had been minimised in school largely on the basis of him having suffered rejection by his mother, with the previous work undertaken by the social services department focusing on trying to improve their relationship.

To date the Stop and Think programme has only been used with young boys, originally as a groupwork programme, and subsequently on an individual basis. For this reason, only boys will be referred to when describing the model and its practical implementation. This is not to say that this approach cannot be used with girls.

Theoretical background

Sexual aggression can be a behavioural manifestation of early traumatic sexualisation (Finkelhor, 1986). However, whilst many young children who become sexually aggressive have been sexually abused themselves, others have learned to behave in this way through exposure to pornography or developmentally inappropriate sexual materials or behaviour.

The cognitive-behavioural theoretical model of the development of psychological problems integrates learning theory, particularly the influence of conditioning, contingencies, and models in the environment, with the impact of cognitive factors (Kendall and Braswell, 1985). This model can be applied to explain the development and maintenance of sexually aggressive behaviour in young children through a mixture of classical conditioning (Pavlov, 1927), operant conditioning (Skinner, 1953), and vicarious learning or modelling (Bandura, 1969). For example, particular stimuli or triggers can become associated with a particular response (in this case a sexually aggressive act) through classical conditioning and may then be maintained through processes of positive and negative reinforcement.

Many sexually aggressive children come from violent backgrounds where aggression is the norm; their home environments are often chaotic, with few boundaries, and the children have developed few internal controls, tending to be generally impulsive and aggressive. Research shows that the model of self-control children develop is influenced by the models they observe (Bandura, 1969). Some sexually aggressive children come from backgrounds where their emotional needs are not met, and have learned to meet their emotional needs for comfort and nurture through sexuality. Those who have been abused may also have become confused between ordinary caregiving affection and sexuality, particularly if their abuser was an attachment figure.

Assessment

The Stop and Think work undertaken with young boys who are sexually aggressive has taken place in the context of a busy Child and Adolescent Mental Health Service, with the usual range of referrals for emotional, behavioural and psychological problems, rather than in a specialist unit dealing with abused and abusing children. While a number of the young boys were referred specifically for overtly sexually aggressive behaviour, others were referred originally because they displayed extreme sexualised behaviour or language, or disturbed behaviour, such as touching animals in sexual ways. When a detailed assessment was carried out, some of these children were found to have committed previously unidentified sexually aggressive acts towards children, or acts of sexual aggression that had been minimised or dismissed as normal sexual curiosity. In the context of the known association between sexual aggression and prior sexual abuse, this fits with a number of studies which have shown that increased sexualised behaviour is a common feature of children who have been sexually abused (Williams and New, 1996) and that sexual behaviour with animals is correlated with a history of sexual abuse (Friedrich, 1993).

To distinguish between behaviour that is exploratory, sexualised or sexually aggressive requires careful assessment of the child and their environment (see chapter 6). Lane (1991) suggests that issues of power and consent provide the basis to distinguish between behaviours that are sexually abusive and those reflecting normal curiosity and exploration. Behaviour described as abusive is normally described as calculated, power-based, or subtly coercive behaviour which normally involves elements of secrecy and which, if the child had been of the age of criminal responsibility, would have been considered a sexual offence.

Assessment framework

Assessment should involve gathering information from multiple sources (Kendal-Tackett et al., 1993) – it is as important to assess the child in the school setting as it is at home, given the frequency with which worrying behaviours are often displayed in that setting. Information should be obtained from all the significant people in the child's life including any social worker or other support workers involved.

Assessment interviews with carers

As with carers of adolescents, it is vital to help carers deal with feelings such as shock, distress, self-blame or disbelief that they may be experiencing in order that they can participate meaningfully in what will be a detailed, essentially ongoing and often upsetting assessment process. In order to achieve this, it is extremely useful to explain how sexually aggressive behaviour often develops, and give them some reassurance that effective help for their child is available.

Detailed assessment should cover such areas as:

- precise details of the sexually aggressive acts;
- the responses of adults and other children to those acts;
- people's attributions regarding what has happened;
- protective measures already taken or planned;
- any other sexual behaviour problems;
- family beliefs around sexuality.

This specific information should be considered in the context of the more general information gathered from a full developmental history of the child, a family history and an assessment of current family functioning and other potential stressors, such as domestic violence.

Assessment interviews with the child

It is important to remember that a young child coming to see professionals may be frightened that they are going to get an angry response because they are bad, or that they will be sent away, on the basis that the adults in the child's life have often already expressed anger or disgust regarding the incident(s) of sexual aggression that have occurred. The child also needs to understand that they have come to a place where it is safe to talk about the things that they have done. However, it is also vital to state at the outset that, if information reveals someone being hurt, including themselves, that information would be passed on to ensure safety.

The interviews should be conducted in a way that is appropriate to the child's level of development using drawings, puppets, small figures and other materials that can be used to represent people and situations in a concrete way.

It is useful to explore with the child:

- precise details of the sexually aggressive acts;
- the child's attributions regarding the events;
- any history of other sexually aggressive thoughts or behaviours;
- their understanding of the other child/ren's perspective;
- the strategies they used to involve and/or silence the other child/ren;
- their motivation for future sexual aggression;

- their understanding of the likely future consequences of their actions.

Interviews such as this are very difficult for young children and it is important to affirm with the child how well they have done by talking about difficult and embarrassing matters in a way that has helped the professionals to understand what happened. Finally many children have experienced great relief at having their sexually aggressive acts separated from them as a person. This can be achieved by explaining that although they have got some things wrong and hurt another child, this does not make them a bad person (as they may have been told), but rather someone who needs to work hard to become a safer person.

Treatment issues

A number of issues should be thought through carefully in relation to working with sexually aggressive children.

Safety and protection issues

Safety and protection issues must be addressed prior to beginning any work with sexually aggressive children, for their own protection as well as that of other children. Interventions with children who are sexually aggressive are usually complex and should involve work with the child, their non-abusing carer and the wider system. It is not appropriate to work with a young child who is not in a safe placement, or who does not have emotional and psychological support from a carer. If these protective factors are not in place, the priority should be on achieving a safe and supportive environment before treatment starts.

At the beginning of treatment, it is unlikely that the full extent of the child's inappropriate behaviour will be known, nor the degree of impulsivity involved. It is therefore most important to agree safety rules and establish some practical arrangements with those adults in regular contact with the child to ensure that he is not put in situations that increase his own or other children's vulnerability.

There is a natural tendency for concern to diminish as treatment progresses and someone else is seen to be working on the problem behaviour. At that time significant adults may become less vigilant, and so maintaining contacts with carers, school staff and any sessional workers throughout the treatment process remains important. At various points in the treatment programme, it may be necessary to share information to ensure the safety of other children, for example, if it becomes apparent that a strong stimulus to being sexually aggressive is present in a particular situation. Planning may be required initially to enable this situation to be avoided, or later in the treatment programme, to deal with the situation under close supervision.

It can be helpful to arrange for the child not to have to return to school immediately after a Stop and Think session because there is an increased risk, particularly at the beginning of the work, that memories may have been triggered which increase the likelihood of the child behaving in sexually aggressive ways.

Working with non-abusing carers

It is crucial to involve the child's non-abusing carer(s) in treatment, as without their support and involvement treatment will be unsuccessful (Vizard *et al.*, 1995). When working with problematic behaviour in children generally, it is important that this is done in conjunction with the carer (Wolfe *et al.*, 1993), so that the child is not expected to change in an unchanging environment. When working with sexually aggressive children, carers are critical in ensuring the safety of the child while treatment is being carried out. Furthermore, if carers are not involved, they can feel excluded and may consciously or unconsciously undermine treatment progress. Lastly and possibly most importantly, carers can be our best resource to help the child practise their developing skills in real-life situations. It is therefore important to continue the engagement process begun during assessment by training carers to become co-workers in the work with the child. Maintaining this relationship is time-consuming but pays dividends as the work progresses.

A psycho-educational component is a critical part of the work with the carer. For most carers, this is their first experience of working with children who have been sexually aggressive towards other children and they may have a range of feelings about the child's behaviour. This can result in an initial rejection of the child or a minimisation of events, or feelings of anger and blame towards the system – and individuals – who have identified the problems and who may continue to do so when the carer would prefer to forget what has taken place. If the child has been removed or rejected by their family and accommodated elsewhere, a false assumption is often made that things are safe now that the child is away from the influences of their previous environment and that treatment is not needed!

Many people prefer not to think that young children can be sexually aggressive and carers seldom have much understanding as to how their child became sexually aggressive in the first place. If carers understand the ways in which young children learn to behave generally, this general understanding can then be applied specifically to the issues related to the child's having learned to be sexually aggressive. Understanding the processes by which such behaviours are learned and maintained helps the carers to accept that this behaviour can be changed or unlearned and to maintain this perspective when the process of change is slow. Carers can be encouraged to be alert to areas of possible risk in their environment, to establish appropriate boundaries and to avoid inadvertently putting the sexually aggressive child, or other children, at risk. Using knowledge of how behaviour is learned, maintained and changed, the carer can also be helped to develop, if necessary, behavioural management skills (Patterson, 1982; Herbert, 1991) to reduce sexual aggression and increase pro-social behaviour.

This educative work may be undertaken in a number of different ways: in sessions which involve the carer alone or the carer and child together; through regular network meetings that include the carer, the child's school teacher, social worker or sessional worker; or, if running a children's group, by having a carer's group running in parallel to the children's group. It is extremely helpful to provide carers with simple handouts covering session material so that they can review the ideas as necessary in their own time.

Issues arising during treatment

When working with a child who is both a victim of sexual abuse and a victimiser of other children, the order in which issues are dealt with in treatment is less clear-cut than when working with adolescents or adults. It has been recommended when working with adolescents and adults (Salter, 1988) that treatment focuses on offending behaviour prior to addressing victimisation issues, to avoid the possibility that the abuser's own victimisation is used as an excuse for sexually abusing others. Experience of working with young children shows that it is not always easy for them to separate out their own victimisation from their sexual aggression to others, as one is so often a re-enactment of the other. For this reason, work on their own abuse and on their sexual aggression often takes place interchangeably, with one aspect informing the other as the work progresses.

During the course of treatment, some sexually aggressive children disclose verbally that they have been sexually abused. With others where it is known that they have been abused themselves, it can become apparent that their sexually aggressive behaviour is a re-enactment of their own known victimisation. For children not known to have been abused, the suspicion may grow that they have been. On occasion it happens that, as the work progresses and the realisation dawns that what they have done to another child is wrong, the child begins to think that what has happened to them was also wrong. This complicates matters, as often the child will not want this information shared. The preparatory work on limited confidentiality is therefore helpful.

If a disclosure occurs during the course of treatment, then a child protection agency will need to be informed to ensure the child's safety. A risk assessment may need to be undertaken depending on the child's situation, and a joint social services/police investigation interview (Memorandum of Good Practice, 1992) may be necessary as the sexually aggressive child has now been identified as both a victim and a victimiser. Before continuing with treatment, it is important to confer with colleagues from the police and crown prosecution service regarding matters of evidence. Practice varies nationally regarding what is regarded as permissible in terms of treatment prior to the completion of any criminal proceedings. The views of the various agencies involved at this point in time may differ regarding the child's therapeutic needs versus the needs of the legal system and so this decision should not be taken in isolation. Whatever the decision reached, it is important that the child understands what is happening and why.

The Stop and Think programme

Introduction

Many of the treatment programmes that have been used with sexually aggressive children have been based on programmes designed for adults and so have not satisfactorily addressed developmental issues. Conversely effective cognitive-behavioural therapy (CBT) approaches with children, such as the intervention programmes for impulsive, attention-disordered children developed by Spivak and Shure (1974) and Kendall and Braswell (1985) were not designed for use with children who were sexually aggressive. CBT for children comprises various techniques that teach them cognitive mediational strategies to guide their behaviour and increase their adjustment (Durlak et al., 1991). It can be used effectively with quite young children provided that their cognitive-developmental level is taken into account and abstract concepts are translated into concrete terms that are accessible to the child (Ronen, 1995). The younger the child, the more concrete must be the methods used. Braswell et al. (1985) argue that verbal methods of inducing cognitive change are weakest with younger children, and that demonstrations of self-efficacy produce the most change.

For the Stop and Think programme, therefore, interventions from the field of sexual abuse have been adapted to a form that is understandable and usable by young children, combining these interventions with CBT concepts and treatment techniques used with children who are generally impulsive and aggressive. The programme provides the child with opportunities to acquire skills that they lack and gives opportunities to practise in naturalistic settings. The programme was developed initially as a groupwork programme (Elliott and Butler, 1994) and then subsequently modified for individual work with sexually aggressive children and their carers.

A major tension in this approach is that while the material needs to be repeated many times for learning to be effective, the children often have a short attention span and get bored easily. This repetition therefore needs to be carried out in a variety of ways to sustain interest, using creative material that is age-appropriate and appealing. A range of games, quizzes, cartoons, mnemonics, situation cards and role-plays have been developed and used to practise problem-solving skills. Thus considerable effort is expended to make the work interesting and fun for the children wherever possible and, by and large, children and their carers do express their enjoyment of the programme as well their appreciation of the benefits it brings. Interestingly, Himeleign and McElrath (1996) have noted that the acquisition of problem-solving skills and the development of a sense of humour increase the resilience of abused children.

The Stop and Think model

The treatment programme is designed to help a child inhibit impulsive behaviour and organise his thoughts and feelings in relation to appropriate behaviour and is based around the Stop and Think model, a problem-solving technique, which is organised into four steps:

Step 1: What's the problem? This requires the child to inhibit his initial response and accurately identify the problem.

Step 2: What can I do? Here, the child brainstorms possible solutions to the identified problem.

Step 3: What might happen? Now the child needs to think consequentially in predicting as best he can possible outcomes for the different solutions he generated.

Step 4: Decide and do This last step requires the child to pick a course of action, carry it out and then evaluate its effectiveness.

Effective use of this model requires a child to follow through the complete sequence of steps, which of course will be impossible if they do not have the skills necessary to perform each individual stage. For this reason, the basic skills that underpin the programme are covered with the child to ensure that they have been acquired before the formal model is presented in its integrated sequential format.

Laying the foundation for the Stop and Think model

Throughout this stage, many varied activities are used to help the child acquire the necessary component skills, some of which are outlined below. In relation to Step 1, going beyond initial, sometimes mistaken perceptions to accurately identify the nature of a 'problem' may necessitate analysis of thoughts, feelings and behaviours for the child and any others involved in what may be a complex sequence of events. Initial work therefore focuses on developing the child's capacity to achieve these skills. Similarly, the child begins to address the requirements of Step 2 using activities in which he learns to generate ideas as to what he or someone else might do in particular situations. Step 3 involves predicting future outcomes for particular courses of action and so requires an understanding of increasingly complex issues in social interaction such as perspective-taking, reciprocity and cause and effect. Moving towards the presentation of the model involves progressively linking the preparatory work together in larger and more complex sequences. More recently, this has involved a more detailed stage dealing specifically with the links between cognition, emotion and behaviour.

Think–Feel–Do

Experience has shown that sexually aggressive children often have particular difficulty understanding their own and other people's emotions and so this part of the programme involves considering emotions in a more detailed way. Extensive input is provided to help the child first to identify their own and other people's feelings and extend their emotional language, second to identify associated thoughts and finally to link feelings, thoughts and behaviours in situational contexts. The importance of this is derived from the central premise in CBT that cognitions, emotions and behaviours are highly interdependent and that an intervention that targets one of these areas indirectly affects the others (Deblinger and Heflin, 1996).

Initial work can involve using games, quizzes and cartoons to identify emotions and having the child practise 'spotting feelings' with their carer as a homework task. The child is then helped to detect and use verbal and non-verbal information to read other people's emotions more accurately. Using an emotion that they are familiar with, such as anger, children can be helped to identify the physical sensations that accompany their different feelings which facilitates their understanding of their own feelings and their learning to handle them differently.

Because of the child's developmental stage, it is helpful to make the experience of emotion more concrete and this can be done by drawing the child (life-size is usually fun) and helping them to map out the different parts of their body in which they experience various emotions, using colours or drawings.

> Billy's body map showed an angry fist coloured in red, a sad heart containing a drawing of someone he had lost from his life, and a tummy that felt wobbly when he was scared.

As the child learns to think about the times and places and the people with whom they have experienced the various emotions, the links between these emotions, cognitions and behaviours can be developed in increasing complexity by adding 'thought bubbles' to the map, in which the child can describe his thoughts in relation to the emotions he has mapped and the behaviours which may be associated with them.

This section of the work is completed by presenting the interrelationship between cognitions, emotions, and behaviours in the form of a 'Think–Feel–Do' triangle, with a thought bubble representing 'Think', a heart representing 'Feel' and a hand representing 'Do', as illustrated in figure 11.1. A child's thoughts, feelings and behaviours are written or drawn on the diagram initially for general incidents and then later for specific incidents of sexually aggressive acts, thoughts or feelings.

Introducing the Stop and Think model

When the child is ready to move on to learning the Stop and Think model, the model is introduced formally to the child and their carer. As the content of the steps will be familiar from the preparatory work, what is being learned at this stage is essentially how the skills they have been practising fit together in the problem-solving sequence. The model is used initially to practise problem-solving with general everyday problems before tackling the more difficult problems of sexual aggression.

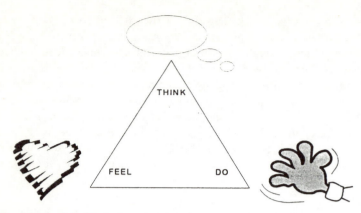

Figure 11.1 A basic starting triangle

Source: Adapted from Hackett and Marsland

As soon as possible, the child and the carer are encouraged to identify real-life problems to practise problem-solving in sessions and then at home and in school.

> Billy interrupted his carer constantly. She found this extremely annoying, as she never got to finish a sentence; she felt as if he did not want to listen. When the model was used Billy's responses were as follows:
>
> *Step 1: What's the problem?* His carer got angry with him because she thought he didn't want to hear what she had to say.
>
> *Step 2: What can I do?* Carry on interrupting, shut up, listen.
>
> *Step 3: What might happen?* If he continued interrupting, he would be sent to his room. If he shut up or listened his carer would not get angry; he might hear something interesting.
>
> *Step 4: Decide and do.* He decided to try to interrupt less. This was practised initially in the session and then worked on as a homework task, with his carer, with the outcome reviewed in the next session.

Since habitual behaviour is difficult to change, Billy was not able to stop interrupting all at once, simply by having sorted out what to do using the model. In order to help him continue to make progress towards the final goal of not interrupting at all, the process was broken down into smaller, achievable steps. It was agreed with his carer that he would be rewarded initially for catching himself interrupting, then for attempting to inhibit his initial interrupting response, and then for interrupting less frequently, rather than for not interrupting at all; he was always congratulated for trying. Over several months, his carer continued to help him work on reducing the frequency of interrupting by reminding him to 'Stop and Think' and follow the problem-solving process.

Through this stage of applying the model, opportunities are taken whenever possible to role-play inter-personal problems that arise during sessions. Carers are encouraged to bring incidents that have occurred at home or school in order to have salient examples for in-session work.

Using the Stop and Think model with sexually aggressive behaviour

When the child is able to problem-solve general everyday problems using the Stop and Think model, albeit often still with help, the Stop and Think model is used to work on problem-solving the more complex issues connected to sexually aggressive behaviour. Again several issues are worth mentioning.

Language

Young children usually feel more comfortable using the names for body parts and acts that they are familiar with in their family and as long as it is not abusive or pejorative language, this seems to be helpful to the child and their carer. If the Stop and Think work is taking place in a group setting, then it is helpful to agree terms for body parts and acts early on in the programme.

Sex education

Many sexually aggressive young children have been sexually abused themselves (Cantwell, 1995), which means that they have had experiences of which young children are not normally aware. These experiences are often distressing and young children may not have the cognitive or emotional ability to deal with them. Often they have little or no basic sex education and no idea of what would be considered 'normal' sexual behaviour, (which is sometimes a deliberate choice by their abuser to keep them ignorant and therefore less likely to realise that what was happening to them was abusive). It is therefore helpful for the child to acquire some developmentally appropriate knowledge, perhaps using some of the very useful sex education material available. For example, it can be helpful for the child to know that it is acceptable to masturbate in private if they need to do so but that it isn't acceptable to do so in public. Establishing appropriate sexual boundaries will also help the child not to signal vulnerability.

Practical work

To begin working on sexual aggression, it is helpful to return to an incident that was discussed during the assessment period. Often the child is reluctant to do this and may need motivating by being reminded that this is to give them the opportunity to apply their newly acquired knowledge to become safer.

> Billy had assaulted a 5-year-old girl in a playing field. The sequence of events described at assessment was that Billy threatened the girl with a knife if she did not comply, pinned her to the ground with one hand, pulled her knickers down with the other hand, and then squeezed her 'bottom' until she cried. He then stopped and let her go, issuing a warning not to tell or he'd get her again. When helped to go beyond the behaviour that was described at assessment and to look at the incident in a more complex way, he identified that, when he *did* the 'rude things' to the little girl, he *felt* 'scared and excited'; he *thought* 'why shouldn't I do this?' because he'd seen other older boys doing it to older girls and nothing bad had happened to them!

Using whatever material was gathered in the assessment, the child is reminded of the behavioural description of the incident. He is then facilitated in describing the sorts of feelings he was experiencing and the thoughts he had at the time. It can be helpful here to use a 'Think–Feel–Do' exercise sheet to help the child make the connections between their thoughts, feelings and behaviours explicit in a concrete way that is developmentally appropriate.

Billy was enabled to identify that he felt angry because
he had been left out again. He thought 'why does my
little sister get all the love?'; he wanted to hurt his sister,
or someone who reminded him of her. He felt scared in
his tummy and excited in his 'willy', and he did some
rude things and hurt the little girl in the park.

Subsequently the same techniques can be used to look at the planning of the sexually aggressive act and to identify the child's thoughts
and feelings prior to it. During this process, more detail is often added
to the original assessment materials. For example, developing a sequence
of drawings describing the process of the act may help the child begin
to identify thoughts and feelings linked to sexually aggressive behaviours,
again reinforcing the links between thoughts, feelings and behaviours
in a concrete way.

Returning to the material used to explain how different emotions
are experienced in the body can help the child to understand the
confusion of experiencing competing emotions, for example, that
'scared' feeling in his tummy at the same time as that 'excited' feeling
in his penis. As a child becomes familiar with this process and begins to
understand the connections, he may be able to identify that, for
example, some of his feelings were angry and some of his thoughts
were about hurting someone smaller or younger because he was
hurting himself. In this way, the triggers that stimulate a sexually
aggressive response are gradually identified and made overt in a way
that the child understands. Later in the programme this
'Think–Feel–Do' approach can be used to develop victim empathy by
looking at the impact of the child's behaviour on other people's
thoughts, feelings and behaviours.

Being able to identify precursor thoughts and feelings to being
sexually aggressive is an important basis for learning to inhibit the
initial response by 'Stopping' and then changing the behaviour, by
thinking and doing something different. By moving through the range
of emotions and gradually developing the ability to identify how each
emotion is experienced physically as well as emotionally, the child
develops the basis for making the important link between his feelings,
thoughts and the behaviour that follows. This provides some basic
material to use in the problem-solving module.

Precursors

Enabling the child to think about the emotional, cognitive or situational triggers that are precursors to his sexual aggression and to decide what alternative behaviours might be more appropriate begins to develop the possibility of learning to do something different. This also contributes to making the environment safer by providing information about high-risk situations for the child, information which enables the adults to organise a more protected environment. This reduces the likelihood of setting the child up to fail by placing them in situations that may trigger a sexually aggressive response.

The trigger may be:

- a cognition ('no one cares about me', 'people hurt me, so I'm going to hurt someone else');
- an image (of being hurt or hurting someone);
- an emotion (feeling sad, afraid, or lonely);
- a situation (being alone with a child who reminds them of a previous victim);
- a sensation (such as a smell, or a non-sexual touch that the child has eroticised).

Several triggers may occur simultaneously or at close intervals. Through the process of making the triggers overt, the child begins to see the connection between them and his sexually aggressive behaviour and is able to start working on alternative responses to the triggers.

> Once, when in the waiting room with his carer, Billy insisted on going to wait in the corridor outside the waiting room. He revealed later that this was because a small child had come in to the room who reminded him of his little sister he had abused from her babyhood. As he said, he 'Stopped to Think' and did something different, using one of his agreed coping strategies developed in earlier treatment sessions – namely, to get out of a situation where he became aware of a trigger to sexual aggression, and then talk to someone about it.

Impulsivity and consequential thinking

Children who are sexually aggressive tend to be impulsive, acting first and thinking later. This is not to say that there is no degree of planning in some of their sexual aggression. Some quite young children will select a victim who is less likely to tell and a situation in which they are less likely to be caught. Much impulsivity is learned behaviour, as the children often come from environments that are chaotic and sometimes violent, where they have observed family members behaving in impulsive and aggressive ways. For this reason, getting the child to 'Stop' is crucial, as it gives the child the space and opportunity to then think about possible consequences *before* acting. Once the initial impulsivity is inhibited, the child has an opportunity to use some of the cognitive-mediational skills they have developed to think consequentially. The Stop and Think problem-solving model is then used to look at the various triggers that the child has identified and responds to, and at the consequences of various responses, initially for them, which may include consequences for people that they care about. As the work progresses, the same process can be used to look at the consequences for the child victim.

> Billy's view of the consequences for himself were as follows. The little girl told her mum, who told the police; then he had to talk to social workers, his mum cried and shouted at him; there was a meeting about him and he thought he might have to go into a home. He felt sad because no one liked him any more, he got into loads of trouble, he's grounded and he had to come here and talk about the rude things he did.

The Stop and Think model can now be used to look not only at what *did* happen, but what *might* have happened if he had 'Stopped to Think' at different stages in the process of being sexually aggressive towards the little girl.

Generalisation and maintenance

It is not sufficient for the child to be able to 'Stop and Think' in therapy sessions. Given how difficult it is for young children to generalise any changes achieved in treatment sessions to their everyday environment and to maintain them over time, the continued support and involvement of the significant people involved in their network is crucial. It is helpful, towards the end of treatment, to use the meetings with carers, teachers and social workers to remind them of the child's progress, discuss how they can continue to help the child practise the model, be vigilant regarding any areas of continuing risk and to look at relapse prevention for when treatment is discontinued.

There is no point in teaching impulsive children the theory only: they need to be given many opportunities to practise at the point of performance, that is, where the theory needs to be put into practice. Therefore the carer's involvement becomes increasingly important in helping the child generalise their behaviour from treatment sessions to using the model in naturalistic settings. This is why, in order to help the child practise outside treatment sessions, carers need to be comfortable with the model themselves. The words 'Stop and Think' progressively become a more frequent part of the vocabulary in the child's home and not just in treatment sessions.

At the appropriate time, it is important to provide the child with opportunities to practise the Stop and Think approach in real-life higher-risk situations, without placing him or other children at risk. This can be achieved by extensive preparation in treatment sessions, including imaginal rehearsal, and then helping the child to 'Stop and Think' in those actual higher-risk situations, in the context of appropriate levels of supervision to ensure safety. The child can also be encouraged to 'Stop and Think' at specified times of the day and in situations that spontaneously arise. Hopefully at this stage the child is identifying risky situations himself and is 'Stopping to Think' and problem-solve events, either outside treatment sessions with their carer or in sessions.

Billy, who was playing in a 'ball pool' at a children's play area, while under the careful supervision of his carer, noticed a little girl who appeared to be stuck in one of the climbing frames. He decided to help her down, and his initial thought was to lift her down by the bottom half of her body (which would have been in reality the most obvious and natural way to help her). However, the boy knew that he was not supposed to touch little girl's bottoms for a number of reasons, which included getting into trouble and little girls not liking it. He 'Stopped to Think' and tried to lift the little girl down using her upper body, which turned out to be quite awkward! The little girl's parent/carer told him to leave her alone and the little boy became angry and responded in a cheeky way to the woman. Fortunately, the boy's carer saw what happened and was able to talk the event through with him later, congratulating him for stopping to think and not touching the girl's bottom, while being sympathetic with him because he had been told off when he was trying to be helpful. His carer was aware that while he needed to understand that he should not be cheeky to adults, she should not be too punishing to him because he had in fact 'Stopped to Think'.

As with more general problem-solving, it is important to continue to praise the child's attempts to inhibit their initial responses by 'Stopping to Think', rather than rewarding complete successes only. Children may not always get the process quite right but they need to be rewarded for trying and encouraged to continue stopping to think. Awarding 'Stop and Think' certificates at specific points in treatment has proved to be an attractive reward for many children. In addition, their subsequent proud display of the certificate at home has obvious potential benefits as a stimulus for maintenance of change.

By this stage in treatment, much should be known about the child's precursors to being sexually aggressive, allowing for the identification of real high-risk situations that are likely to occur in the future. A simple form of relapse rehearsal can then be undertaken (Pithers et al., 1988b), problem-solving around those situations by helping the child to rehearse how they might deal with their precursor thoughts and feelings in ways that did not involve hurting another child.

Victim empathy

Developing victim empathy is known to be an important factor in successful relapse prevention but it is also one of the most difficult aspects for young children to develop. Aside from cognitive-developmental issues related to perspective-taking, long-standing emotional issues often hinder the child's progress in this area. Many sexually aggressive children have attachment problems with caregivers, and they may find it difficult to understand the impact their behaviour has on others emotionally when their own emotional needs are unmet. It can also be difficult for young children to deal with the emotional impact of realising the pain that their victimisation of another child has caused, if their own experience of victimisation has not been addressed.

In practical terms, what often happens when working with young children is that aspects of victim empathy are addressed during the process of treating the sexual aggression (for example when the child is learning how to choose between different possible solutions to a problem) but then returned to in more detail towards the end of treatment. The child is encouraged to apply the Stop and Think model to the various incidents of sexual aggression that have already been worked on but with a much stronger emphasis on the victim's perspective. Sometimes it is helpful to use some of the emotional impact of the child's own experiences as a victim to help them achieve this.

Although desirable in terms of relapse prevention, with some young children it is not possible to achieve victim empathy because of their stage of cognitive or emotional development. In that case, the focus needs to be on helping the child think consequentially about the impact any future sexually aggressive behaviour will have on them and on people of significance to them, rather than by trying to get them to look at the hypothetical impact of sexual aggression from a future victim's perspective.

Conclusions

With some severely damaged children, treatment to change sexually aggressive behaviour can involve seeing the child at least weekly for up to a year, as well as regular meetings with all those in the child's social network. In addition, 'top-ups' are likely to be required at various stages of the child's development, such as at key transition periods like moving schools or changes of placement. As the work is emotionally demanding as well as intensive and long term, two workers should ideally be involved (especially in groupwork), and if possible a male and female dyad who can work together to deal with gender issues that may arise and to model appropriate male–female relationships.

In terms of timing, it is crucial to begin working with the child before the onset of puberty if this is at all possible, before the inappropriate behaviours and distorted cognitions that the child displays are confounded with the normal physical and emotional changes of adolescence related to sexuality. This helps the child, their carers and teachers to cope with an early onset of puberty, which can happen with some children who have been seriously sexually abused.

The literature on evaluated treatment programmes for dealing with sexual aggression is sparse. The Stop and Think programme addresses some key areas that research has shown to be helpful in changing behaviour in young children, both in general and specifically relating to sexual aggression. These include working closely with non-abusing carers and the child's social network (Deblinger and Heflin, 1996; Vizard *et al.*, 1995; Wolfe *et al.*, 1993) to implement aspects of the treatment programme in the child's environment and helping the child decrease inappropriate behaviours and increase appropriate behaviours through the learning of new coping skills (Durlak *et al.*, 1991; Kendall, 1991; Ronen, 1992). By working on the cognitive and emotional events that occur between triggers and behavioural responses, the programme helps the child develop self-regulation skills (Braswell, 1991; Himeleign and McElrath, 1996).

12

EVALUATION OF ADOLESCENT SEXUAL ABUSERS

Richard Beckett

Introduction

Adolescent sexual abusers are a highly heterogeneous group and, compared with adult abusers, there is a paucity of research to guide evaluation, decision-making and risk prediction. The chapter is divided into three main sections. The first considers what is known about sexual and general recidivism in adolescents. It argues, on the basis of currently available research, that with adolescents the risk of both violent and general re-offending appears greater than the risk of sexual recidivism. Well-designed and standardised assessment measures are the central building blocks of effective evaluation. Because of this, the next section provides a brief guide to some of the main issues of psychological test design. It is hoped that this section will help practitioners to be mindful of the current limitations of test designs, and select and critically evaluate tests and measures for their own use. The third section describes the evaluation of some of the main factors, both static (fixed) and dynamic (changeable), which are relevant to the assessment of risk in adolescent abusers.

The focus will be on the evaluation of males, partly because the large majority of adolescent sexual offending is committed by young men and partly because this is the focus of most research to date in the area of evaluation.

Risk of re-offending

One of the main purposes of assessment is to identify adolescent sexual offenders who are at high risk of recidivism. In assessing risk, we are interested in both short-term risk and in the likelihood that sexually abusive behaviour may continue through adolescence into adulthood.

The question also arises as to whether the risk is of further sexual, violent or non-sexual offending and the relative likelihood that any of these might occur. Risk of violent offending is of concern, not only because it creates victims but also because, with adult offenders at least, risk of sexual recidivism is increased in those individuals with backgrounds of violence and non-sexual convictions (Thornton and Travers, 1991).

There are a number of obvious benefits to being able to identify adolescent abusers at high risk of re-offending. Firstly, where treatment resources are limited, it is important to concentrate resources on high-risk adolescents with low-risk individuals given less costly interventions. This strategy is in keeping with treatment efficacy literature (Andrews, 1995) which shows that treatment and supervision is most effective when applied to higher-risk cases. Moreover, as seems likely, if the demand for monitoring, surveillance and notification of sexual offenders increases, then it is the high-risk individuals who should be the priority for such activity. Applying registration and long-term notification to low risk adolescent sexual offenders is not only potentially costly, but risks stigmatising young people and increasing their vulnerability to ostracisation and vigilante attention. This not only goes against the current philosophy of juvenile justice, but high level surveillance or public notification of low-risk abusers might increase their likelihood of sexual offending by alienating them, disrupting their peer relationships and restricting their social and employment opportunities (see chapter 3).

Sexual recidivism in adolescents

Compared to the study of recidivism in adult sexual offenders where a number of developmental, historical and criminological characteristics have been identified as contributing to risk prediction (Quinsey *et al.*, 1995; Prentky *et al.*, 1997; Hanson and Bussière, 1996, our knowledge of, and ability to predict, sexual recidivism in adolescents is still in its infancy. In the only study in which untreated adolescent sexual offenders have been tracked into adulthood (Elliot, 1994) sixty-six self-reported and largely undetected adolescent rapists were followed up over an approximate fifteen-year period. During this time 22 per cent of subjects self-reported a further sexual offence, and 78 per cent a further non-sexual offence. The remaining, relatively few, adolescent reconviction studies all report following up adolescents discharged from treatment programmes. For the most part they suffer from the methodological problems that have previously impeded our understanding of adults' sexual recidivism. These include an over-reliance on sexual reconvictions as opposed to actual rates of re-abuse; a lack of untreated and matched comparison groups; small sample sizes and short follow-up periods. Moreover, studies of adolescent sexual abusers suffer from mixing adolescents who abuse children with those who assault peers or adult women. As a result, differences in re-offence rates which might be reasonably expected to exist between different sub-groups of adolescent abusers cannot be identified.

Weinrott (1996) has conducted what is probably the most thorough review of adolescent sexual offender recidivism studies. He examined twenty-two treatment studies, the majority of which followed up subjects for under five years. Subjects across studies ranged from adolescents who had committed relatively minor behaviours or offences (excessive masturbation, indecent exposure, voyeurism and 'immorality') through to serious sexual assaults. The treatment interventions ranged from prosecution in open court combined with 'sex hygiene guidance' and 'reorientation' (Doshay, 1943), through to more familiar cognitive-behavioural interventions (e.g. Becker, 1990; Scram et al., 1991; Milloy, 1994).

Weinrott's review showed that relatively few adolescents were charged with subsequent sexual crimes, though the reasons for this were not possible to determine, and it should be borne in mind that no study used untreated control groups. Two-thirds reported sexual re-offence rates of under 10 per cent. Furthermore, where sexual and non-sexual re-offence rates were reported, adolescent sexual offenders were at least twice as likely to receive a non-sexual, as opposed to a further sexual conviction. For a five–ten year period following conviction, most boys who assaulted children did not appear to sexually re-offend. More tentatively, Weinrott also concluded that for adolescents whose only offence was sexual, further non-sexual convictions were uncommon and that, overall, adolescent sexual offenders were less likely than delinquents to generally re-offend.

Unfortunately, because there are so few follow-up studies on adolescent sexual offenders there is no reliable guide to the relative sexual recidivism rates of adolescents who abuse males as opposed to females; whether extrafamilial as opposed to intrafamilial abusers have higher recidivism rates; nor indeed whether adolescents who sexually abuse multiple victims as opposed to single victims have higher rates of reconviction. There is, however, at least some evidence regarding short-term re-offending rates of treated adolescent rapists and child abusers. Hagen and Cho (1996) reported on a sample of fifty adolescent child abusers, and fifty adolescent rapists who were discharged from a juvenile correction facility, having undergone cognitive-behavioural and adjunctive therapies. At the two-year follow-up point, 10 per cent of the rapists and 8 per cent of the child abusers have been convicted of a further sexual offence. Neither this difference, the difference in non-sexual re-offending (child abusers 54 per cent versus rapists 38 per cent), nor the seriousness of new offences were significant.

Predicting the persistence of sexual offending into adulthood

As yet there are no adequate prospective studies which enable us to identify those characteristics which predict which adolescent sexual offenders will continue their sexual offending into adulthood. We do, however, have information from retrospective studies of adult sexual offenders. Abel *et al.* (1986) reported on 561 adult sexual offenders and, through confidential interviews, found that 53.6 per cent of abusers reported the onset of at least one deviant sexual interest prior to the age of 18. This study has been used, as evidence, not only that adult sexual offending is preceded by early onset of sexual deviancy, but also that deviant sexual interest in adolescence predicts the emergence of sexually deviant behaviour in adulthood.

Caution, however, must be applied when interpreting this study. Most importantly, the study was retrospective and could give no indication as to what proportion of adolescents show deviant sexual interests but do not go on to be sexual offenders. Moreover, whilst these offenders reported deviant interests in adolescence, the authors did not claim that these men acted on those interests by committing sexual assaults. Because of the high profile of the Abel clinic an unrepresentative group of particularly deviant and persistent adult sexual offenders may have been recruited, a disproportionately large number of whom may have developed their deviant sexual interest in adolescence. Although similarly high levels of early onset of deviant sexual interest were found in the Laws adult sexual offender programme (1986), this was not found to be the case when Marshall and Barberee (1990) examined their own clinical files on men referred to their service.

In a sophisticated study Prentky and Knight (1993) conducted clinical interviews and examined file data on 131 adult rapists and child abusers and compared those who had committed their first sexual assault in either adulthood, adolescence or as a child. The authors found that all three groups had similarly high levels of deviant sexual fantasy and behaviour. As such this study did not support the hypothesis that those who begin sexual abusing in childhood or adolescence have higher levels of sexual pathology, including sexual deviant interest, than those who begin their sexual offending in adulthood.

Given these contradictory findings, the role of deviant sexual interest in adolescents as a predictor for adult sexual offending has yet to be resolved. The Prentky and Knight study did, however, identify a number of characteristics which were more often present in abusers who began their offending in adolescence as opposed to adulthood. Adolescents who continued to sexually abuse into adulthood were much more likely to have a history of impulsive, antisocial behaviour than those who first abused as adults. This was the case for both rapists and child abusers. Secondly, those who did not begin their offending until late adolescence or adulthood were found to be much more socially competent than individuals who began offending during adolescence. Again, this was true for both rapists, and particularly for child abusers.

These findings are consistent with the general literature of antisocial and criminal behaviour. Individuals who present with behavioural problems at school, and who show lifestyle impulsivity, delinquent and antisocial behaviour, who get into fights and are generally assaultative, are much more likely to develop chronic patterns of offending in adulthood (Farrington, 1973; Hanson et al., 1984; Loeber, 1990; Knight and Prentky, 1993). The study found that adults who had begun their sexual assaulting in adolescence as opposed to adulthood were more likely themselves to have been sexually abused as a child. Finally, child abusers who began assaulting during adolescence were more likely to be physically abused, whereas more physical neglect was found in the backgrounds of rapists who began their offending in adolescence.

Persistence of delinquency into adult criminality

It is now recognised that there are two types of adolescent who show antisocial behaviour: those whose antisocial behaviour is temporary and limited to adolescence, and those whose antisocial behaviour starts in childhood as conduct disorder and persists through adolescence and into adulthood (Moffitt, 1993). The concept of adolescent-limited delinquency is based on the recognition that offence rates in general peak by the age of 17 and then decline markedly as adulthood approaches (Blumstein et al., 1988). Whilst a majority of male teenagers engage in some form of delinquent behaviour during adolescence (Elliott et al., 1983) there is a small group of adolescents whose antisocial behaviour remains stable and persistent from childhood to adolescence, into adulthood. This group, approximately 5 per cent of males, are responsible for about half of all crimes committed (Farrington *et al.*, 1986), and are regarded as 'life course persistent'.

Elkins *et al.* (1997) reported on five recent longitudinal studies on adolescents, and examined those characteristics which distinguished adolescent-limited delinquents from those who persisted in antisocial behaviour into adulthood. The studies reviewed were longitudinal studies conducted in the UK, North America and New Zealand. The findings generally supported the predictions of Moffitt (1993) that adolescent-limited and life-course persistent antisocial behaviour have different aetiologies and histories. Delinquents who ceased their criminal behaviour as they entered adulthood were found, in many respects, to be similar to non-antisocial adolescents, although they did tend to be more impulsive and less conventional. In contrast, delinquents who become adult criminals were distinguished by low IQ and poor school attainment.

Life-course-persistent criminals were also found to have a range of personality difficulties. These included being more aggressive and hostile, impulsive and thrill-seeking in their orientation to life, and more responsive to frustration with negative emotions (angry and destructive behaviour). High levels of alcohol and drug abuse are also linked to persistent antisocial behaviour. Farrington and Hawkins (1991) found, for example, that heavy drinking at the age of 18 was a good predictor of persistence of antisocial behaviour into adulthood. Furthermore, Elkins *et al.* (1997) found that lifetime persistent criminals were more likely to start drinking earlier, and to get intoxicated younger than non-criminals, and adult criminals who did not have a delinquent history. Blumstein and Cohen (1987) found that amongst criminal offenders who used drugs, frequency of crimes were six times as high during periods of heavy drug use.

The preceding section has discussed what is known about the prediction of sexual, violent and general offending. Two main themes emerge from this discussion. The first is that whilst research informs our prediction of sexual and non-sexual recidivism in adult offenders, and while there are factors known to increase risk that delinquents will become adult criminals, we do not have information to guide the prediction of sexual recidivism in adolescent sexual abusers. The second theme to emerge is that the majority of factors found to predict sexual recidivism are historical or extremely stable. Historical variables such as history of abuse, conduct disorder and so on are fixed and cannot be changed through treatment. Similarly, deviant sexual arousal and psychopathy, both of which, when present in adults, strongly predict sexual recidivism, are in practice very resistant to treatment change. In contrast recent studies of general adult criminality have found that although static variables remain important in predicting recidivism, dynamic variables such as procriminal-thinking are increasingly emerging as more powerful predictors of recidivism (Gendreau *et al.*, 1996).

To date, however, these dynamic factors, which are the target of cognitive-behavioural treatment, have not emerged from large reviews as predictors of sexual recidivism (Furby *et al.*, 1989; Hall, 1995; Quinsey *et al.*, 1995; Hanson and Bussière, 1996). There are several reasons for this. First, large-scale reviews include many studies which did not examine dynamic variables. Moreover, it is only relatively recently that adequate measures have been developed to assess dynamic variables which are the core targets of sexual offender treatment such as victim empathy, cognitive distortions, relapse prevention knowledge and skills. Consequently, there is scant research on the link between treatment changes in dynamic variables and subsequent recidivism. Furthermore, risk is by its nature a dynamic phenomenon influenced not just by the psychological characteristics of an individual abuser, but also by, for example, the availability of victims, situational circumstances, level of the support and monitoring given to offenders. There is little research which addresses the fluctuating nature of risk, but where it has been undertaken the role of dynamic factors, potentially amenable to treatment change, appear more prominent (Pithers *et al.*, 1988a; Hanson *et al.*, 1997).

In summary, although research on adolescent sexual abusers is at an early stage, particularly with regard to who becomes an adult abuser, there is now a known constellation of characteristics evident during childhood and adolescence, which predict the persistence of violent and non-violent criminality in adulthood. If we are concerned to identify adolescent sexual abusers at risk of persisting in general and violent antisocial behaviour as well as sexual re-offending we should give treatment priority to those individuals with risk factors as described above. These can be summarised as follows:

1   A history of frequent physical abuse (in adolescent child abusers) and for adolescent rapists, a history of childhood neglect;
2   Childhood Conduct Disorder as defined by verbal and physical assaults on peers at school and aggression against teachers, cruelty to animals and other people, severe destructiveness, firesetting, stealing, repeated lying, truancy and running away from home (ICD-10 Classification of Mental and Behavioural Disorders, 1992);

3   In adolescence, antisocial behaviour, delinquency, vandalism, aggression and high impulsivity. High scores on the adolescent version of the Psychopathy Checklist (Hare, 1991);

4   For adolescent sexual offenders, low social competence as shown by poor social skills, assertiveness deficits, and isolation from peers.

Assessing adolescent abusers – developing assessment scales

The assessment of adolescent abusers and their response to treatment cannot be undertaken without an understanding of normal adolescence. Primarily there needs to be an appreciation of adolescence and the complexities inherent in its definition. The onset of adolescence represents a point in a continuum of an individual's development. From a biological perspective males undergo a number of physical developments in response to underlying hormonal processes. The changes in secondary sexual characteristics which mark adolescence (growth of genitals, appearance of pubic hair, increased muscle growth, voice deepening and the appearance of facial hair) occur in the same sequence for all individuals. However, there are wide differences in the timing and rate of these. For boys, such changes start between the ages of 9 to 14, and take between two and four and a half years to complete (Grunbach, 1980).

These signs of physical maturation are accompanied by other changes across a number of dimensions. Changes in physical appearance affect self-concept and the response of family and peers, which are accompanied by changes in social role, for example, in expectations of greater autonomy and independence. The senses of sexual self and sexual behaviour which have been developing during childhood take on new meaning, and boys must learn to deal with increasingly strong sexual desires. Consequently, not only does the onset of adolescence vary considerably between individuals, but at any point in time individual adolescents may vary along a number of dimensions, for example, in self-perception, moral reasoning, sexual awareness, social perception and peer relationships.

In order to assess adolescent abusers properly, whether through direct behavioural observation or through self-report, valid and reliable measures must be developed. Good psychological tests have a number of psychometric properties, details of which can be found in many texts (for example, Coolican, 1996). Psychological measures must be valid, that is, genuinely measure what they purport to do, and also be reliable along a number of dimensions. These dimensions include having questionnaire items which inter-relate to focus on the central construct under investigation (internal consistency). They must also be stable over time (test–retest reliability), and where direct behaviour observations are made, independent observers should have a good level of agreement as to what is taking place (inter-rater reliability). With questionnaires, items should be constructed in such a way that the 'correct' answers are not transparently obvious since if they are the measure is vulnerable to faking. Where questionnaires are used to evaluate treatment progress, tests selected should give stable scores with untreated subjects, yet also be sensitive to change when such changes take place as a result of treatment intervention. Furthermore, although follow-up studies are required to determine this, changes in test scores should have predictive validity. That is, for example, improvement in victim empathy, or reduction in cognitive distortions should be associated with a reduced risk of sexual offending.

Socially desirable responding, giving answers which are incorrect but which cast the individual in the most favourable light, can also be a problem. This is especially the case with questionnaires investigating themes, for example antisocial or sexual behaviour, where, if true answers were given, the subject anticipates disapproval or fears embarrassment. Consequently, tests should be chosen which have investigated vulnerability to faking and socially desirable responding. Where this is not the case, we should routinely include scales to detect such problems and be prepared to adjust questionnaire results accordingly. Questionnaires designed to detect socially desirable responding include the Marlow-Crowne Scale (Crowne and Marlow, 1960), the Personal Reaction Inventory (Greenwald and Satow, 1970), and the Balanced Inventory of Desirable Responding (Paulhus, 1984).

As well as detecting faking and socially desirable responding we also need to know how open an adolescent is prepared to be about their sexual drives and interests. The less open a person is about their general sexual behaviour the less likely they are to disclose deviant thoughts and behaviour. The Social Sexual Desirability Scale of the Multiphasic Sex Inventory (Nichols and Molinder, 1984) provides such a measure, but it requires standardisation on non-offending youths before it can be reliably used with adolescent abusers.

In addition to the above, there are also a number of general issues which need to be taken into consideration when using questionnaires with adolescents. Firstly, age-appropriate language should be used. In this regard, during the piloting stage questionnaires can be discussed with young people to ensure the appropriateness of language used. This may be necessary, for example, when adapting measures developed in

North America. When adapting adult measures for use with adolescents language may need to be simplified and, for example, double negative questions removed to avoid confusion. When using questionnaires focusing on sexual, especially abusive or deviant, behaviour care needs to be taken to ensure that adolescents are not exposed to sexual practices which are beyond their realm of experience and which could be viewed as corrupting.

Psychological tests cannot be adequately interpreted without reference to control and comparison groups. The lack of comparative studies has been a major problem in the study of adolescent abusers to date. Standardising tests on normal adolescents provides a range of scores against which to compare adolescent abusers. Without information on normal adolescents it is not possible, for example, to determine whether particular cognitive distortions or lack of sexual knowledge are abnormal or typical for a particular adolescent age group. Standardising questionnaires on normal subjects not only enables judgement as to whether an adolescent is different from his peers, but also provides targets for treatment change. For example, when therapy is targeted on improving victim empathy, the goal set might be to improve an adolescent abuser's appreciation of victim harm to a standard found in the general non-offending adolescent population.

Because such considerable change takes place during the course of adolescence, it is important to standardise measures on a range of age groups, for example, 11–13, 14–16, 17–19. Standardising psychological tests on different age groups not only allows more accurate test interpretation but also enables adolescents who receive treatment over an extended period to be compared with the appropriate age groups, both before and after treatment. This helps ensure that changes, for example, in perspective taking, or sexual knowledge, that take place as a result of treatment, can be distinguished from those which occur as part of a normal maturation process. Given that apprehended adolescent abusers tend to come from social classes 3–5, it is also important to ensure that when tests are standardised, that this is done on the appropriate social class groups. Finally it is also important to bear in mind that it is not appropriate to use North American norms when interpreting the test scores of British adolescents.

In addition to standardising measures on normal adolescents, it is highly desirable to standardise measures on other adolescent offenders. First this helps distinguish those characteristics which are unique to adolescent abusers from those which are shared by general antisocial youth. Second, where adolescent sexual abusers are found to share characteristics with high-risk adolescent offenders this improves risk prediction. For example, where adolescent abusers are found to share significant characteristics with violent delinquents (e.g. high levels of impulsivity and generalised aggression), this increases the likelihood that they are also at risk of violent offending.

Evaluating static and dynamic factors relevant to the assessment of risk in adolescent sexual abusers

Social competence

Ideally multiple sources of information should be used to assess an adolescent's social skills and competence. Reports from parents, teachers and peers are all potentially rich sources of information on an adolescent's ability to behave in a socially competent manner. Practitioners can devise their own questionnaires which might include questions focused upon the extent to which the adolescent has close friends or is solitary, engages in recreational activities, has the ability to co-operate, whether he is shy or socially anxious, popular or unpopular, bullied or aggressive.

Role-play exercises can also be used to assess not only social competence across a range of situations (e.g. making requests, coping with criticism), but also provide an opportunity to examine non-verbal social skills (e.g. eye contact, body posture and interpersonal distancing). Testing individuals before and after treatment in standard role-play scenarios can be used to measure treatment change, as can changes in the reports of teachers, peers and parents. Of the self-report measures available, questionnaires such as the Fear of Negative Evaluation Scale (Watson and Friend, 1969) can be adjusted for use with adolescents and used to investigate underlying beliefs which can undermine social competence. Where problems in the accurate perception of emotional expression are suspected Spence (1980) has developed a test to investigate such problems.

With regard to more global assertiveness skills, a range of measures are available, some of which have been developed particularly for adolescents and standardised on appropriate samples. An example is the Child Assertive Behaviour Scale (Mitchelson and Wood, 1982) which has been standardised on (North American) children and adolescents and correlates well with teachers' ratings of pupils' social competence and social skills. This questionnaire does, however, require standardisation on British adolescents, and its vulnerability to socially desirable responding has yet to be reported.

Dating skills and sexual knowledge

As well as exploring issues of sexual confidence and knowledge at interview an examination of the adolescent's pattern of friendships and dating success can indicate whether problems may exist in this area. Sexual knowledge and apprehension can also be examined through the use of questionnaires. The Math Tech Sex Education Test (Kirby, 1984) has a range of questions designed to examine adolescents' attitudes and beliefs towards sex and relationships, and has good psychometric qualities. It also has the advantage of already having its use reported with adolescent sexual offenders (Kaplan *et al.*, 1991). Another relevant scale is the Sex Knowledge and Attitude Test for Adolescents (Keif *et al.*, 1990). This scale has three main sections covering sexual knowledge, attitudes and behaviour, and includes items of particular relevance to adolescent sexual abusers. For younger adolescents, and adolescents with limited ability, a briefer scale has been developed by Fisher and Hall (1988). Finally, the Multiphasic Sex Inventory (MSI) (Nichols and Molinder, 1984) contains items which directly explore an adolescent's feelings of sexual competence and apprehension, although this scale has yet to be adequately standardised. The MSI also has a sexual knowledge questionnaire which has been retained from the adult version of the questionnaire. This scale is, however, of limited use, being too biologically focused and omitting key areas of adolescent concern and confusion, for example, contraception and sexual diseases.

Self-esteem

Of the self-esteem questionnaires available, the Coopersmith Self-Esteem Inventory (Coopersmith, 1967) has been used with adolescent abusers, though it has been argued (Harter, 1985) that it may not be understandable or applicable for use with adolescents and children. Of the dedicated child and adolescent self-esteem inventories, the Piers-Harris Children's Self-Concept Scale (Piers and Harris, 1969) has the disadvantage of being time-consuming to complete, difficult to understand and complex in its scoring. The Harter Self-Esteem Questionnaire (Harter, 1985) was designed to overcome these aforementioned problems, and has the advantage of being standardised on British schoolchildren (Hoare *et al.*, 1993). In addition to items measuring global self-esteem, this 36-item questionnaire has separate sub-scales focusing on scholastic performance, social acceptance, athletic competence, physical appearance and behaviour.

Emotional loneliness

We may reasonably suspect problems of emotional loneliness in young people who have difficulty making friends, who are bullied or rejected by peers, have behavioural problems which interfere with them relating successfully to others, or have been emotionally rejected by their parents. As well as self-report and those of parents regarding the young person's pattern of friendships, questionnaires can also be used to assess this potential problem area. The UCLA Emotional Loneliness Scale (Russell *et al.*, 1980) was developed to detect emotional loneliness in adults that occur in everyday life and has good psychometric properties. This scale can potentially be adapted and restandardised for adolescent abusers.

Intelligence and academic achievement

There are two principal reasons for assessing this area. First, low IQ and poor scholastic achievement have been identified as characteristics which predict the persistence of adolescent antisocial behaviour into adulthood (Elkins *et al.*, 1997). Second, intellectual and reading ability are major considerations when matching individuals to types of treatment programmes.

Assessment of intelligence is a specialised task undertaken by psychologists. Standard intelligence tests typically provide not only a measure of verbal and non-verbal intellectual functioning, but are also used alongside other specialist tests to investigate possible neurological impairments. As well as clinical psychologists, educational psychologists frequently assess intellectual functioning in making their assessment for a Statement of Special Educational Need. A range of formal tests are also available to assess reading ability. In the absence of formal psychological assessment, teachers' reports provide a valuable and reliable guide to a young person's level of overall intellectual functioning, including the level of concentration, comprehension and academic performance.

Personality

Certain personality traits are now known to be associated with serious delinquent behaviour and violent behaviour and the persistence of delinquency into adult criminality. These traits include high impulsivity (Loeber, 1990), negative emotionality, alienation, aggression and inability to cope with stress (Moffitt *et al.*, 1995; Elkins *et al.*, 1997) and psychopathy (Hare, 1991; Hart, 1998).

The presence of any of the above traits is best identified through a combination of parental, teacher and self-report. The Revised Child Behaviour Checklists (RCBC) (Achenbach, 1992) provide checklists of problem behaviours for both parents and teachers. These question-naires have good psychometric properties and sub-scales related to aggression and delinquent behaviour. The Revised Behaviour Problem Checklist (RBPC) (Quay and Peterson, 1987) can also be used with parents of adolescents to identify aggressive, delinquent and impulsive behaviour. As with the RCBC it discriminates between violent and non-violent delinquents (Blaske *et al.*, 1989) and predicts serious offence history and delinquency (Hanson *et al.*, 1984). With regard to self-report measures the Reactions to Provocation Questionnaire (Novaco, 1991) includes a number of sub-scales relevant to the assessment of negative emotionality (hostility and suspicion) as well as aggression and impulsivity. The State-Trait Anger Expression Inventory (Speilberger, 1991) also contains items assessing propensity to act aggressively. The Multi-dimensional Personality Questionnaire (Tellegen, 1982), although not appropriate for younger adolescents, has been used with older adolescents (Krueger *et al.*, 1994) and has good psychometric properties. It contains scales assessing aggression, alienation, ability to cope with stress (negative emotionality) and impulsivity. Finally, adolescent abusers may be assessed according to the criteria of the Psychopathy Checklist (Hare, 1991). In general, adolescents who assault peers or older adults, as opposed to children, are more likely to score highly on this measure.

Delinquent behaviour

The extent to which an adolescent abuser has a history of non-sexual crime, and engages in delinquent behaviour is relevant to the assessment of risk of future criminal behaviour and, in the field of general delinquency, Young (1996) has developed a scale which predicts the likelihood of non-sexual reconviction for British delinquents.

Examination of an adolescent abuser's previous patterns of convictions and cautions is essential to any evaluation of risk. Because many accusations do not result in caution or conviction it is important to ask the adolescent and his parents whether previous accusations have been made but not proceeded with. Moreover, even though they are vulnerable to dissimulation, the use of self-report delinquency inventories should not be ignored since criminologists have made significant advances in the design and use of such inventories over recent years (Moffitt *et al.*, 1995). Such inventories include those developed by

Elliot *et al.* (1985) for the National Youth Survey, and the Farrington and West Inventory of Delinquent Behaviour (Farrington, 1973).

Drug and alcohol abuse

There is little agreement in the literature as to the extent of alcohol and drug involvement in juvenile sexual offending (Lightfoot and Barbaree, 1993). Given what is known about juvenile and adult offending in general one would expect that high levels of drug and alcohol abuse would be seen more often in adolescent sexual offenders who are older, delinquent, and whose offending is associated with overt violence. As discussed above, delinquents who abuse alcohol, particularly from an early age, are at greater risk of becoming adult criminals.

Ideally self-report combined with the report of others, particularly parents, should be used in assessing alcohol and drug use. The extent to which alcohol abuse is relevant to a particular offence may also be deduced from victim reports, who may describe the abuser as intoxicated, smelling of alcohol, or 'high'.

Questionnaires designed to assess drug and alcohol use include The Adolescent Drinking Index (Harrell and Wirtz, 1994), the Michigan Alcohol Screening Test (Seltzer, 1971), the Substance Abuse Relapse Assessment (Schonfeld *et al.*, 1993), and the Drug Abuse Screening Test (Skinner, 1982).

Denial and minimisation

Denial and minimisation can be assessed through information derived at interview and questionnaires. At interview, comparing the offender's account with that of the victim's is the most common way of assessing the abuser's willingness to admit, at least with regard to known victims, the extent of his sexually abusive behaviour. Such assessments can be improved by studying victim statements, listing the range of abusive behaviour which took place, and using this as a checklist ('which of the following things did you do to your victim') before and after treatment (see also chapter 6). Practitioners' attention is particularly drawn to the work of Kaufman *et al.* (1996) who have systematically investigated adolescent abusers' *modus operandi*. Their work provides a detailed structure within which adolescent abusers' patterns of denial/admittance of planning, grooming and assault can be evaluated.

The assessment of denial of fantasy and planning, particularly with young abusers, is more problematic. With adult abusers it is generally assumed, especially where a victim has been repeatedly abused or there are multiple victims, that the abuse was planned and accompanied by increasingly strong levels of sexual preoccupation. Whereas this may also be true for some of the older adolescents, it may not be so for younger abusers. Questionnaires developed for adult abusers may, therefore, misrepresent the true patterns of denial and minimisation in younger abusers. For example, both the Sex Offender Attitude Questionnaire (Proctor, 1994) and the denial and minimisation scales of the Multiphasic Sex Inventory (Nichols and Molinder, 1984) are both constructed on assumptions about the role of fantasy and planning in the committing of sexual assaults. Although these and other similar scales can be adjusted for use with adolescents, without careful restandardisation on appropriate control and comparison groups the risk of misinterpretation is considerable.

Justifications and cognitive distortions

Although the range of adult justifications and cognitive distortions has been well documented (Beckett et al., 1994; Beech et al., 1999), and tests designed to assess these, the equivalent systematic work has not been undertaken with adolescent abusers. It is not inconceivable that the type of justifications used, particularly by younger adolescents, may be different from those seen in adult abusers. With regard to cognitive distortions, younger abusers are less likely to show entrenched distortions, though some older adolescent abusers may have justifications and cognitive distortions indistinguishable from adult abusers.

Justifications and cognitive distortions commonly emerge when abusers are asked to provide a detailed account of their abusive behaviour. Having been elicited such statements can be recorded, made into simple scales, and used as a baseline to assess treatment change. For example, if an adolescent abuser makes a statement: 'I touched my cousin's vagina because she didn't mind and enjoyed it', this statement could be represented to the adolescent with a scale ranging from Very True/Not Sure/Very Untrue.

With regard to questionnaires, few adolescent scales have been published. One exception is the Adolescent Cognition Scale (Hunter et al., 1991). The extent to which this questionnaire is biased to socially desirable responding has not been reported, and unfortunately this measure has not been found to discriminate between adolescent abusers and non-offenders. This is not, however, an absolute objection to its use. With adult child abusers only those who are fixated on children have levels of cognitive distortions which distinguish them from non-offending males (Beckett *et al.*, 1994) and this may well also be the case with adolescent abusers.

A number of adult scales offer potential for use with adolescents. These include the Molest Scale (Bunby, 1996) and the Cognitive Distortion scale of the Children and Sex Questionnaire (Beckett, 1994b). Both scales have good psychometric characteristics, lack of social desirability bias and sensitivity to treatment change. Finally, the Justifications Scale of the Multiphasic Sex Inventory (Nichols and Molinder, 1984) is another scale recommended for development with adolescent abusers. All these scales require standardisation on adolescent samples before their utility with adolescent sexual abusers can be determined.

Rape prone attitudes and beliefs

Of the currently available adult scales, the following are candidates for modification and use with adolescent abusers. Burt (1980) has developed several scales to measure attitudes that directly and indirectly support aggression against women. These include: Adversarial Sexual Beliefs, Acceptance of Interpersonal Violence, Sex Role Stereotyping, and Rape Myth Acceptance. The Hypermasculinity Inventory (Mosher and Sirkin, 1984) was designed to measure various components of 'macho' personality, and comprises three scales: calloused sex attitudes towards women; a conception of violence as manly; and a view of danger as exciting. In adults these scales are associated with alcohol abuse, drug taking, delinquency and aggression. Another relevant rape scale is that of Bunby (1996). This scale, when used with adult rapists, has good psychometric characteristics, low social desirable response bias and sensitivity to treatment change.

Victim empathy

Although not all sexual offenders show general deficits in empathy there is strong evidence that both child abusers and rapists lack empathy for their own particular victims (Beckett, 1994b; Marshall *et al.*, 1995; Hanson and Scott, 1995; Beech *et al.*, 1999). While the last few years have seen considerable work devoted to the study of empathy deficits in adult sexual offenders, the equivalent work has not been undertaken with adolescent abusers.

A number of approaches can be used when assessing empathy in young abusers. With younger children, teachers' ratings of children's empathy have been found to highly correlate with ratings of helpfulness, co-operativeness and caring (Roberts and Strayer, 1994). Information gathered from others (teachers, family and friends) can also provide evidence of a young person's ability to form caring relationships, and whether their behaviour (for example, cruelty to animals, bullying and violence) suggests a lack of sympathy or compassion for others. Such information can be incorporated into rating scales such as the Psychopathy Checklist: Youth Version (Forth and Burke, 1998).

Empathy and emotional responsiveness may also be assessed by observing and asking abusers to report their reactions to reading material about sexual abuse and videotapes of victims talking. Abusers can then rate the distress and other effects suffered by the victim on simple scales, which can then be used as a baseline for measuring subsequent change. Writing victim 'apology' letters or accounts of the abuse from the victim's perspective are also a means of examining an abuser's ability to accept victim fear and harm and can be used as baselines against which to measure therapeutic change.

A variety of adult questionnaires can, in principle, be adjusted for use with adolescents. For the assessment of general empathy, the Interpersonal Reactivity Scale (Davis, 1980) contains subscales on both perspective-taking and empathic concern. Where problems in the perception of emotion in others is of concern this can be explored using the Emotional Perception Test (Spence, 1980). The Victim Empathy Scale (Beckett and Fisher, 1994) has been standardised on non-offending men and adult child abusers, and is adaptable for younger subjects. Its usefulness with rapists, however, has yet to be determined. With adult rapists, the Empathy for Women test (Hanson, 1998) shows promise. It contains fifteen vignettes describing interactions between men and women depicting a range of interactions from the ambiguous through to the abusive, and subjects are asked to make judgements as to how the women feel in the situations described. The test has three dimensions: measuring a subject's tendency to 'fake good'; impute hostile motives to a woman; and underestimate a woman's distress by overestimating the level of the woman's sexual interest and motives.

All the scales described above will, however, need to be restandard-ised on appropriate control and comparison groups before their utility as reliable adolescent measures can be determined.

Deviant sexual arousal

With adult sexual offenders, particularly child abusers, deviant sexual arousal is one of the strongest predictors of sexual recidivism (Quinsey et al., 1995; Hanson and Bussière 1996; Prentky et al., 1997).

However, the relationship between deviant sexual arousal and sexual recidivism in adolescent abusers has yet to be clarified. Hunter *et al.* (1991), for example, found less correlation between adolescent sexual offenders' measured sexual arousal and their offence histories than has been reported in the literature of adult offenders and cautioned against interpreting adolescent sexual arousal patterns in the same way as one might interpret adult data. None the less it is likely that as research progresses the presence of deviant arousal to children or to non-consenting sex will emerge as an important factor in the prediction of sexual recidivism in some adolescent abusers.

There are three approaches to the assessment of deviant interest in adolescent abusers: clinical interviews; psychological tests; and phallo-metric (PPG) assessment (see also chapter 6). Although clinical interview is widely used to assess adolescents' deviant sexual interest and behaviour, information divulged by the adolescent is of question-able reliability, because of denial and minimisation.

With regard to psychological tests, the two most widely used measures are the Multiphasic Sex Inventory (MSI) (Nichols and Molinder, 1984) and the Adolescent Sexual Interest Cardsort (ASIC) (Becker, 1993). The juvenile form of the MSI is widely used in North America, though there are no published studies on the use of this scale with adolescent sexual abusers. Within the twenty-one clinical scales of the MSI there are three which ask direct questions about deviant sexual fantasies, planning and sexual assaults, and it is not uncommon for adolescent abusers to admit more deviant sexual thoughts and behaviour on this questionnaire than is disclosed at interview. While the MSI is particularly valuable in measuring changes in admittance/denial of deviant fantasy and behaviour, some question-naire items are inappropriate and ethically problematic for younger or less serious abusers (for example, questions on sadomasochism and sex with animals). The ASIC is a self-report measure of sexual interest, and consists of a series of sexual vignettes which the adolescent rates on a three-point scale, indicating whether he is aroused to thoughts of engaging in that behaviour. The vignettes variously describe sexual assaults against male and female adults, peers and children, as well as consenting sex and certain paraphilic behaviours (voyeurism, frottage and exhibitionism). Although the ASIC has good internal consistency and retest reliability, it does not significantly correlate with phallo-metric measures (Hunter *et al.*, 1991). This finding again highlights the problem that with juveniles, as with adult sexual offenders, dissim-ulation is a major limitation for any self-report measure of sexual interest.

The final approach to the measurement of deviant sexual arousal is phallometric assessment. Although the penile plenthysmograph (PPG) is widely used in North America for the assessment of both adult and adolescent sexual abusers, there is scant research on the utility of phallometric assessment with adolescent sexual offenders (Becker, 1998). Penile plenthysmography involves presenting sexual stimuli to the subject whilst their penile tumescence is measured via a penile transducer: a strain gauge placed around the penis. Research (e.g. Hunter and Becker, 1994) has highlighted a complex relationship between deviant sexual arousal and behaviour in adolescent abusers, the problems of using phallometrically derived measures of sexual arousal to predict risk and the need for further research in this area.

Relapse prevention knowledge and skills

A detailed relapse prevention plan is one of the products of successful cognitive-behavioural treatment for sexual offenders. Relapse prevention plans not only identify the internal psychological processes which lead to relapse, but also those external signs that might indicate a person is at risk.

The extent to which a young person accepts the possibility of future risk, and can identify their high-risk thoughts, feelings and behaviours, is typically determined during the course of treatment. Such knowledge can also be evaluated by giving the young person a structured relapse prevention questionnaire or interview. Beckett et al. (1997) have described such a questionnaire developed for use with adult sexual offenders which can also be used to structure a relapse prevention interview. Such questionnaires are most appropriately used by therapists who have a detailed knowledge of an abuser's actual pattern of offending, since without this it is not possible to judge whether an individual's relapse prevention plan is appropriate and realistic. Although such questionnaires can assist in evaluating relapse prevention skills, given the discrepancy which exists between self-report and real behaviour, they are not a substitute for direct behavioural observation. Asking the young person to demonstrate in a role play, for example, how they would cope with a particular risk situation, is a far superior test of whether a skill has been learned. Similarly, the reports of parents gives a more accurate guide to whether a young person has changed their behaviour, for example, within the home, than simply relying upon the young person's self-report.

Conclusions

Despite the substantial progress that has been made in our under-standing of general delinquency, the development of reliable evaluation methods and in the prediction of recidivism risk, the equivalent work has yet to be undertaken with adolescent sexual abusers. As early as 1987 Davis and Leitenberg highlighted the methodological inadequa-cies of research in this area. These included the lack of reliable measures to assess those key areas believed to be of relevance in sexual re-offending and the failure of treatment studies to use treated comparison groups. Ten years on, similar problems continue to impede our attempts to evaluate adolescent sexual abusers (Vizard *et al.*, 1995; Weinrott, 1996). The majority of studies published continue to use unstandardised measures, to report on small samples, mix different types of adolescent abusers together and follow up subjects for rela-tively short periods of time. Not surprisingly, we have yet to develop reliable typologies of adolescent abusers and risk prediction scales.

Moreover, despite the recognition that much adolescent sexual abuse occurs within the family, little progress has been made in devel-oping measures to systematically evaluate family context variables, for example, parental attitudes to sexual abuse. Furthermore, virtually no work has been undertaken to develop systematic and reliable measures to evaluate pre-pubescent children who abuse (see chapter 11). Similarly the area of female juvenile sexual offenders remains largely uninvestigated (see chapter 10).

Despite the aforementioned problems, available evidence suggests that important distinctions exist between male juvenile and adult offenders. Studies to date suggest most adolescents who sexually abuse will cease this behaviour by the time they reach adulthood, especially if they are provided with specialised treatment and supervision. Particularly for adolescent child abusers, poor social competency and deficits in self-esteem rather than paraphilic interests and psychopathic tendencies currently appear to offer the best explanation as to why they commit sexual assaults. The challenge is to develop measures to iden-tify high-risk adolescent abusers, to develop treatment programmes which accurately target their crimeogenic needs, and to evaluate the impact of treatment programmes through long-term follow-up.

13

EMPOWERED PRACTICE WITH YOUNG PEOPLE WHO SEXUALLY ABUSE

Simon Hackett

Introduction

> The starting point with a client is never 'simply where the client is' but rather where both the client and the ... worker are.(Abramson, 1996, p. 200)

Preceding chapters of this book have set out a variety of practice approaches to work with young people who have sexually abused across a wide range of therapeutic and service delivery contexts. In this sense, we have seen the young person's 'starting point' and have identified ways of helping him or her to move to a different and non-abusive position. Throughout this chapter young people who abuse are referred to as both male and female. This is done in order to stress that sexual abuse is a gendered problem and that gender-specific considerations are crucial in the field. Indeed, to adequately extend professional consciousness to include the existence of female abusers, we must not only acknowledge their existence, but also maintain an undistorted perspective on the fact that it is overwhelmingly males who perpetrate sexual violence and that sexual violence is bound up with issues about masculinity.

This final chapter addresses the personal and professional context of working with young people who have sexually abused: the parallel journey of the practitioner. In a field which embraces both criminal justice and child protection systems, the same practitioner can be law enforcer and advocate, as well as resource allocator, risk manager and vehicle for therapeutic change. Although 'the practitioner' is an *implicit* ingredient in the interpersonal exchange with young people who have abused, he or she has often been the missing *explicit* dynamic in theoretical understanding and practice debate. All too often this area of practice has been proposed as scientific, gender-free, impersonal: 'offence-focused work' is what the young person has to 'do' in order to 'satisfy the demands' of the legal order he or she is subject to. The practitioner is the 'officer' charged with the task of 'supervising' this work. The focus on the practitioner's starting point and its impact upon the young person's progress, as well as the complexity of the interpersonal exchange between the worker and client has been limited. Questions such as 'what does it mean for me to be working in this field?' and 'what impact do I have upon the young people with whom I work and they upon me?' do not readily fit such an approach.

The essential premise of this chapter is that in order to be effective as practitioners we need to engage interpersonally with young people to empower change. We can only do this if we, in turn, are empowered by the framework of theory and knowledge we hold, and by the structures and remit of the organisations within which we practise. As a result, this chapter seeks to identify the necessary components in building practice which is empowered. Consideration is therefore given to the nature of impact in this work, potential areas of impact for the individual are highlighted and a model proposed for the practitioner to better understand his or her responses to the work. A set of factors associated with worker empowerment is then identified and the organisational contribution to empowered practice is considered.

Encounters with ourselves: understanding impact issues in work with young people who sexually abuse

> Experience in treating sexually abusive youth has demonstrated there may be significant personal and emotional impacts upon those who work with this population. Providers must be aware of the personal risks they take, seek peer support, and obtain professional counselling when indicated.
> (National Task Force on Juvenile Sexual Offending, 1993. p. 60)

Conceived within a politically charged and ambiguous societal frame, working with young people who sexually abuse is not a neutral area of practice. We should not be untouched, nor on occasions untroubled, by our work. At the same time, the work should challenge us, inspire us, fire our creativity and lead us to new and positive personal and professional understandings. Morrison (1997) likens the process of engaging in this work to a personal journey, whose endpoint is often unknown or unanticipated. This journey 'may involve encounters with self and sexuality that prove rewarding, enlightening and liberating, but it may for some reveal aspects of our own sexual development and sexual values which are unresolved' (p. 24).

Whilst it is impossible to predict how one will respond to a certain set of experiences, practitioners can build knowledge and a set of skills with which they can better deal with personal issues. The range of negative and positive personal consequences of engaging in this work can be considered within the inclusive term 'impact'. As such, impact embraces more specific theoretical constructs such as transference (Preston-Shoot and Agass, 1990) and counter-transference reactions (Mitchell and Melikian, 1995), and stress responses (Hopkins, 1998). In order to deal constructively with impact in this field of practice, workers need:

- knowledge about common impact responses;
- a model for understanding how impact issues arise;
- ways of dealing appropriately with these issues.

Common impact issues in work with young people who sexually abuse

With notable exceptions (Erooga, 1994; Hoghughi *et al.*, 1997) only limited attention has been paid within the existing British literature to the impact of working with sex offenders. Erooga (1994) draws upon the wider literature relating to stress in the helping professions and draws out a number of important themes which can occur in work with sex offenders. Although these are not specific to work with young people, many of the themes apply directly to this area of practice. Elsewhere, Polson and McCullom (1995), writing from a North American perspective, suggest that clinicians treating sex offenders can face both individual and societal difficulties. Community criticism and ostracism as well as isolation and disapproval from other professional groupings are documented (Barnard *et al.*, 1989, National Taskforce, 1993). These issues have also affected UK practitioners, who have striven over recent years to have colleagues within their own organisations and within the multi-agency network recognise both the seriousness of issues presented by young abusers and the legitimacy of treatment work (Print and Morrison, in press). On a more personal level, difficulties can arise as a result of a practitioner becoming 'consumed' by work, and therefore giving up intimate personal relationships (National Taskforce, 1993).

A wide range of individual emotional responses to work with adolescent and adult sex offenders has been noted, including: anger and hatred (Haugaard and Reppucci, 1988) and sadistic feelings and retaliatory impulses (Mitchell and Melikian, 1995). The North American National Taskforce's revised report (1993) highlights how practitioners can come to feel psychologically victimised by young people who abuse due to unresolved issues of victimisation from their own past or over-identification with victims. This can lead to paranoia and fear (National Taskforce, 1993) or feeling 'dirtied' or sullied by the work (Hoghughi *et al.*, 1997).

Erooga (1994) states that feelings of powerlessness and a desire for control are common affective responses in adult sex offender work. Equally, being exposed to issues of control and the abuse of power in respect of young people who abuse can lead to irrational thinking, over-identification with offenders or helplessness (National Taskforce, 1993). Power issues are of particular importance in work with young people given that, developmentally, adolescents are both behaviourally and emotionally unpredictable and often seek out conflict with authority. Many young people who abuse, by virtue of their behaviour, enter into work on an involuntary basis, further exacerbating these normative adolescent presentations. We are well aware from our clients that being disempowered breeds cognitive distortions and can lead to compensatory maladaptive behaviours. As practitioners, we too can take on a wide range of distortions about our work, our clients and ourselves. Given the all-pervasive nature of the power issues in our work, the distortions that can be generated are often related to power, powerlessness and responsibility. Practitioners can feel overly responsible for their clients' behaviour (Morrison, 1997), or falsely hold themselves personally accountable for organisational deficiencies (National Taskforce, 1993).

Perhaps the most difficult area of impact for practitioners to acknowledge is the potential impact of this work upon their own sexual functioning. In this area of work, we are, whatever the context of our own sexual histories, forced into making an associative link between children, sex and abuse. The constant focus upon issues of sex can create sexual tension (Hoghughi *et al.*, 1997) and can highlight workers' own sexual histories and sexual interests. Hyper-awareness of arousal patterns and fantasies are possible (National Taskforce, 1993), leading in some cases to sexual dysfunction and interference in sexual relationships. In my own study of male social workers engaged in sexual abuse work (Hackett, 1997), men described a wide range of sexual impact issues which included:

- an inability to talk to partners about sex, about work or about the connections between the two;
- sexual dysfunctions, including arousal problems and lack of interest in sex;
- a heightening of the importance of sex in personal relationships;
- over-sensitisation to sex; with sex becoming a compulsive way of self-soothing, coping with the stress of the work or 'ridding oneself' of particularly distasteful images from casework;
- intrusive flashbacks to details of case work whilst engaged in sexual activity;
- feelings of sexual corruption; a sense of being dirtied by hearing and having to listen to such 'sordid' sexual material;
- avoidance/fear of entering a new relationship due to the sexual content of the work.

A final major area of impact is that of gender and personal identification. As a result of the constant struggle to encourage young people to look critically at their masculinity or femininity, both men and women can experience feelings of loss and grief regarding aspects of their gendered identity which they are themselves forced to review. Male practitioners, in particular, can experience a gender crisis, feelings of gender shame (Hackett, 1997) or guilt (Erooga, 1994). This kind of personal reappraisal can be a painful process, but can also lead to new levels of positive personal awareness.

The interactional dynamics of impact model

As seen above, there is a wide-ranging set of potential areas of personal impact to which practitioners may be subject. Whilst we should accept the inevitability of a personal response of some nature (Morrison, 1990, 1997), one of the difficulties is why some people respond in certain ways to aspects of the work and others in vastly different ways. It may, for example, be helpful to highlight that men who work with other men who have committed sexual crimes may feel anger towards the offender for the 'sullying' of the male gender. However if I, as an individual male practitioner do feel this sense of anger, then this awareness does not in itself help me to understand the complex dynamics of why I feel like this and what the consequences are both for me and for my clients. On the other hand, if I do not feel like this, then I may be left wondering what is wrong with me as a man and what have I missed. Clearly, it is too simplistic to generalise and prescribe how groups of individual practitioners will respond to aspects of the work. In doing so, we can easily replicate unhelpful and stereotypical gender, race and sexuality assumptions. In this way, impact is an *interactional* phenomenon, influenced by a complex set of variables.

The literature on stress provides a useful parallel example here. Whilst stress was previously seen in terms of a force which exists externally, something out in the world which exerts pressure upon the individual (for example, moving house or changing jobs), more recent work on stress emphasises the importance of examining the complex relationship between environmental stress stimuli (stressors) and the individual's reactions (Morrison, 1990; Preston-Shoot and Braye, 1991). Such interactional models perceive the individual in a transactional relationship with the environment. Stress occurs when there is a misfit between the characteristics of the person and that of the environment.

'Impact' is a wider concept than stress, embracing, as outlined above, the whole range of possible positive and negative responses to an experience or set of experiences. Nevertheless, the relevance of an interactional framework is clear. A model which helps to explain the *dynamics of impact* in relation to our work will help us to move beyond simplistic assertions such as 'he's not/I'm not cut out for this job' into an understanding of:

- how an individual's responses are influenced by a set of variables;
- how we can understand these variables and,
- what we can do to overcome any negative or undesirable impact responses.

Within the sexual abuse field, Finkelhor and Browne (1985) have proposed the traumagenic dynamics model of sexual abuse. This model, which examines the long-term consequences of sexual abuse upon abuse survivors, will be familiar to many practitioners and its strength is precisely due to its interactional, rather than linear, perspective. The authors divide the effects of sexual abuse into four traumagenic, or trauma-causing, categories, each of which are seen as 'clusterings of injurious influences with a common theme' (Finkelhor and Browne, 1985, p. 33). For each category, the authors highlight the potential impact of abuse in relation to (a) the dynamics of the abuser–victim contact, (b) the psychological impact upon the victim and (c) the behavioural consequence for the victim.

In the same way, we can understand the 'impact' of working with abusers as a dynamic process with complex influences. These include *pre-existing factors*: the thoughts, values, prior life experiences, gender and race status that the worker and the client both bring to the encounter. These are mitigated and influenced by the *environment* within which the work takes place, as well as current life events of all concerned. 'Impact' itself works on *cognitive, affective* and *behavioural* levels, thus mirroring the cognitive-behavioural framework of our practice with young people who have sexually abused. This interactional model of impact can be represented diagrammatically as in figure 13.1. To make use of the model in analysing one's responses to an experience or a set of experiences, practitioners will need to ask themselves the following set of questions:

Pre-existing influences

- In what way do my previous life and professional experiences influence my responses to young people and their families?
- How do my values, particularly in relation to sexuality and abuse, affect the way in which I conduct the work and make sense of my role in the task?
- What are my previous experiences of practice in this field? How do they influence my approaches and responses?

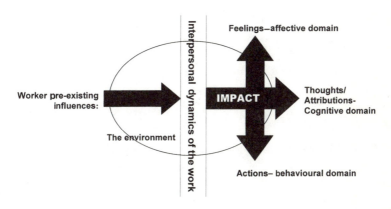

Figure 13.1   The interactional dynamics of the impact model

The environment

- What is happening in my external life/personal life currently?
- How does the environment I work in contribute to, or influence, the impact of my experience?

The interpersonal dynamics

- What are the minute details of the interpersonal exchange I have with my clients?
- What are the particular themes and struggles associated with my direct contact with young people?

Impact affective domain

- What feelings are promoted in me as a consequence of the work about me, my work and my world view?
- What patterns and links can I trace in the web of feelings that emerge?

Impact cognitive domain

- What particular scripts and schemas are being projected upon me?
- In what ways are my thoughts, beliefs and attitudes being changed, eroded or strengthened through the experience of the work?

Impact behavioural domain

- What is different now about my behaviour than when I first engaged in this work?
- To what degree are my behaviours appropriate and effective ways of coping?
- To what extent are my behaviours, thoughts and feelings congruent to each other?

Table 13.1 uses the model outlined above to describe more fully some of the common impact issues for practitioners arising from work with young people who sexually abuse. This is not meant to be a comprehensive list, but includes many factors from the literature as well as from contact with other practitioners. These are ordered, as in Finkelhor and Browne's model, into clusterings, in this case into three broad impact areas: sex and sexuality; gender and personal identification; and power and powerlessness. There is, of course, a degree of overlap across these categories. Significantly, impact issues are not represented in two separate gender-specific tables for male and female practitioners, but points of particular gender significance are highlighted within the table. Representing the impact issues in this way reflects a belief that there is an overwhelming degree of commonality, as well as some important elements of difference, in the way that men and women experience the impact of this work.

To make use of this table, individuals are advised to identify, trace and add their own particular impact 'threads' through the different layers described. This exercise could usefully be incorporated into personal preparation, consultation or supervision, or into debriefing sessions with co-workers following client contact.

Building worker empowerment

Worker empowerment is the cornerstone on which effective practice with young people is built. At its simplest level, being an empowered practitioner means having the skills and knowledge, the remit and the support structures necessary to undertake this emotionally demanding area of work. Becoming an empowered practitioner therefore means being prepared to look critically at oneself, as well as the organisations within which one practises. Empowered practice in relation to young people who sexually abuse can therefore be represented diagrammatically as in figure 13.2.

Personal preparation and worker qualities

Within the context of service delivery across disciplines in Britain there is no single route into work with young people who sexually abuse. The inter-disciplinary basis to the field means that there is a real diversity in professional cultures and backgrounds and, in many cases, practitioners have found themselves practising in this area without even rudimentary preparation or specialist training in sexual aggression. Nor is there an agreed set of desirable personal qualities or professional competence for those engaging in this complex area of practice.

Personal preparation provides the essential foundation upon which workers can deal with impact issues as they practise. Erooga (1994) describes a useful building-blocks approach to staff care, which considers essential factors in worker preparation at personal, agency, professional and co-work levels. On a personal level, practitioners are encouraged to scrutinise their motivations for entering the work, the

Table 13.1 The interactional dynamics of impact in work with young people who abuse

Dynamics	Impact area		
	Affective domain	Cognitive domain	Behavioural domain
SEX AND SEXUALITY Worker is bombarded by sexual stimuli in the work	Repulsion by sexual issues	Re-evaluation of sexual values	Sexual abstinence
Worker listens to accounts of abusive sexuality	Worker feels victimised sexually	Distorted views of sexual normality (abuse = the norm, or all sex = abuse)	Questioning of sexual identity (positive and negative connotations)
Worker subject to sexually deviant fantasies	Worker feels like an abuser	'Reading sex into everything' – over-salience of sex in cognitive schema	Over-emphasis on sex
Young person's sexual behaviours force the worker to make an association between sex, children and abuse	Fear of being perceived an abuser	Sexual imagery intrudes into sexual experiences – affective flashbacks to the work/ an account of abuse, esp. during sex	Sexual fixation and increased sexual drive
	Own sexual development and experiences highlighted	Development of deviant fantasies	Arousal problems
	Unresolved feelings about own victimisation experiences resurface		Consensual sex becomes a behavioural fix – a way of 'cleansing' self from influence of work
	Feeling that all sex is dirty and sordid		Relationship strain and break-up
GENDER AND PERSONAL IDENTI-FICATION Worker subject to overwhelming accounts of male sexual and non-sexual violence	Feelings of gender confusion	Distorted sense of responsibility for actions of all men	Career revision to cope with gender role strain
Abuser attempts to recruit workers into exaggerated gender stereotypes; e.g. men into collusion to distortions about women, women into submissive roles, etc.	Feelings of loss; of innocence, of self, of elements of gender socialisation	Distorted view of masculine and feminine roles	Exaggerated behavioural attempts to distance self from identification as 'abuser'

	Dynamics	Impact area		
		Affective domain	*Cognitive domain*	*Behavioural domain*
		Anger at abusers for damaging own gendered identity and gender assumptions	Review of self and own socialisation, leading to negative or positive new self-awareness	Reluctance to engage in certain professional or personal life activities/roles; e.g. bathing children
		Fear of being associated as an abuser through commonality of gender or other personal aspect	Male worker experiences a 'gender crisis'	Review of external life activities; e.g. protection of own children
		Self-guilt and gender shame (men)	Sense of distance from members of same gender (esp. men)	
		Pride in new gender awareness		
		Personal isolation		
POWER AND POWER-LESSNESS	Abuser engages worker in power struggle	Worker feels overwhelmed by extent of young person's unmet need	Distorted sense of own power	Punitive behaviours towards others
	Worker is required to exercise an uncomfortable level of power and control over young person	Feelings of exaggerated power – euphoria	Increased self-confidence and increased level of self-esteem	Increased respectful behaviours within own relationships
	Young person projects overwhelming level of need upon worker	Feelings of exaggerated powerlessness – depression	Non-abusive relationships given added value	New-found assertiveness
		Deep cynicism about society and the denial of sexual abuse issues		
		Desire for revenge – wish to right wrongs of victim		

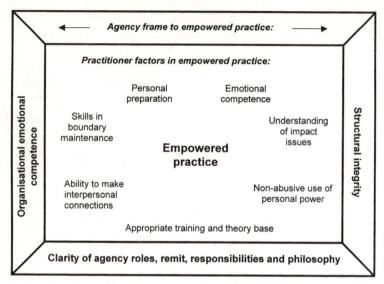

Figure 13.2   Contributions to empowered practice

resonance the work is likely to have due to one's previous life experiences, as well as to consider the meaning of the work given one's current life experiences.

The National Taskforce Report (1993) identifies a series of desirable personal characteristics of the practitioner. These include emotional well-being, respect for self and others and personal behaviour that is value-directed. Blanchard (1995) states that the following are essential characteristics of a skilled therapist with people who have sexually abused:

- congruence: between thoughts, feelings, values and actions;
- authenticity: being genuine, spontaneous and trustworthy;
- warmth: compassionate responsiveness to others;
- equality: ownership of our power and a desire to use this to constructive ends;
- vulnerability: acknowledgement of own 'raw spots' which adds to one's wholeness;
- humour: which, when appropriately directed becomes the natural extension of an authentic and healthy personality;
- compassion: a willingness to attempt understanding of the sex offender's emotional condition and life situation.

Awareness of personal power

The empowered practitioner is aware of his or her own personal power and develops skills in the use of self-knowledge in an appropriately empowering and non-abusive way. In a field where the abuse of power is a central issue, it is important for practitioners to assess and understand the various sources of their own power and examine how these various elements may conflict at times. Figure 13.3, adapted from Hackett and Marsland (1997), highlights how power results from a complex interlinking of personal as well as professional factors. Within this model, power is not seen as a static personality trait, but is derived from dynamic variables that may change over time and according to the interface with other people's 'power triangles'. Most important is that the individual is committed to the non-abusive use of personal power, which involves attention to:

- personal acknowledgement of the existence of power imbalances within one's relationships with others;
- a readiness to focus on how one's own power is used and experienced;
- an ability to maintain critical openness about oneself and others;

Agency / political power

**policy and social context to
young abusers
positional status within agency
the legislative framework**

Personal power

**background
personal experiences
gender
race
sexuality
disability
age**

Professional identity power

**training
experience of practice
professional status within
multi-agency network**

Figure 13.3 Sources of power triangle

Source: Adapted from Hackett and Marsland

- recognition of others' 'difference' and a willingness to validate and value this in contact with others;
- scrutiny of personal values and behaviour, with specific regard to sex, sexuality and gender.

Whilst workers benefit from a clear set of principles and ethics upon which to build practice (Hackett *et al.*, 1998), principles in themselves are passive expressions of intent. Abramson (1996) describes the process of owning and mobilising principles into practice as 'knowing oneself ethically'. Having and using ethical self-knowledge is a corner-stone in building worker empowerment. In particular, it allows the practitioner to 'move from an understanding of his or her own attitude toward fate and responsibility to an appreciation of why he or she believes that a particular client should be treated in a manner different from how another client is treated' (Abramson, 1996. p. 198).

Abramson describes this process of gaining ethical self-knowledge as involving a number of distinct stages, which are summarised as:

- understanding one's own world view;
- knowing what makes one feel good about oneself and one's practice;
- ascertaining and monitoring how one uses and prioritises ethical principles in practice.

Using Abramson's model, each stage poses a number of important questions for workers who wish to build and practise empowerment with young people who sexually abuse. The following exercise, adapted from Abramson's work, can be considered by the individual practitioner alone or within the context of supervision, co-work or consultation.

Developing ethical self-knowledge – an exercise for practitioners

STAGE 1

Understanding my own world view:

- What do I know and recognise of myself in terms of race, ethnicity, gender, class, sexuality, disability status?
- What do I recognise of my own personal and value system, biases, experiences, stereotypes and agenda that are derived from my own personal and cultural history?

- How do these factors inform my perspectives on sexual violence, young people and their families?

Knowing what makes me feel good about my practice and myself:

- What is it about my work with young people who sexually abuse that generates self-esteem and self-approval in me?
- What is my image of a competent sex offender therapist/practitioner?
- What is my perception of a good therapist in terms of professional standards and ethics?
- What makes me feel a responsible member of the team/organisation that I work for?
- What is it about my work that makes me feel that I have done a good job or made a valid contribution – to my organisation, the community, victims of sexual abuse, young people who abuse.

Ascertaining and monitoring how I use and prioritise ethical principles in my practice:

- Where do I stand on issues such as autonomy, justice, victim/abuser rights?
- How important are these principles to me?
- How do I resolve conflicts that arise between these principles in my practice with young people, particularly in relation to empowerment and control?
- What is my view on the way that 'justice' is served/not served in relation to the sexual behaviour of young people? How does this influence my practice?
- How far are my judgements about what young people deserve from others and from me based on my own attributions of moral responsibility?
- When an individual young person's rights and needs come into conflict with the community's rights and needs, how do I resolve this? Under what circumstances am I more likely to sympathise with one or the other?

SIMON HACKETT

Skills in managing stress

Whilst we should anticipate stress as an inevitable factor in work with child abuse (Morrison, 1990), rather than a symptom of personal inadequacy or incompetence, it is not always easy to predict when and how stress reactions will occur. Understanding and using the Interpersonal Dynamics Model described above is an important step in managing an individual's stress experience. Additionally however, the empowered practitioner requires a range of strategies to deal with stress reactions when they occur.

The National Taskforce revised report (1993) distinguishes between preventive and renewal strategies to avoid practitioner burn-out. *Preventive strategies* relate largely to the strengthening of a worker's personal and professional supports. The authors also advise workers to maintain professional exposure to non-sex offender clients. Whilst this is a useful way of maintaining a reality check and preventing the adoption of distortions from constant exposure to abusers' distortions, there may equally also be problems associated for some practitioners who are expected to work with sexually aggressive behaviour infrequently. The challenge is for the practitioner to find 'caseload congruence' to integrate work with abusers into the variety of professional roles and to seek a helpful balance between these various aspects. *Renewal strategies* relate to the building into practice of ways of seeking help when stress occurs. Strategies include the constructive use of supervision, consultation or counselling. Self-care routines are also helpful.

An ability to make interpersonal connections

One of the failings of much of the practice literature in relation to sex offenders in general, and young people who have abused in particular, is the combative characterisation of the work. Whilst the orthodoxy of treatment justifies this as being about 'breaking down' denial, this is more often a reflection of the practitioner's own needs to express feelings of anger or frustration or to remain in control (Sheath, 1990). Of course, it is correct that the focus of intervention is put on the young person to demonstrate evidence of behavioural and cognitive change. It is also right to highlight that it is the responsibility of the young person as the abuser to change his behaviour, not his family, his victims or the practitioner who is working with him. However, we should not use this attribution of responsibility as a way of not accepting responsibility for our own practice behaviour, nor to excuse distanced

240

disinterest in the young person as an individual. 'Because so many sex offenders have experienced dysfunctional and abusive primary relationships, an essential element of restoration lies in the healing power of interpersonal relationships – particularly the relationship with the therapist' (Blanchard, 1995, p. 10).

This point is perhaps all the stronger in relation to young people, many of whom come into the intervention process with no prior experiences of positive, nurturing or caring relationships. To meet this with a distanced, angry or disinterested approach simply confirms to young people the perceived lack of self-worth which has been such a feature of how others have dealt with them in the past.

Theory can also be used to contribute to defensive and uncreative practice. This is not a criticism of the cognitive-behavioural basis to our work, but more of the uncritical tendency to see the teaching of theoretical constructs as ends in themselves, rather than as means to an end. Blanchard (1995) warns against the 'mechanisation of treatment'. Rich states that the cycle of sexual assault can easily restrict and constrain insight rather than expand it (Rich, 1998). At worst, the practitioner becomes a distant, stagnant figure for the young person. The worker opens the workbook at the correct page, the next treatment exercise or psychometric test is completed, the reality of the young person's external world is kept separate from the therapy session and both the practitioner and young person remain largely untouched by the whole experience. This is therapeutic defensiveness of the worst kind and would be unimaginable, for example, in work with abuse survivors. Clearly, practitioners should not collude with the young person, blind to risk factors and ineffectual in the crucial risk management and monitoring role. Nevertheless, as workers we need to conceive of ourselves as the most powerful therapeutic tool and best resource for young people, not a piece of paper with a photocopied circle on it.

The ability to model empathic concern

Working with offenders to look at the nature of difference and oppression are important aspects of the *content* of intervention. If the message is that oppression is not to be tolerated and that sexual abuse is a fundamental expression of disrespect and oppressive behaviour, then the *delivery* also has to model this in every way. There is, for example, no way that we can begin to help our clients manage anger constructively, if the message they receive from us every time we meet is that, as powerful people, we are entitled to be angry and disrespectful towards them. Blanchard (1995) states that the therapist must be personally adaptable (and this must include a willingness to adapt theoretical material) as well as modelling care and respect for the offender. Hoghughi *et al.* (1997) feel that young people who sexually abuse are not the most attractive client group to work with and seem to highlight the benefit to society as the only acceptable motivation for conducting the work. However, the practitioner who cannot experience a sense of empathic concern and warmth towards young people who abuse, should not engage in this work. Of course, this does not mean that we should condone or collude with young people's abusive behaviour, nor that we cannot express empathy towards the young person's victims.

The ability to maintain appropriate boundaries

Sometimes, working in the field of sexual aggression feels like having one's personal and professional boundaries bombarded on all sides. We are bombarded by our clients, whose wide-ranging needs are projected onto us in the hope that here, at last, is somebody who can make a difference. We are bombarded by the anxiety and demands of the communities within which we practise and sometimes live. We are also often overwhelmed by the demands of the inadequate systems and structures within which we work. Finally, we bombard ourselves with unrealistic expectations and responsibilities to make things better, safer and healthier. Understanding the pressures on, and maintaining, appropriate boundaries without becoming over-enmeshed or distanced is a fundamental skill in empowering practice. Once more, the constructive use of supervision or consultation is crucial.

The organisational commitment to worker empowerment

The parallel impact upon practitioners of organisational deficits to that of the abuser–child relationship in child sexual abuse has been outlined by a number of authors across child protection contexts. Adapting Roland Summit's model of Child Sexual Abuse Accommodation Syndrome (1983), Morrison (1990, 1996), has written persuasively about how workers, like the abused child, can accommodate to emotionally incompetent systems in their own behaviours and emotional responses. Elsewhere, I have reflected upon how social workers can abuse power within the context of practice placements within child protection settings (Hackett and Marsland, 1997). It is equally clear that the field of sexual aggression is far from immune from these dynamics (Spencer, 1997).

Whilst a detailed discussion of the organisational context for practice in this field is beyond the scope of this chapter and is more the subject of chapter 2, the following are essential organisational contributions to worker empowerment and anti-oppressive practice:

- staff support mechanisms, designed to promote individual and organisational emotional competence;
- structural integrity of remit, roles and mandate;
- established lines of accountability and supervision, including the possibility of specialist external consultation;
- an organisational framework which promotes partnership and values difference in all interactions with young people and their families;
- written aims and objectives to services with young people who abuse and an explicit philosophy, agreed at organisational level, to underpin practice;
- a clear and unambiguous policy on exchange of information and the limited nature of confidentiality;
- an anti-oppressive statement, which has as its core prevention and protection of actual and potential victims, but which defines young people's rights;
- an agreed organisational risk management policy in respect of young people who abuse.

Summary

This chapter has discussed a range of impact issues relating to work with young people who sexually abuse others and has proposed a model of empowered practice. It is hoped these concepts will be used and further developed by those working in the field. Engaging with young people with sexual aggression problems remains a complex and challenging area. The practitioner's 'parallel journey', which often proceeds silently and unobserved alongside that of young people, frequently involves painful lessons and difficult experiences. Yet it can bring significant opportunities for new and heightened personal awareness and professional development. Both the chapter and the book ends therefore with a plea: that as we continue to develop our practice models and theoretical understandings, so we continue to share our experiences and learn from each other.

REFERENCES

Abel, G., Becker, J., Cunningham-Rathner, J., Kaplan M. and Reich, J. (1984) *The Treatment of Child Molesters*, New York: Columbia University.

Abel, G., Mittelman, M., Becker, J. (1985) 'Sexual offenders: results of assessment and recommendations for treatment', in H. Ben-Aron, S. Hucker and C. Webster (eds), *Clinical Criminology*, Toronto: M M Graphics.

Abel, G., Becker, J.V., Cunningham-Rathner, J., Rouleau, J., Kaplan, M. and Reich, J. (1986) *The Treatment of Child Molesters – A Manual.* [Available from SBC-Tm, 722 West 168th Street, Box 17, New York, NY 10032.]

Abramson, M. (1996) 'Reflections on knowing oneself ethically: toward a working framework for social work practice', *Families in Society: The Journal of Contemporary Human Services*, April 1996: 195–202.

Achenbach, T.M. (1992) 'New developments in multiaxial empirically based assessment of child and adolescent psychopathology', in J.C. Rosen and P. McReynolds (eds), *Advances in Psychological Assessment*, 8, 75–102, New York: Plenum Press.

ACOP (1996) *Sex Offender Survey*, London: ACOP.

Ageton, S. (1983) *Sexual Assault Among Adolescents*, Lexington, MA: Lexington Books.

Allam, J.A. and Browne, K.D. (1998) 'Evaluating community-based treatment programmes for men who sexually abuse children', *Child Abuse Review* 7: 13–29.

Alvarez, A. (1990) 'Child sexual abuse – The Need to remember and the need to forget', in J. Ouston (ed.), *The Consequences of Child Sexual Abuse*. Occasional Papers No. 3. [Association for Child Psychology and Psychiatry, St Saviour's House, 39/41 Union Street, London, SE1 1SD.]

Alvarez, A. and Phillips, A. (1998) 'The importance of play: a child psychotherapist's view', *Child Psychology and Psychiatry Review* 3(3): 99–103.

Andrews, D. (1995) 'The psychology of criminal conduct and effective treatment', in J. McGuire (ed.), *What Works: Reducing Reoffending: Guidelines from Research and Practice*, Chichester: Wiley.

Araji, S. (1997) *Sexually Aggressive Children – Coming to Understand Them*, Thousand Oaks, CA: Sage.

ATSA (1997) *Position on the Effective Legal Management of Juvenile Sexual Offenders*, ATSA, Suite 26, Beaverton, Oregon.

Audit Commission (1998) *Misspent Youth '98 The Challenge for Youth Justice*, London: Audit Commission Publications.

Avis, J. and Myers, (1988) 'Deepening awareness: a private guide to feminism and family therapy, *Journal of Psychotherapy and the Family* 3: 15–46

Awad, G. and Saunders, E.B. (1989) 'Male adolescent sexual assaulters', *Journal of Interpersonal Violence* 6: 446–60.

Bacon, R. (1988) 'Counter transference in a case conference', in G. Pearson, J. Treseder, M. Yelloly (eds) (1988) *Social Work and the Legacy of Freud*, London: MacMillan.

Bandura, A. (1969) *Principles of Behaviour Modification*, New York: Holt, Rinehart and Winston.

Bannister, A. and Gallagher, E. (1996) 'Children who sexually abuse other children', *The Journal of Sexual Aggression* 2: 87–98.

Barbaree, H., Marshall, W. and McCormick, J. (1998) 'The development of deviant sexual behaviour amongst adolescents and its implications for prevention and treatment', *Irish Journal of Psychology* 19(1): 1–31.

Barber, J.G. (1992) 'Relapse prevention and the need for brief social interventions', *Journal of Substance Abuse Treatment* 9: 157–68.

Barnard, M., Fuller, S., Robbins, E., and Shaw, M. (1989) *The Child Molester*, New York: Plenum Press.

Bateson, G. (1972) *Steps to an Ecology of Mind*, London: Paladin Granada Publishing.

Becker, J. (1988) cited in A. Bentovim and B. Williams (1998) 'Children and adolescents: victims who become perpetrators', *Advances in Psychiatric Treatment* 4: 101–7.

—— (1990) 'Treating adolescent sexual offenders', *Professional Psychology Research and Practice* 21: 362–5.

—— (1993) 'Adolescent sexual interest card sort', in G.C.N. Hall (ed.), *Sexual Aggression*, Bristol, PA: Taylor and Francis.

—— (1998) 'The assessment of adolescent perpetrators of childhood sexual abuse', *Irish Journal of Psychology* 19(1): 82–92.

Becker, J. and Abel, G. (1985) 'Methodological and ethical issues in evaluating and treating adolescent sex offenders', in E.M. Odey and G.D. Ryan (eds), *Adolescent Sex Offenders: Issues in Research and Treatment.* [Rockville, M D: NI Mt, Department of Health and Human Services (Publication No. ADM-85–1396).]

Becker, J. and Kaplan, M. (1988) 'The assessment of adolescent sex offenders', *Advances in Behavioral Assessment of Children and Families* 4: 97–118.

—— (1993) 'Cognitive behavioural treatment of the juvenile sex offender', in H. Barbaree, W. Marshall and S. Hudson (eds), *The Juvenile Sex Offender*, New York: The Guilford Press.

Becker, J., Kaplan, M. and Kavoussi, R. (1988) 'Measuring the effectiveness of treatment for the aggressive adolescent sexual offender', *Annals of the New York Academy of Sciences* 528: 215–22.

Beckett, R. (1994a) 'Cognitive-behavioural treatment of sex offenders', in T. Morrison, M. Erooga and R. Beckett (eds) (1994) *Sexual Offending Against Children: Assessment and Treatment of Male Abusers*, London: Routledge.

—— (1994b) 'The Children and Sex questionnaire' unpublished manuscript, in print.

Beckett, R. and Brown, S. (in process) 'Evaluating the effectiveness of treatment'.

Beckett, R., Beech, A., Fisher, D. and Fordham, A.S. (1994a) *Community-Based Treatment For Sex Offenders: An Evaluation Of Seven Treatment Programmes*, London: Home Office.

Beckett, R.C., Fisher, D., Mann, R. and Thornton, D. (1997) 'The relapse prevention questionnaire and interview', in H. Eldridge, *Therapist's Guide for Maintaining Change: Relapse Prevention Manual for Adult Male Perpetrators of Child Sexual Abuse*, Thousand Oaks, CA: Sage.

Beech, A., Fisher, D. and Beckett, R. (1999) *STEP 3: An Evaluation of the Prison Sex Offender Treatment Programme*, London. [Home Office Publications Unit, 50 Queen Anne's Gate, London SW1H 9AT.]

Bengis, S. (1986) *A Comprehensive Service Delivery System with a Continuum of Care for Adolescent Sexual Offenders*, Orwell, Vermont: Safer Society Press.

Bentovim, A. (1991) 'Children and young people as abusers', in A. Hollows and H. Armstrong (eds), *Children and Young People as Abusers*, London: National Children's Bureau.

—— (1992) 'Family violence: explanatory models to describe violent and abusive families', in D. Campbell and R. Draper (eds), *Trauma Organised Systems. Physical and Sexual Abuse in Families*, Systemic Thinking and Practice Series, London: Karnac Books.

—— (1996) 'Trauma-organised systems', *Clinical Child Psychology and Psychiatry* 1: 513–24.

—— (1998) 'Family systematic approach to work with young sex offenders', *The Irish Journal of Psychology* 19(1): 119–25.

Bentovim, A. and Williams, B. (1998) 'Children and adolescents: victims who become perpetrators', *Advances in Psychiatric Treatment* 4: 101–7.

Berkowitz, R. and Leff, J. (1984) 'Clinical teams reflect family dysfunction', *Journal of Family Therapy* 6(2): 79–90.

Blanchard, G. (1995) *The Difficult Connection: The Therapeutic Relationship In Sex Offender Treatment*, Vermont: Safer Society Press.

Blaske, D.M., Borduin, C.M., Henggeler, S.W. and Mann, B.J. (1989) 'Individual, family, and peer characteristics of adolescent sex offenders and assaultive offenders', *Developmental Psychology* 25, 846–55.

Blumstein, A. and Cohen, J. (1987) 'Characterizing criminal careers', *Science* Aug. 237: 985–91.

Blumstein, A., Cohen, J. and Farrington, D.P. (1988) 'Criminal career research: its value for criminology', *Criminology* 26, 1–35.

Bolton, F.G., Morris, L.A. and MacEachron, A.E. (eds) (1989) *Males at Risk*, Thousand Oaks, CA: Sage.

Boscolo, L. and Bertrando, P. (1993) *The Times of Time: A New Perspective in Systemic Therapy and Consultation*, London, Norton Press.

Boscolo, L., Cecchin, G., Hoffman, L. and Penn, P. (1987) *Milan Systemic Family Therapy: Conversations in Theory and Practice*, New York: Basic Books.

Bourke, M.L. and Donohue, B. (1996) 'Assessment and treatment of juvenile sex offenders: an empirical review', *Journal of Child Sexual Abuse* 5(1): 47–70.

Brandon, M. and Lewis, A. (1996) 'Significant harm and children's experiences of domestic violence', *Child and Family Social Work* 1(1): 333–42.

Braswell, L. (1991) 'Involving parents in cognitive-behavioral therapy with children and adolescents', in P.C. Kendall (ed.), *Child and Adolescent Therapy: Cognitive-Behavioral Procedures*, New York: Guilford.

Braswell, L., Koehler, C. and Kendall, P.C. (1985) 'Attributions and outcomes in Child Psychotherapy', *Journal of Social and Clinical Psychology* 3: 458–65.

Bremer, J.F. (1991) 'Intervention with the juvenile sex offender', *Human Systems: The Journal of Systemic Consultation and Management* 2(3 and 4): 235–46.

Briggs, D., Doyle, P., Gooch, T. and Kennington, R. (1998) *Assessing Men who Sexually Abuse: A Practice Guide*, London: Jessica Kingsley Publications.

British Crime Survey (1988) in *Criminal Statistics, England and Wales 1990*, Cmmd. 1935, 1991.

Britton, R. (1981) 'Re-enactment as an unwitting professional response to family dynamics', in S. Box, B. Copley, J. Magagna and E. Moustaki (eds), *Psychotherapy With Families: An Analytic Approach*, London: Routledge and Kegan Paul.

Brown, A. (1995) *Developing and Running a County Wide Programme: Account and Audit of the Shropshire Adolescent Sexual Offences Programme, 1987–1994*, Alvechurch: The Lucy Faithfull Foundation.

Bruner, J. (1986) *Actual Minds, Possible Worlds*, Cambridge, MA: Harvard University Press

Bunby, K.M. (1996) 'Assessing the cognitive distortions of child molesters and rapists: development and validation of the molest and rape scales', *Sexual Abuse: A Journal of Research and Treatment* 8: 37–54.

Burnham, J. (1986) *Family Therapy: First Steps Towards a Systemic Approach*, London, Tavistock Publications

—— (1992) 'Approach–Method–Technique: making distinctions and creating connections', *Human Systems: The Journal of Systemic Consultation and Management* 3: 3–26.

—— (1993) 'Systemic supervision: the evolution of reflexivity in the supervisory relationship', in 'Voices from the training context' a special edition of *Human Systems: The Journal of Systemic Consultation and Management* 4(3 and 4): 349–81.

—— (1999) 'Internalised other interviewing: evaluating and enhancing empathy', *Clinical Psychology Forum*, forthcoming.

Burnham, J. and Harris, Q. (1996) 'Emerging ethnicity: a tale of three cultures', in K.N. Dwivedi and V.P. Varma (eds), *Meeting the Needs of Ethnic Minority Children*, London: Jessica Kingsley Publications.

Burt, M.R. (1980) 'Cultural myths and supports for rape', *Journal of Personality and Social Psychology* 38: 217–30.

Burton, D.L., Nesmith, A.A. and Badten, L. (1997) 'Clinician's views on sexually aggressive children and their families: a theoretical exploration', *Child Abuse and Neglect* 21(2): 157–70.

Butterworth, J. (1993), *Straight Talk – How to Handle Sex*, London: Macmillan.

Byrne, N.R and McCarthy, I.C. (1995) 'Abuse, risk and protection: a fifth province approach to an adolescence sexual offence', in C. Burk and B. Speed *Gender, Power and Relationships*, London: Routledge.

Campbell, D. (1998) 'Branded', *Guardian* 11 August.

Canter, D. (1989) 'Offender profiling', *The Psychologist* 2: 12–16.

—— (1994) *Criminal Shadows: Inside the Mind of the Serial Killer*, London: Harper Collins.

Cantwell, H.B. (1995) 'Sexually aggressive children and societal response', in M. Hunter (ed.), *Child Survivors and Perpetrators of Sexual Abuse: Treatment Innovations*, Thousand Oaks, CA: Sage.

Carr, A. (1989) 'Counter-transference to families where child abuse has occurred', *Journal of Family Therapy* 11(1): 87–97.

Carrell, S. (1993) *Group Exercises for Adolescents: A Manual for Therapists*, Thousand Oaks, CA: Sage.

Cavanagh-Johnson, T. (1989), 'Female child perpetrators – children who molest other children', *Journal of Child Abuse and Neglect* 13: 571–85.

Cavanagh-Johnson, T. and Gill, E. (1993) *Sexualised Children, Assessment and Treatment of Sexualised Children and Children Who Molest*, Maryland: Launch Press.

Cecchin, G. (1987) 'Hypothesizing – circularity – neutrality revisited: an invitation to curiosity', *Family Process* 26: 405–13.

Cecchin, G., Lane, G. and Ray, W.A. (1994) *The Cybernetics Of Prejudices In the Practice of Psychotherapy*, London: Karnac Books.

Clare, I. (1993) 'Issues in the assessment and treatment of male sex offenders with mild learning disabilities', *Sexual and Marital Therapy* 8: 167–80.

Clark, S. (1997) 'Immune Systems', *Community Care* 22–28 May.

Cleveland Inquiry (1988) *Report of the Inquiry into Child Abuse in Cleveland 1987*, London: HMSO.

Cohen, S.L. (1997) 'Working with resistance to experiencing and expressing emotions in group therapy', *International Journal of Group Psychotherapy* 47(4): 443–58.

Coolican, H. (1996) *Research Methods and Statistics in Psychology*, London: Hodder and Stoughton.

Coopersmith, S. (1967) *The Antecedents of Self-Esteem*, San Francisco: W.H. Freeman.

Corder, B.F., Whiteside, L. and Haizlip, T.M. (1981) 'A study of the curative factors in group psychotherapy with adolescents', *International Journal of Group Psychotherapy* 31: 345–54.

Cowburn, M. (1996) 'The black male sex offender in prison: images and issues', *The Journal of Sexual Aggression* 2(2): 122–42.

Craissati, J. and McClurg, G. (1997) 'The challenge project: a treatment program evaluation for perpetrators of child sexual abuse', *Child Abuse and Neglect* 21 (7): 637–48.

Crawford, D.A. and Howells, K. (1982) 'The effect of sex education with disturbed adolescents', *Behavioural Psychotherapy*, Oct. 10(4): 339–45.

Cronen, V. and Lang, P. (1994) 'Language and action: Wittgenstein and Dewey in the practice of therapy and consultation', *Human Systems: The Journal of Systemic Consultation and Management* 5(1 and 2): 5–44.

Cronen, V.E. and Pearce, W B (1985) 'Toward an explanation of how the Milan Method works: an invitation to a systemic epistemology and the evolution of family systems', in D. Campbell and R. Draper (eds), *Applications of Systemic Therapy: The Milan Approach*, London: Grune and Stratton.

Crowne, D.P. and Marlow, D. (1960) 'A new scale of social desirability independent of psychopathology', *Journal of Consulting Psychology* 24: 349–54.

Cullen, J.E. and Seddon, J.W. (1981) 'The application of a behavioural regime to disturbed young offenders', *Personality and Individual Differences* 2: 285–92.

Davis, G.E. and Leitenberg, H. (1987) 'Adolescent sex offenders', *Psychological Bulletin* 101(3): 417–27.

Davis, M.H. (1980) 'A multidimential approach to individual differences in empathy', *JSAS Catalog of Selected Documents in Psychology* 10(A).

Deblinger, E. and Heflin, A. H. (1996) *Treating Sexually Abused Children and their Non-offending Parents: A Cognitive Behavioural Approach*, Thousand Oaks, CA: Sage.

Department of Health (1991a) *The Children Act 1989 Guidance and Regulations: Volume 4, Residential Care*, London: HMSO.

—— (1991b) *Working Together under the Children Act 1989. A Guide to the Arrangements for Inter-agency Co-operation for the Protection of Children from Abuse*, London: HMSO

—— (1992) *A Strategic Statement on Working with Abusers*, London: HMSO.

—— (1995a) *Children and Young People on Child Protection Registers*, London: Government Statistical Service.

—— (1995b) *Child Protection: Messages from Research*, : London: HMSO.

—— (1998) *Working Together to Safeguard Children: New Government Proposals for Inter-Agency Co-operation. Consultation Paper*, London, DOH.

Department of Health and Social Security (DHSS) (1988) *Diagnosis of Child Sexual Abuse: Guidance for Doctors*, London, HMSO.

DeRisi, W.J. and Butz, G. (1975) *Writing Behavioural Contracts*, Champaigne, IL: Research Press.

Dimmock, B. and Dungworth, D. (1985) 'Beyond the family: using network meetings with statutory child care cases', *Journal of Family Therapy* 7(1): 45–68

Dobash, R.P., Carnie, J. and Waterhouse, L. (1993) 'Child sexual abusers: recognition and response', in L. Waterhouse (ed.), *Child Abuse and Abusers: Protection and Prevention*, London: Jessica Kingsley Publications.

Doshay, L.J. (1943) *The boy sex offender and his later career*, Montclair, NJ: Patterson Smith.

Doughty, D. and Schneider, H. (1987) 'Attribution of blame in incest among mental health professionals', *Psychological Reports* 60: 1,159–65.

Douglas, T. (1995) *Survival In Groups: The Basics Of Group Membership*, Buckingham: Open University Press.

Duboust, S. and Knight, P. (1995) *Group Activities for Personal Development*, Bicester: Winslow Press.

Durlak, J., Furnham, T. and Lampman, C. (1991) 'Effectiveness of cognitive-behavioral therapy for maladapting children: a meta-analysis', *Psychological Bulletin* 110(2): 204–14.

Dwivedi, K.N. (ed.) (1993) *Groupwork with Children and Adolescents: A Handbook*, London: Jessica Kingsley.

Dziuba-Leatherman, J. and Finkelhor, D. (1994) 'How does receiving information about sexual abuse influence boys' perceptions of their risk?', *Child Abuse and Neglect* 18: 557–68.

Edleson, J. (1997) 'Charging battered mothers with failure to protect is often wrong', *APSAC Advisor* 10: 2–3.

Eldridge, H. (1998) *Therapist Guide for Maintaining Change: Relapse Prevention for Adult Male Perpetrators of Child Sexual Abuse*, Thousand Oaks, CA: Sage.

Elkins, I.J., Iacono, W.G., Doyle A.E. and McCue, M. (1997) 'Characteristics associated with the persistence of antisocial behaviour: results from recent longitudinal research', *Aggression and Violent Behaviour* 2(2): 101–24.

Elliot, D.S. (1994) 'The developmental course of sexual and non-sexual violence: results from a national longitudinal study', presentation at the 13th Annual Research and Treatment Conference of the Association of Sexual Abusers, San Francisco.

Elliott, C. E. and Butler, L. (1994) 'The Stop and Think Group: changing sexually aggressive behaviour in young children', *The Journal of Sexual Aggression* 1: 15–28.

Elliot, D.S., Dunford, F.W. and Huzinga, D. (1983) 'The identification and prediction of career offenders utilizing self-reported and official data', unpublished manuscript, Boulder, CO: Behavioural Research Institute.

Elliot, D.S., Huizinga, D. and Ageton, S.S. (1985) *Explaining Delinquency and Drug Use*, Thousand Oaks, CA: Sage.

Elliott, M. (ed.) (1993) *Female Sexual Abuse of Children: The Ultimate Taboo*, London: Longmans.

Epps, K.J. (1997a) 'Managing risk', in M. Hoghughi, S. Bhate and F. Graham (eds), *Working with Sexually Abusive Adolescents*, Thousand Oaks, CA: Sage.

—— (1997b) 'Pointers for carers', in M.C. Calder, *Juveniles and Children who Sexually Abuse: A Guide to Risk Assessment*, Lyme Regis, Dorset: Russell House Publishing.

Erooga, M. (1994) 'Where the professional meets the personal', in T. Morrison, M. Erooga, and R.C. Beckett (eds), *Sexual Offending Against Children Assessment and Treatment of Male Abusers*, London: Routledge.

Evans, J. (1993) *Adolescent and Pre-Adolescent Psychiatry*, London: Academic Press.

—— (1998) *Active Analytic Psychotherapy for Adolescents*, London: Jessica Kingsley.

Farmer, E. (1998) 'Fostering and residential care for sexually abused and abusing children', paper presented at the British Association for the Study and Prevention of Child Abuse and Neglect National Study Day, Services for Children in Need with Practical Solutions to Help Them, Bristol, England, March.

Farmer, E. and Pollock, S. (1998) *Sexually Abused and Abusing Children in Substitute Care*, Chichester: John Wiley.

Farrington, D.P. (1973) 'Self-reports of deviant behaviour: predictive and stable?', *Journal of Criminal Law and Criminology* 64: 99–110.

Farrington, D.P. and Hawkins, J.D. (1991) 'Predicting participation, early onset and later persistence in officially recorded offending', *Criminal Behaviour and Mental Health* 1: 1–33.

Farrington, D.P., Ohlin, L.E. and Wilson, J.Q. (1986) *Understanding and Controlling Crime*, New York: Springer.

Fehrenbach, P.A., Smith, W., Monastersky, C. and Deisher, R.W. (1986) 'Adolescent sexual offenders: offender and offence characteristics', *American Journal of Orthopsychiatry* 56: 225–33.

Finkelhor, D. (1979) *Sexually Victimised Children*, New York: Free Press.

—— (1984) *Child Sexual Abuse: New Theory and Research*, New York: Free Press.

—— (1986) *A Source Book on Child Sexual Abuse*, New York: Free Press.

Finkelhor, D. and Browne, A. (1985) 'The traumatic impact of child sexual abuse: An update', *American Journal of Orthopsychiatry* 55: 530–41.

—— (1986) 'Initial and long-term effects: a conceptual framework' in D.A. Finkelhor, *Sourcebook on Child Sexual Abuse*, Beverley Hills, CA: Sage.

Finkelhor, D. and Russell, D. (1984) 'Women as perpetrators', in D. Finkelhor (ed.), *Child Sexual Abuse: New Theory and Research*, New York: Free Press.

Fisher, N. (1991) *Boys about Boys*, London: Pan.

Fisher, T.D. and Hall, R.G. (1988) 'A scale for the comparison of the sexual attitudes of adolescents and their parents', *Journal of Sex Research* 24: 90–100.

Forth, A.E., and Burke, H.C. (1998) 'Psychotherapy in adolescence: assessment, violence and developmental precursors', in D.J. Cooke, A.E. Forth and R.D. Hare (eds), *Psychopathy: Theory, Research and Implications for Society*, NATO ASI Series, Netherlands: Kluwer Academic Publishers.

251

Forth, A.E., Kosson, D.S. and Hare, R.D. (1994) 'The Psychopathy Checklist: Youth Version', unpublished test manual.

Freud, S. (1905) *Three essays on the Theory of Sexuality. I. The Sexual Aberrations*, in J. Strachey (ed.), *The Standard Edition of the Complete Psychological Works of Sigmund Freud*, London: The Hogarth Press and The Institute of Psycho-analysis.

Friedrich, W. (1997) 'Psychotherapy with sexually abused boys in child abuse', in D.A. Wolfe, R.S. McMahon and R.D. Peters (eds), *New Directions in Prevention and Treatment across the Lifespan*, Thousand Oaks, CA: Sage.

——. (1993) 'Sexual victimization and sexual behaviour in children: a review of recent literature', *Child Abuse and Neglect* 17: 59–66.

Fromuth, M.E., Jones, C.W. and Burkhart, B.R. (1991) 'Hidden child molestation: an investigation of perpetrators in a non-clinical sample', *Journal of Interpersonal Violence* 6(3): 376–84.

Frugerri, L. (1992) 'Therapeutic process as social construction', in S. McNamee and K.J. Gergen (eds), *Therapy as Social Construction*, Thousand Oaks, CA: Sage.

Furby, L., Weinrott, M.R. and Blackshaw, L. (1989) 'Sex offender recidivism: a review', *Psychological Bulletin* 105: 3–30.

Furniss, T. (1991) *The Multi-professional Handbook of Child Sexual Abuse: Integrated management, Therapy and Legal Intervention*, London: Routledge

Garland, J.A. (1992) 'The establishment of individual and collective competency in children's groups as a prelude to entry into intimacy, disclosure and bonding', *International Journal of Group Psychotherapy* 42(3): 395–405.

Gelsthorpe, L. and Morris, A. (eds) (1990) *Feminist Perspectives in Criminology*, Milton Keynes: Open University Press.

Gendreau, P., Little, T. and Goggin, C. (1996) 'A meta-analysis of the predictors of adult offender recidivism: what works', *Criminology* 34: 575–607.

Gilbert, N. (1988) 'Teaching children to prevent sexual abuse', *The Public Interest* 93: 3–15.

Glasgow, D. (1988) 'Structured assessment of sexual offenders', unpublished manuscript.

Glasser, M. (1979) 'Some aspects of the role of aggression in the perversions', in L. Rosen (ed.), *Sexual Deviations*, Oxford: Oxford University Press.

GMC (1997) *Confidentiality In Duties of a Doctor*, Guidance from the General Medical Council. [178–202 Great Portland Street, London WIN 6JE.]

Graham, F., Richardson, G. and Bhate, S. (1997) 'Cognitive-based practice with sexually abusive adolescents', in M. Hoghughi, S. Bhate and F. Graham (1997) *Working with Sexually Abusive Adolescents*, Thousand Oaks, CA: Sage.

Graves, R.B. (1993) 'Conceptualizing the youthful male sex offender: a meta-analytic examination of offender characteristics by offence type', unpublished doctoral dissertation, Utah State University: Logan.

Greenwald, H.J. and Satow, Y. (1970) 'A short social desirability scale', *Psychological Reports* 27: 131–5.

Groth, A.N. (1979) *Men Who Rape: The Psychology of the Offender*, New York: Plenum.

Guardian (1998) See extensive coverage of the trial of four 10-year-old boys accused of raping a female classmate in the school toilets, 16 January and 6 February.

Hackett, S. (1997) 'Men protecting children? A study of male social workers' experiences of working in child sexual abuse', unpublished MA Thesis, University of Manchester.

Hackett, S. and Marsland, P. (1997) 'Perceptions of power: an exploration of the dynamics in the student–tutor–practice teacher relationship within child protection placements', *Social Work Education*16(2): 44–62.

Hackett, S., Print, B. and Dey, C. (1998) 'Brother nature?: Therapeutic intervention with young men who sexually abuse their siblings', in A. Bannister (ed.), *From Hearing to Healing: Working with the Aftermath of Child Sexual Abuse*, second edition, Chichester: Wiley.

Hagen, M.P. and Cho, M.E. (1996) 'A comparison of treatment outcomes between adolescent rapists and child sexual offenders', *Journal of Offender Therapy and Comparative Criminology* 40(2): 113–22.

Hall, G.C. (1995) 'Sexual offender recidivism revisited: a meta-analysis of recent treatment studies', *Journal of Consulting and Clinical Psychology* 63(5): 802–9.

Hanks, H. (1997) ' "Normal" psychosexual development, behaviour and knowledge', in M Calder, *Juveniles and Children who Sexually Abuse. A Guide to Risk Assessment*, Lyme Regis: Russell House

Hanson, C.L., Henggeler, S.W., Haefele, W.F. and Rodick, J.D. (1984) 'Demographic, individual and family relationship correlates of serious and repeated crime amongst adolescents and their siblings', *Journal of Consulting and Clinical Psychology* 52: 528–38.

Hanson, R.K. (1998) 'The Empathy for Women Test – version 2', unpublished manuscript. [Available from Corrections Research, Department of the Solicitor General of Canada, 340 Laurier Avenue, West, Ottawa, Canada, K1A 0PB.]

Hanson, R.K. and Bussière, M.T. (1996) 'Predictors of sexual offender recidivism: a meta-analysis', *User Report No. 1996–04*, Ottawa: Solicitor General Canada.

Hanson, R.K. and Scott, H. (1995) 'Assessing perspective-taking amongst sexual offenders, non-sexual criminals and non-offenders', *Sexual Abuse: A Journal of Research and Treatment* 7: 259–77.

Hanson, R.K., Harris, A., Gray, G.A., Forouzan, E., McWhinnie, A.J. and Osweiler, M.C. (1997, October) 'Dynamic predictors of sexual reoffence project 1997', presentation at the 16th Annual Research and Treatment Conference of the Association for the Treatment of Sexual Offenders, Arlington, VA.

Harnett, P. (1997) 'The attitudes of female and male residential care workers to the perpetrators of sexual and physical abuse, *Child Abuse and Neglect* 21(9): 861–8.

Harrell, A.V. and Wirtz, P.W. (1994) *Adolescent Drinking Index*, Odessa, FL: Psychological Assessment Resources.

Harrington, R. (1994) 'Affective disorders', in M. Rutter, E. Taylor and L. Hersov (eds), *Child and Adolescent Psychiatry Modern Approaches*, Oxford: Blackwell.

Harrison, H. (1993) 'Female abusers – what children and young people have told childline', in M. Elliott (ed.), *Female Sexual Abuse of Children The Ultimate Taboo*, Longman.

Hart, S.D. (1998) 'Psychopathy and risk for violence', in D.J. Cooke, A.E. Forth and R.D. Hare (eds), *Psychopathy: Theory, Research and Implications for Society*, NATO ASI Series D, Vol. 88, London: Kluwer.

Harter, S. (1985) *Manual for the Self-Perception Profile for Children*, Denver, CO: University of Denver.

Hartjen, C.A. (1978) *Crime and Criminalisation*, 2nd edition, New York: Preagar.

Haugaard, J. and Reppucci, N. (1988) *The Sexual Abuse of Children: A Comprehensive Guide to Current Knowledge and Intervention Strategies*, San Francisco, CA: Jossey-Bass.

Hawkes, C., Jenkins, J.A. and Vizard, E. (1997) 'Roots of sexual violence in children and adolescents', in V. Varma (ed.), *Violence in Children and Adolescents*, London: Jessica Kingsley Publishers.

Hedderman, C. and Sugg, D. (1997) 'Does treating sex offending reduce reoffending?', *Home Office Research and Statistics Directorate* No. 45, London: Home Office.

Herbert, M. (1991) *Clinical Child Psychology: Social Learning, Development and Behaviour*, Chichester: Wiley.

Herington, S. (1990) 'Constructivism and child abuse', *Human Systems: The Journal of Systemic Consultation and Management* 1(1): 75–82.

Himeleign, M.J. and McElrath, J.A.V. (1996) 'Resilient child sexual abuse survivors: cognitive coping and illusion', *Child Abuse and Neglect* 20(8): 747–58.

Hirst, J. (1994) *Not in Front of the Grown-ups. A Study of the Social and Sexual Lives of 15 and 16 year olds*, Sheffield: Pavic Publications.

HM Inspectorate of Probation (1998) *Exercising Constant Vigilance: The Role of the Probation Service in Protecting the Public from Sex Offenders. Report of a Thematic Inspection*, London: Home Office.

HMSO (1998) *Crime and Disorder Act*, London: HMSO.

Hoare, P., Elton, R., Greer, A. and Kerley, S. (1993) 'The modification and standardisation of the Harter self-esteem questionnaire with Scottish school children', *European Child and Adolescent Psychiatry* 2(1): 19–33.

Hobbs, C.J. and Wynne, J.M. (1993) 'The evaluation of child abuse', in C.J. Hobbs and J.M. Wynne (eds), *Child Abuse, Clinical Paediatrics, International Practice and Research* 1(1): 1–29.

Hodges, J., Lanyado, M. and Andreou, C. (1994) 'Sexuality and violence: preliminary clinical hypotheses from psychotherapeutic assessments in a research programme on young sexual offenders', *Journal of Child Psychotherapy* 20(3): 283–308.

Hoghughi, M., Bhate, S. and Graham, F. (1997) *Working with Sexually Abusive Adolescents*, Thousand Oaks, CA: Sage.

Holmes, E. (1983). 'Psychological assessment', in M. Boston and R. Szur (eds), *Psychotherapy with Severely Disturbed Children*, London: Routledge and Kegan Paul.

Home Office (1995) *Criminal Statistics for England and Wales 1994*, London: Home Office.

—— (1998) *Criminal Statistics for England and Wales 1997*, Cmd. 4162, London: Home Office.

—— (1998a) *Draft Guidance on Establishing Youth Offending Teams. Circular 122/98 Task Force on Youth Justice*, London: Home Office.

—— (1998b) *No More Excuses: A New Approach to tackling Youth Crime in England and Wales*, White Paper, Home Office Juvenile Offenders Unit, London.

Hopkins, J. (1998) 'Secondary abuse', in A. Bannister (ed.), *From Hearing to Healing: Working with the Aftermath of Child Sexual Abuse*, 2nd edition, Chichester: Wiley.

Horne, L., Glasgow, D., Cox, A. and Calam, R. (1991) 'Sexual abuse of children by children', *Journal of Child Law* 3(4): 147–51.

Hunter, J.A. and Becker, J.V. (1994) 'The role of deviant sexual arousal in juvenile sexual offending: etiology, evaluation and treatment', *Criminal Justice and Behaviour* 21: 132–49.

Hunter, J.A., Becker, J.V. and Kaplan, M.S. (1991) 'The reliability and discriminative utility of the adolescent cognitions scale for juvenile sex offenders', *Annals of Sex Research* 4(3 and 4): 281–6.

ICD-10 Classification of Mental and Behavioural Disorders (1992) *Clinical Descriptions and Diagnostic Guidelines*, Geneva: World Health Organisation.

Insoo Kim Berg (1991) *Family Preservation – A Brief Therapy Workbook*, London: Brief Therapy Press.

James, A. and Jenks, C. (1996) 'Perceptions of childhood criminality', *British Journal of Sociology* 47(2): 315–31.

Jenkins, A. (1990) *Invitations to Responsibility – The Therapeutic Engagement of Men Who Are Violent and Abusive*, Adelaide: Dulwich Centre Publications.

Johnson, T.C. (1988) 'Child perpetrators – children who molest other children: preliminary findings', *Child Abuse and Neglect* 12: 219–29.

—— (1989) 'Female child perpetrators: children who molest other children', *Child Abuse and Neglect* 13: 571–85.

Justice, R. and Justice, B. (1993) 'Child abuse and the law: how to avoid being the abused or the abuser', *Transactional Analysis Journal* 23(3): 139–45.

Kahn, T.J. (1990) *Pathways – A Guided Workbook for Youth Beginning Treatment*, Vermont: Safer Society Press.

Kahn, T.J. and Chambers, H. (1991) 'Assessing reoffence risk with juvenile sexual offenders', *Child Welfare* 70 (3).

Kaplan, M.S., Becker, J.V. and Tenke, C.E. (1991) 'Assessment of sexual knowledge and attitudes in an adolescent sex offender population', *Journal of Sex Education and Therapy* 17(3): 217–25.

Karpman, S. (1968) 'Fairy tales and script drama analysis', *Transactional Analysis Bulletin* 7(26): 39–43.

Kaufman, K.L. and Hilliker, D.R. and Daleiden, E.L. (1996) 'Subgroup differences in the modus operandi of adolescent sexual offenders', *Child Maltreatment* 1: 17–24.

Kavoussi, R., Kaplan, M. and Becker, J. (1988) 'Psychiatric diagnoses in juvenile sex offenders', *Journal of the American Academy of Child and Adolescent Psychiatry* 27: 241–3.

Keif, H.I., Fullard, W. and Devlin, S.J. (1990) 'A new measure of adolescent sexuality: SKAT-A', *Journal of Sex Education and Therapy* 16(2): 79–91.

Kelly, L., Regan, L. and Burton, S. (1991) *An Exploratory Study of the Prevalence of Sexual Abuse in a Sample of 16–21 year olds*, North London Polytechnic: CSAU.

Kelly, L., Burton, S. and Regan, L. (1992) ' "And what happened to him?": Policy on sex offenders from the survivor's perspective', in Prison Reform Trust, *Beyond Containment: The Penal Response to Sex Offending*, London: Prison Reform Trust.

Kendall, P.C. (1991) 'Guiding theory for therapy with children and adolescents', in P.C. Kendall (ed.), *Child and Adolescent Therapy: Cognitive-Behavioral Procedures*, New York: Guilford.

Kendall, P.C. and Braswell, L. (1985) *Cognitive-Behavioural Therapy for Impulsive Children*, New York: Guilford Press.

Kendal-Tackett, K.A., Williams, L.M. and Finkelhor, D. (1993) 'Impact of sexual abuse on children: a review and synthesis of recent empirical studies', *Psychological Bulletin* 113: 164–80.

Kennel, R. and Agresti, A. (1995) 'Effects of gender and age on psychologists' reporting of child sexual abuse', *Professional Psychology: Research and Practice* 26(6): 612–15.

Kirby, D. (1984) *Sexual Education: An Evaluation of Programmes and Their Effects*, Santa Cruz, CA: Network.

Klein, M. (1946) 'Notes on some schizoid mechanisms', in Masud R. Khan (ed.), *Envy and Gratitude and Other Works (1946–1963). The Writings of Melanie Klein, Volume III*, The International Psycho-Analytical Library No. 104, London: The Hogarth Press and the Institute of Psychoanalysis.

Knight, R.A. and Prentky, R. (1993) 'Exploring characteristics for classifying juvenile sex offenders', in H.E. Barbaree, W.L. Marshall and S.M. Hudson (eds), *The Juvenile Sex Offender*, New York: Guildford.

Knopp, F.H., Freeman-Longo, R. and Stephenson, W.H. (1992) *Nationwide Survey of Juvenile and Adult Sex Offender Treatment Program and Models*, Orwell, VT: Safer Society Program Publications.

Kraft, P. (1993) 'Sexual knowledge among Norwegian adolescents', *Journal of Adolescence* 16: 3–21.

Krueger, R., Schmutte, P.S., Caspi, A., Moffitt, T., Campbell, K. and Silva, P.A. (1994) 'Personality traits are linked to crime: evidence from a birth cohort', *Journal of Abnormal Psychology* 103: 328–38.

Lab, S.P., Shields, G. and Schondel, C. (1993) 'Research note: an evaluation of juvenile sexual offender treatment', *Crime and Delinquency* 39(4): 543–53.

Lamb, S. (1991) 'Acts without agents: an analysis of linguistic avoidance in journal articles on men who batter women', *Journal of Orthopsychiatry* 61(2): 250–7.

Lane, S. (1991a) 'Special offender populations', in G. Ryan, and S. Lane (eds), *Juvenile Sexual Offending: Causes, Consequences and Corrections*, Lexington, MA: Lexington Books.

—— (1991) 'The sexual abuse cycle', in G. Ryan, and S. Lane (eds), *Juvenile Sexual Offending: Causes, Consequences and Corrections*, Lexington, MA: Lexington Books.

—— (1997) 'The sexual abuse cycle', in G. Ryan and S. Lane (eds), *Juvenile Sexual Offending Causes, Consequences and Corrections*, San Francisco: Jossey-Bass.

Lane, S. with Lobanov-Rostovsky (1997) 'Special populations: children, females, the developmentally disabled, and violent youth', in G. Ryan and S. Lane (1997) *Juvenile Sexual Offending. Causes, Consequences and Corrections*, 2nd edition, San Francisco: Jossey-Bass.

Lane, S. and Zamora, P. (1978) 'Syllabus materials from inservice training – closed adolescent treatment centre', cited in G. Ryan and S. Lane (1991), *Juvenile Sexual Offending – Causes, Consequences and Corrections*, Lexington, MA: Lexington Books.

—— (1982, 1984) cited in S. Lane (1997) 'The sexual abuse cycle', in G. Ryan and S. Lane (eds), *Juvenile Sexual Offending Causes, Consequences and Corrections*, San Francisco: Jossey-Bass.

Lang, W.P., Little, M. and Cronen, V. (1990) 'The systemic professional: domains of action and the question of neutrality', *Human Systems: The Journal of Systemic Consultation and Management* 1(1): 39–56.

Laws, D.R. (1986) 'Prevention of relapse in sex offenders', paper presented at the NIMH Conference at the 12th Annual Meeting of the International Academy of Sex Research, Amsterdam.

—— (ed.) (1989) *Relapse Prevention with Sexual Offenders*, New York: Guilford Press.

Laws, D.R. and Marshall, W.L. (1990) 'A conditioning theory of the etiology and maintenance of deviant sexual preference and behavior', in W.L. Marshall, D.R. Laws, and H.E. Barbaree (eds), *Handbook of Sexual Assault: Issues, Theories, and Treatment of the Offender*, New York: Plenum.

Le Doux, J.E. (1994) 'Emotion, memory and the brain', *Scientific American* June: 50–7.

Lee, D.G. and Olender, M.B. (1992) 'Working with juvenile sex offenders in foster care', *Community Alternatives: International Journal of Family Care* 4: 63–75.

Lightfoot, L.O. and Barbaree, H.E. (1993) 'The relationship between substance use and sexual offending in adolescents', in H.E. Barbaree, W.L. Marshall and S.M. Hudson (eds), *The Juvenile Sex Offender*, London: Guildford.

Limentani, A. (1989) *Between Freud and Klein. The Psychoanalytic Quest for Knowledge and Truth*, London, Free Association Books.

Little, L. and Hamby, S. (1996) 'Impact of a clinician's sexual abuse history, gender, and theoretical orientation on treatment issues related to child sexual abuse', *Professional Psychology: Research and Practice* 27(6): 617–62.

Loeber, R. (1990) 'Development and risk factors of juvenile antisocial behaviour and delinquence', *Clinical Psychology Review* 10: 1–41.

Longo, R. and Groth, N. (1983) cited in Bentovim and Williams, 1998.

Loughlin, B. (1992) 'Supervision in the face of no cure – working on the boundary', *Journal of Social Work Practice* 6(2): 111–16.

Madanes, C. (1990) 'The therapy of a juvenile sex offender', in C. Madanes, *Sex, Love and Violence: Strategies for Transformation*, London: Norton Publications.

Malan, D. (1979) *Individual Psychotherapy and the Science of Psychodynamics*, London: Butterworth-Heinemann.

Malekoff, A. (1997) *Group Work with Adolescents: Principles and Practice*, New York: Guilford Press.

Maletzky, B. (1991) *Treating the Sexual Offender*, Thousand Oaks, CA: Sage.

Marlatt, G.A. and Gordon, J.R. (eds) (1985) *Relapse Prevention: Maintenance Strategies in the Treatment of Addictive Behaviours*, New York: Guilford Press.

Marshall, P. (1996) *Reconvictions of Sexual Offenders in England and Wales*, Research and Statistics Directorate, Home Office, London: HMSO.

Marshall, W.L. (1989) 'Invited essay: intimacy, loneliness and sexual offenders', *Behaviour Research and Therapy* 27: 491–503.

Marshall, W.L. and Barbaree, H.E. (1990) 'Outcome of comprehensive cognitive-behavioural treatment programmes', in W.L. Marshall, D.R. Laws and H.E. Barbaree (eds), *Handbook of Sexual Assault: Issues, Theories and the Treatment of the Offender*, London: Plenum.

Marshall, W.L., Hudson, S.M. and Ward, T. (1992) 'Sexual deviance', in P. H. Wilson (ed.), *Principles and Practice of Relapse Prevention*, London: Guilford Press.

Marshall, W.L., Hudson, S.M., Jones, R. and Fernandez, Y.M. (1995) 'Empathy in sex offenders', *Clinical Psychology Review* 15(2): 99–113.

Mason, B. (1993) 'Towards positions of safe uncertainty in voices from the training context', a special edition of *Human Systems: The Journal of Systemic Consultation and Management* 4(3 and 4): 189–200.

Masson, H. (1995) 'Children and adolescents who sexually abuse other children: responses to an emerging problem', *Journal of Social Welfare and Family Law* 17(3): 325–36.

—— (1997) 'Researching policy and practice in relation to children and young people who sexually abuse, *Research, Policy and Planning* 15(3): 8–16.

Masson, H. and Erooga, M. (1989) 'The silent volcano – groupwork with mothers of sexually abused children', *Practice Journal* 3(1): 24–41.

Masson, J. (1992) *The Assault on Truth. Freud and Child Sex Abuse*, London: Fontana.

Matthews, J.K. (1993) 'Working with female sex abusers', in M. Elliott, *Female Sexual Abuse of Children The Ultimate Taboo*, Longman.

Matthews, R., Hunter, J.A. and Vuz, J. (1997) 'Juvenile female sexual offenders – characteristics and treatment issues', *Sexual Abuse – A Journal of Research and Treatment* 9(3): 187–99.

Matthews, R., Matthews, J.K. and Spelz, K. (1989) *Female Sexual Offenders. An Exploratory Study*, Vermont: Safer Society Press.

Maturana, H.R. and Varela, F.J. (1987) *The Tree of Knowledge: The Biological Roots of Human Understanding*, Boston and London: New Science Library.

Mavasti, J. (1986) 'Incestuous mothers', *American Journal of Forensic Psychiatry* 7: 63–9.

Mayer, A. (1988) *Sex Offenders*, Holmes Beach, FL: Learning Publications Inc.

—— (1992) *Women Sex offenders – Treatment and Dynamics*, Holmes Beach, FL: Learning Publications Inc.

Maynard, C. and Wiederman, M. (1997) 'Undergraduate students' perceptions of child sexual abuse: effects of age, sex and gender-role attitudes', *Child Abuse and Neglect* 21(9): 861–8.

McClune, N. (1995) 'Adolescent perpetrators of sexual abuse long term outcome of treatment', *Child Care in Practice: Northern Ireland Journal of Multi-Disciplinary Child Care Practice* 1(3): 26–38.

McDougall, J. (1990) *Plea for a Measure of Abnormality*, London, Free Association Books.

McNamee, S. and Gergen, K.J. (eds) (1992) *Therapy as Social Construction*, Thousand Oaks, CA: Sage.

Memorandum of Good Practice (1992) *Video Recorded Interviews with Child Witnesses for Criminal Proceedings*, London: HMSO.

Menzies, l. (1970) *The Functioning of Social Systems as a Defence Against Anxiety*, London: Tavistock Institute of Human Relations.

Milan, M.A. (1987) 'Basic behavioural procedures in closed institutions', in E.K. Morris and C.J. Braukmann (eds), *Behavioural Approaches to Crime and Delinquency: A Handbook of Application, Research and Concepts*, New York: Plenum Press.

Miller, A. (1984) *Thou Shalt Not Be Aware. Society's Betrayal of the Child*, London: Pluto Press.

Milloy, C.D. (1994) *A Comparative Study of Juvenile Sex Offenders and Non-sex Offenders*, Olympia, WA: Washington State Institute for Public Policy.

Mintzer, M. (1996) 'Understanding countertransference reactions in working with adolescent perpetrators of sexual abuse', *Bulletin of the Meninger Clinic* 60(2): 219–27.

Mitchell, C. and Melikian, K. (1995) 'The treatment of male sex offenders: countertransference reactions', *Journal of Child Sexual Abuse* 4(1): 87–93.

Mitchelson, L. and Wood, R. (1982) 'Development and psychometric proper-ties of the Children's Assertiveness Behaviour Scale', *Journal of Behavioural Assessment* 4(1): 3–13.

Moffitt, T.E. (1993) 'Adolescence – limited and life-course-persistence antiso-cial behaviour: a developmental taxonomy', *Psychological Bulletin* 100: 674–701.

Moffitt, T.E., Caspi, A., Silva, P.A., Stouthamer-Loeber, M. (1995) 'Individual differences in personality and intelligence are linked to crime: cross-context evidence from nations, neighborhoods, genders, race and age cohorts', in J. Hayan (ed.), *Current Perspectives on Ageing and the Life Cycle: Vol 4, Delin-quency and Disrepute in the Life-course: Contextual and Dynamic Analyses,* Greenwich, CT: JAI.

Monck, E. and New, M. (1995) *Report of a Study of Sexually Abused Children and Adolescents and of Young Perpetrators of Sexual Abuse who were Treated in Voluntary Agency Community Facilities,* London: HMSO.

Moore, S. and Rosenthal, D. (1993) *Sexuality in Adolescence,* London: Rout-ledge.

Morrison, T. (1990) 'The emotional effects of child protection on the worker', *Practice* 4(4): 253–71.

—— (1994) 'Learning together to manage sexual abuse: rhetoric or reality?', *Journal of Sexual Aggression* 1(1): 29–44.

—— (1996) 'Emotionally competent child protection organisations: fallacy, fiction or necessity', in J. Bates, R. Pugh and N. Thompson (eds), *Protecting Children: Challenges and Change,* London: Arena Books.

—— (1997) 'Where have we come from: where are we going? Managing adolescents who sexually abuse others', *NOTA News* 21: 15–27.

—— (1998) 'NOTA Conference, September 1997: managing risk: learning our lessons', *NOTA News* 25.

Morrison, T. and Print, B. (1995) *Adolescent Sexual Abusers: An Overview,* NOTA, National Organisation for the Treatment of Abusers.

Morrison, T., Erooga, M. and Beckett, R.C. (1994) *Sexual Offending Against Children. Assessment and Treatment of Male Abusers,* London: Routledge.

Mosher, D.L. and Sirkin, M. (1984) 'Measuring a macho personality constella-tion', *Journal of Research in Personality* 18, 150–63.

Multi-media Film Foundation of Canada (undated) *Sex – A Guide for the Young,* video supplied by Educational Media Film and Video Ltd. [235, Imperial Drive, Harrow, Middlesex, England.]

National Children's Homes (1992) *Report of the Committee of Enquiry into Children and Young People who Sexually Abuse Other Children,* London: NCH.

Nichols, H.R. and Molinder, I. (1984) *The MSI Manual.* [Available from Nichols and Molinder, 437 Bowes Drive, Tacoma WA 98466.]

Northern Ireland Research Team (1991) *Child Sexual Abuse in Northern Ireland,* Belfast: Greystone.

North West Treatment Associates (1988) in A. Salter (1988), *Treating Child Sex Offenders and Victims – A Practical Guide,* Beverly Hills: Sage.

NOTA (1993) *Good Practice in the Multi-agency Management of Sex Offenders who Assault Children*, a NOTA Briefing Paper (Policy and Ethics Sub-Committee), Hull: NOTA.

—— (1994) *Working with Adults and Adolescents who exhibit Sexually Abusive Behaviours: The use of Sexually Salient and Pornographic Materials*, a NOTA Briefing Paper (Policy and Ethics Sub-Committee), Hull: NOTA.

Novaco, R. W. (1991) *Reaction to Provocation*, Irvine, CA: University of CA.

Nylund, D. and Corsiglia, V. (1993) 'Internalized other questioning with men who are violent', plus commentary by Alan Jenkins, *Dulwich Centre Newsletter* 2: 29–37.

O'Callaghan, D. and Print, B. (1994) 'Adolescent sexual abusers: research, assessment and treatment', in T. Morrison, M. Erooga and R.C. Beckett (eds), *Sexual Offending Against Children Assessment and Treatment of Male Offenders*, London: Routledge.

O'Hagan, K. (1997) 'The problem of engaging men in child protection work', *British Journal of Social Work* 27(1): 25–42.

O'Hanlon, B. and Beadle, S. (1997) *A Field Guide to Possibility Land: Possibility Therapy Methods*, London: Brief Therapy Press

Olafson, E., Corwin, D. and Summit, R. (1993) 'Modern history of child sexual abuse awareness – cycles of discovery and suppression', *Child Abuse and Neglect* 17(1): 7–24.

Openshaw, D., Graves, R., Erickson, S., Lowry, M., Durso, D., Agee, L., Todd, S., Jones, K. and Scherzinger, J. (1993) 'Youthful sexual offenders: a comprehensive bibliography of scholarly references, 1970–1992, *Family Relations* 42: 222–6.

Palazolli, S., Boscolo, M., Cecchin, G and Prata, G. (1980) 'Hypothesising–circularity–neutrality: three guidelines for the conductor of the session', *Family Process* 19: 3–12.

Patterson, G.R. (1982) *A Social Learning Approach: Vol. 3 Coercive Family Process*, Oregon: Castalia Publishing.

Paulhus, D.L. (1984) 'Two component models of socially desirable responding', *Journal of Personality and Social Psychology* 46: 598–609.

Pavlov, I.P. (1927) *Conditional Reflexes*, London: Oxford University Press.

Pearce, B. (1992) 'A campers guide to constructionisms', *Human Systems: The Journal of Systemic Consultation and Management* 3(3 and 4): 3–27.

Pearce, B. and Cronen, V. (1980) *Communication, Action and Meaning: The Creation of Social Realities*, Praeger: New York.

Penn, P. (1983) 'Circular questioning', *Family Process* 21(3): 267–80.

—— (1985) 'Feedforward: future questions, future maps', *Family Process* 24(3): 299–310.

Perry, B.D. (1994) 'Neurobiological sequelae of childhood trauma: PTSD in children', in M. Murray (ed.), *Catecholamines in Post-Traumatic Stress Disorder: Emerging Concepts*, Washington DC: American Psychiatric Press.

Perry, G. and Orchard, J. (1992) *Assessment and Treatment of Adolescent Sex Offenders*, Sarasota, FL: Professional Resource Press.

Piers, E. and Harris, D. (1969) *The Piers-Harris Children's Self-Concept Scale*, Nashville: Counsellor Recording and Tests.

Pithers, W.D. (1990) 'Relapse prevention with sexual aggressors: a method for maintaining therapeutic gain and enhancing external supervision', in W. L. Marshall, D.R. Laws and H.E. Barbaree (eds), *Handbook of Sexual Assault: Issues, Theories, and Treatment of the Offender*, New York: Press.

Pithers, W. and Gray, A. (1996) cited in Ryan and Lane (1997).

Pithers, W., Marques, J., Gibat, C. and Marlatt, A. (1983) 'Relapse prevention with sexual aggressives', in J. Greer and I. Stuart (eds), *The Sexual Aggressor*, New York: Van Norstrand Reinhold.

Pithers, W.D., Kashima, K. Cummings, G.F., Beal, L.S. and Buell, M. (1988a) 'Relapse prevention of sexual aggression', in R. Prentky and V. Quinsey (eds), *Human Sexual Aggression: Current Perspectives*, New York: New York Academy of Sciences.

Pithers, W.D., Kashima, K.M., Cumming, G.F. and Beal, L.S. (1988b) 'Relapse prevention: a method of enhancing maintenance of change in sex offenders', in A. Salter (ed.), *Treating Child Sex Offenders and their Victims*, Thousand Oaks, CA: Sage.

Polson, M. and McCullom, E. (1995) 'Therapist caring in the treatment of sexual abuse offenders: perspectives from a qualitative case study of one sexual abuse treatment program', *Journal of Child Sexual Abuse* 4(1): 21–43.

Prentky, R.A. and Knight, A.R. (1993) 'Age of onset of sexual assault: criminal and life history correlates', in G.W. Hall, R. Hirschman, J. Graham and M. Zaragoza (eds), *Sexual Aggression: Issues in Aetiology, Assessment and Treatment*, Taylor Francis.

Prentky, R.A., Knight, R.A. and Lee A.F.S. (1997) 'Risk factors associated with recidivism among extra familial child molesters', *Journal of Consulting and Clinical Psychology* 65(1): 141–9.

Preston-Shoot, M. and Agass, D. (1990) *Making Sense of Social Work; Psychodynamics, Systems and Practice*, Basingstoke: Macmillan.

Preston-Shoot, M. and Braye, S. (1991) 'Managing the personal experience of work', *Practice* 5(1): 13–33.

Print, B. and Morrison, T. (in press) 'Adolescents who sexually abuse others', in J. Hanmer and C. Itzin (eds), *Home Truths*, London: Routledge.

Proctor, E. (1994) 'A five year outcome evaluation of a community-based treatment programme for convicted sexual offenders run by the Probation Service', *The Journal of Sexual Aggression* 2(1): 3–16.

Quay, H.C. and Peterson, D.R. (1987) *Manual for the Revised Behaviour Problem Checklist*, Coral Gables, FL: University of Miami.

Quinsey, V.L., Harris, G.T., Rice, M.E. and Harris, G.T. (1995) 'Actuarial prediction of sexual recidivism', *Journal of Interpersonal Violence* 10: 85–105.

Reder, P. (1983) 'Disorganised families and the helping professions: who's in charge of what?', *Journal of Family Therapy* 5(1): 23–36.

—— (1986) 'Multi-agency family systems', *Journal of Family Therapy* 8(2): 139–51.

Reynolds-Mejia, P. and Levitan, S. (1990) 'Countertransference issues in the in-home treatment of child sexual abuse', *Child Welfare* 69(1): 53–61.

Rich, S. (1998) 'A developmental approach to the treatment of adolescent sexual offenders', *The Irish Journal of Psychology* 17(1): 102–18.

Richardson, G., Bhate, S. and Graham, F. (1997) 'Cognitive-based practice with sexually abusive adolescents', in M. Hoghughi, S. Bhate and F. Graham (eds), *Working With Sexually Abusive Adolescents*, Thousand Oaks, CA: Sage.

Roberts, J. (1998) 'Fathering trust', *Community Care* April: 27: 9–15.

Roberts, W. and Strayer, J. (1994) 'Empathy, emotional expressions and prosocial behaviour', Cariboo College, Kamloops, BC: manuscript submitted for publication.

Rogers, C. (1951) *Client-Centred Therapy*, Boston: Houghton Mifflin.

Ronen, T. (1992) 'Cognitive therapy with young children', *Child Psychiatry and Human Development* 23(1): 19–30.

—— (1995) 'Cognitive behavioural therapy with children', in Y. Kasvikis (ed.), *25 years of Scientific Progress in Behavioural and Cognitive Therapies*, Athens: Ellinika Grammata.

Ross, J. and Loss, P. (1987) *Assessment Factors for Adolescent Sexual Offenders*, New London, CT: Ross, Loss and Associates.

—— (1991) 'Assessment of the juvenile sex offender', in G. Ryan and S. Lane (eds), *Juvenile Sexual Offending – Causes, Consequences and Corrections*, Lexington: Lexington Books.

Rowe, J. and Lambert, L. (1973) *Children Who Wait*, London: Association of British Adoption Agencies.

Russell, D., Peplau, L.A. and Cutrona, C.A. (1980) 'The revised UCLA Loneliness Scale: concurrent and discriminant validity evidence', *Journal of Personality and Social Psychology* 39: 472–80.

Russell, M.N. (1995) *Confronting Abusive Beliefs: Group Treatment for Abusive Men*, Thousand Oaks, CA: Sage.

Ryan, G. (1993) 'Workshop notes', Kempe Centre, Denver, Colorado.

—— (1996) 'Goals of group process: the struggle for safety', paper presented at NOTA Conference, Chester, England.

——. (1998) 'The relevance of early life experiences to the behaviour of sexually abusive youth', *Irish Journal of Psychology* 19 (1): 32–48.

Ryan, G. and Lane, S. (1991) *Juvenile Sexual Offending – Causes, Consequences and Corrections*, Lexington: Lexington Books.

—— (1997) *Juvenile Sexual Offending : Causes Consequences and Corrections*, 2nd edition, San Francisco: Jossey-Bass.

Salter, A.C. (1988) *Treating Child Sex Offenders and Victims: A Practical Guide*, Thousand Oaks, CA: Sage.

Sanders, R. and Ladwa-Thomas, U. (1997) 'Interagency perspectives on child sexual abuse perpetrated by juveniles', *Child Maltreatment* 2 (3): 264–71.

Saradjian, J. (1996) *Women Who Sexually Abuse Children – From Research to Clinical Practice*, Chichester: Wiley.

Scaife, J. (1993) 'From hierarchy to heterarchy in systemic therapy', unpublished dissertation from The Diploma in Systemic Therapy, Charles Burns Clinic: University of Birmingham.

Scavo, R. (1989) 'Female adolescent sex offenders – a neglected treatment group', *Social Casework- A Journal of Contemporary Social Work* 70(2):114–17.

Scharff, J.S. and Scharff, D.E. (1994) *Object Relations Therapy of Physical and Sexual Trauma*, London: Jason Aronson Inc.

Schonfeld, L., Octers, R. and Dolente, A. (1993) *Substance Abuse Relapse Assessment*, Odessa, FL: Psychological Assessment Resources.

Schur, E.M. (1971), *Labelling Deviant Behaviour: Its Sociology Implications*, New York: Harper and Row.

Scram D.D., Milloy, C.D. and Rowe, W.E. (1991) *Juvenile Sex Offenders: A Follow-up Study of Reoffence Behaviour*, Olympia, WA: Washington State Institute for Public Policy.

Selekman, M.D. (1993) *Pathways to Change: Brief Therapy Solutions for Difficult Adolescents*, London: Guildford Press.

Seltzer, M. L. (1971) 'The Michigan Alcoholism Screening Test: the quest for a new diagnostic instrument', *American Journal of Psychiatry* 127: 1,653–8.

Selvini Palazolli, M, Boscolo, L, Cecchin, G, and Prata, G., (1980) 'Hypothesizing–circularity–neutrality: three guidelines for the conductor of the session', *Family Process* 19: 3–12.

Sgroi, S.M. and Sargent, N. (1993) 'Impact and treatment issues for victims of childhood sexual abuse by female perpetrators', in M. Elliott, *Female Sexual Abuse of Children The Ultimate Taboo*, London: Longmans.

Sheath, M. (1990) 'Confrontative work with sex offenders: legitimised noncebashing?', *Probation Journal* 37(4): 159–62.

Sheridan, A., McKeown, K., Cherry, J., Donohhoe, E., McGrath, K., O'Reilly, K., Phelan, S. and Tallon, M. (1998) 'Perspectives on treatment outcome in adolescent sexual offending: a study of a community-based treatment programme', *The Irish Journal of Psychology* 19(1): 168–80.

Shoor, M., Speed, M.H. and Bartelt, C. (1966) 'Syndrome of the adolescent child molester', *American Journal of Psychiatry* 122: 783–9.

Shotter, J. (1993) 'Situating social constructionism: knowing from within', in Shotter, J. *Conversational Realities*, Thousand Oaks, CA: Sage.

Sinason, V. (1997a) 'The learning disabled (mentally handicapped) offender', in E.V. Welldon and C. Van Velsen (eds), *A Practical Guide to Forensic Psychotherapy*, London: Jessica Kingsley Publishing.

—— (1997b) 'Stress in the therapist and the Bagshaw Syndrome', in V. Varma (ed.), *Stresses in Psychotherapists*, London: Routledge

Skinner, A. (1997) *A Commitment to Protect. Supervising Sex Offenders: Proposals for More Effective Practice*, Edinburgh: Scottish Office, Social Work Services.

Skinner, B.F. (1953) *Science and Human Behaviour*, London: Collier Macmillan.

Skinner, H.A. (1982) 'The drug abuse screening test', *Addictive Behaviours* 7: 363–71.

Skuse, D. *et al.* (1997) cited in A. Bentovim and B. Williams (1998) 'Children and adolescents: victims who become perpetrators', *Advances in Psychiatric Treatment* 4: 101–7.

Smith, G. (1994) 'Parent, partner, protector: conflicting role demands for mothers of sexually abused children', in T. Morrison, M. Erooga and R. Beckett (eds), *Sexual Offending Against Children: Assessment and Treatment of Male Abusers*, London: Routledge.

Speilberger, C.D. (1991) *Strait-trait Anger Expression Inventory: Revised Research Edition*, Odessa, FL: Psychological Assessment Resources.

Spence, S.H. (1980) *Social Skill Training with Children and Adolescents: A Counselling Manual*, Windsor: NFER.

Spencer, A. (1997) 'I'm not alright, Jack. Looking after our professionals: an invitation to management to accept responsibility and minimise harm', NOTA News 21: 3–8.

Spivak, G. and Shure, M.B. (1974) *Social Adjustment of Young Children: A Cognitive Approach to Solving Real Life Problems*, San Francisco: Jossey-Bass.

Steen, C. and Monnette, B. (1989) *Treating Adolescent Sex Offenders in the Community*, Springfield, IL: Thomas Books.

Stermac, L. and Sheridan, P. (1993) 'The developmentally disabled adolescent sex offender', in H.E. Barbaree, W.L. Marshall and S.M. Hudson (eds), *The Juvenile Sex Offender*, Guildford: Guildford Press.

Stith, S.M. and Bischof, G.H. (1996) 'Communication patterns in families of adolescent sex offenders', in D.D. Cahn and S.A. Lloyd (eds), *Family Violence from a Communication Perspective*, Thousand Oaks, CA: Sage.

Stoller, R.J. (1975) *Perversion. The Erotic Form of Hatred*, London: Maresfield Library, Karnac Books.

STRATA (1997) *Policy on Working with Children and Young People who Sexually Abuse Others*, N. Wales Office: NCH Cymru.

Summit, R. (1983) 'The child sexual abuse accommodation syndrome', *Child Abuse and Neglect* 7: 177–93.

Surrey Children's Services (1998) 'Placement review report', (unpublished).

Taylor, E. (1994) 'Syndromes of attention deficit and overactivity', in M. Rutter, E. Taylor and L. Hersov (eds), *Child and Adolescent Psychiatry Modern Approaches*, Oxford: Blackwell.

Tellegen, A. (1982) *Brief Manual for the Multidimentional Personality Questionnaire*, Minneapolis: University of Minnesota.

Terr, L. (1991) 'Childhood traumas: an outline and overview', *American Journal of Psychiatry* 148: 10–20.

The Centre for Residential Child Care (1995) *Guidance For Residential Workers Caring For Young People Who Have Been Sexually Abused And Those*

Who Abuse Others, Social Work Services Inspectorate, The Scottish Office: Glasgow.

The ICD-10 Classification of Mental and Behavioural Disorders (1992) *Clinical Descriptions and Diagnostic Guidelines*, Geneva: World Health Organisation.

The National Task Force on Juvenile Offending (1993) 'The revised report from the National Task Force on Juvenile Sexual Offending', *Juvenile and Family Court Journal* 44(4): 1–121 (special report edition).

Thomas, J. (1991) 'The adolescent sex offender's family', in G. Ryan and S. Lane (eds), *Juvenile Sexual Offending – Causes, Consequences and Corrections*, Lexington: Lexington Books.

—— (1996) 'Female sexual offenders', Workshop Presentation NAP National Conference, Minneapolis in *Lessons from America – Work With Children and Young People Who Sexually Abuse*, Barnardos.

Thornton D. and Travers, R. (1991) *A Longitudinal Study of Criminal Behaviour of Convicted Sex Offenders*, proceedings of the Prison Psychologists Conference, HM Prison Service, London: Home Office.

Tomm, K. (1987a) 'Interventive interviewing : Part 1: Strategizing as a fourth guideline for the therapist', *Family Process* 26: 3–13.

—— (1987b) 'Interventive interviewing: Part II: Reflexive questioning as a means to enable self-healing', *Family Process* 26: 167–83.

—— (1988) 'Interventive interviewing: Part III: Intending to ask lineal, circular, strategic or reflexive questions, *Family Process* 27: 1–15.

Utting, Sir W. (1997) *People Like Us*, London: The Stationery Office.

Van der Kolk, B. (1987) *Psychological Trauma*, Washington: American Psychiatric Press.

Vizard, E. (1997) 'Adolescents who sexually abuse', in E.V. Welldon and C. Van Velsen (eds), *A Practical Guide to Forensic Psychotherapy*, London: Jessica Kingsley Publishing.

Vizard, E., Monck, E. and Misch, P. (1995) 'Child and adolescent sex abuse perpetrators: a review of the research literature', *Journal of Child Psychology and Psychiatry* 36: 731–56.

Vizard, E., Wynick, S., Hawkes, C., Woods, J. and Jenkins, J. (1996) 'Juvenile sexual offenders: assessment issues', *British Journal of Psychiatry* 168: 259–62.

Watson, D. and Friend, R. (1969) 'Assessment of social evaluation anxiety', *Journal of Consulting and Clinical Psychology* 33, 445–7.

Watzlawick, P., Weakland, J. and Fisch, R. (1974) *Change: Principles of Problem Formation and Problem Resolution*, New York: Norton Press.

Weinrott, M.R. (1996) *Juvenile Sexual Aggression: A Critical Review*, Institute of Behavioural Science: University of Colorado.

Weldon, E.V. (1988) *Mother, Madonna, Whore – The Idealisation and Denigration of Motherhood*, London: Guildford Press.

Wenet, G. and Clarke, T. (1986) 'Juvenile sex offender decision criteria', *The Oregon Report on Juvenile Sex Offenders*, State of Oregon: Department of Human Resources, Children Services Division.

Whitaker, A., Johnson, J., Shaffer, D., Rappoport, J., Kalokow, K., Walsh, B., Davies, M., Brainman, S. and Dolinsky, A. (1990) 'Uncommon troubles in young people: prevalence estimates of selected psychiatric disorders in a non-referred adolescent population', *Archives of General Psychiatry* 47: 487–96.

White, M. and Epston, D. (1991) *Narrative means to Therapeutic Ends* London: Norton Publications.

Will, D. (1994) 'A treatment service for adolescent sex offenders', *Psychiatric Bulletin* 18: 742–4.

Will, D., Douglas, A. and Wood, C. (1995) 'The evolution of a group therapy programme for adolescent perpetrators of sexual abusive behaviour', *The Journal Of Sexual Aggression* 1(2): 69–82.

Williams, B. and New, M. (1996) 'Developmental perspectives on adolescent boys who sexually abuse other children', *Child Psychiatry and Psychology Review* 1(4): 122–9.

Wilson, C. (1998) 'Are battered women responsible for protection of their children in domestic violence cases?', *Journal of Interpersonal Violence* 13: 289–93.

Wolf, S.C. (1984) 'A multifactor model of deviant sexuality', paper presented at Third International Conference on Victimology, Lisbon.

Wolfe, D.A., Werkerle, C., Reitzel-Jaffe, D., Grasley, C., Pittman, A. and MacEachran, A. (1993) 'Interrupting the cycle of violence: empowering youth to promote healthy relationships', in D.A. Wolfe, R.S. McMahon and R.D. Peters (eds), *New Directions in Prevention and Treatment across the Lifespan*, Thousand Oaks, CA: Sage.

Woods, J. (1997) 'Breaking the cycle of abuse and abusing: individual psychotherapy for juvenile sex offenders', *Clinical Child Psychology and Psychiatry* 2(3): 379–92.

Worling, J.R. (1995) 'Sexual abuse histories of adolescent male sex offenders: differences on the basis of the age and gender of their victims', *Journal of Abnormal Psychology* 104: 610–13.

Young, H. (1996) 'A reconviction study of young offenders', internal document, London: HM Prison Services Headquarters.

INDEX

INDEX

Wilde, Oscar 35
Wilson, C. 76
Wittgenstein, Ludwig 152–4
Worling, J. R. 80

YOTs (youth offending teams) 27,
30–1, 46–7

Young Abusers Project 107, 109,
110, 112–14 passim, 118
Young, H. 217
Youth Justice Board 31, 34–5

Zamora, P. 10, 170